He Knew She Was Right

He Knew
She Was Right
The Independent
Woman in the Novels
of Anthony Trollope

Jane Nardin

Southern Illinois University Press
Carbondale and Edwardsville

Copyright © 1989 by the Board of Trustees,
Southern Illinois University

Printed in the United States of America

Edited by Susan H. Wilson

Designed by Joyce Kachergis

Production supervised by Linda Jorgensen-Buhman

92 91 90 89   4 3 2 1

Library of Congress Cataloging-in-Publication Data

Nardin, Jane, 1944–
  He knew she was right : the independent woman in the novels of Anthony
  Trollope / Jane Nardin.
    p.   cm. — (Ad feminam)
  Includes index.
    1. Trollope, Anthony, 1815–1882—Characters—Women.   2. Women in
literature.   3. Sex roles in literature.   4. Feminism in literature.
I. Title.   II. Series.
PR5688.W6N37 1989
823'.8—dc19   88-15786
  ISBN 0-8093-1484-3   CIP

The paper used in this publication meets the minimum requirements of American
National Standard for Information Sciences—Permanence of Paper for Printed
Library Materials, ANSI Z39.48-1984.

For Mary Baron and Gloria Watts

Contents

Ad Feminam:
Women and Literature

Ad Hominem: to the man; appealing to personal interests, prejudices, or emotions rather than to reason; *an argument ad hominem.*
—*American Heritage Dictionary*

Until quite recently, much literary criticism, like most humanistic studies, has been in some sense constituted out of arguments *ad hominem.* Not only have examinations of literary history tended to address themselves "to the man"—that is, to the identity of what was presumed to be the *man* of letters who created our culture's monuments of unaging intellect—but many aesthetic analyses and evaluations have consciously or unconsciously appealed to the "personal interests, prejudices, or emotions" of male critics and readers. As the title of this series is meant to indicate, the intellectual project called "feminist criticism" has sought to counter the limitations of *ad hominem* thinking about literature by asking a series of questions addressed *ad feminam:* "to the woman"—to the woman as both writer and reader of texts.

First, and most crucially, feminist critics ask, What is the relationship between gender and genre, between sexuality and textuality? But in meditating on these issues they raise a number of more specific questions. Does a woman of letters have a literature—a language, a history, a tradition—of her own? Have conventional methods of canon-formation tended to exclude or marginalize female achievements? More generally, do men and women have different modes of literary representation, different definitions of literary production? Do such differences mean that distinctive male- (or female-) authored images of women (or men), as well as distinctly male and female genres, are part of our intellectual heritage? Perhaps most important, are literary differences between men and women essential or accidental, biologically determined or culturally constructed?

Feminist critics have addressed themselves to these problems with increasing sophistication during the last two decades, as they sought to revise, or at times replace, *ad hominem* arguments with *ad feminam* speculations. Whether explicating individual texts, studying the *oeuvre* of a single author, examining the permutations of a major theme, or charting the contours of a tradition, these theorists and scholars have consistently sought to define literary manifestations of difference and to understand the dynamics that have shaped the accomplishments of literary women.

As a consequence of such work, feminist critics, often employing new modes of analysis, have begun to uncover a neglected female tradition along with a heretofore hidden history of the literary dialogue between men and women. This series is dedicated to publishing books that will use innovative as well as traditional interpretive methods in order to help readers of both sexes achieve a better understanding of that hidden history, a clearer consciousness of that neglected but powerful tradition. Reason tells us, after all, that if, transcending prejudice and special pleading, we speak to, and focus on, the woman as well as the man—if we think *ad feminam* as well as *ad hominem*—we will have a better chance of understanding what constitutes the human.

Sandra M. Gilbert

Acknowledgments

I began this study during a sabbatical leave from the University of Wisconsin-Milwaukee. As it progressed, several friends and colleagues provided valuable help. My husband, Terry Nardin, and my friend, Tania Modleski, managed to remain cheerful as they endlessly discussed Trollope's feminism with me—and as they read one version of the manuscript after another. Both intellectually and emotionally, they kept me going. Joseph Guerinot, Janet Jesmok, and Deborah Morse read the manuscript and suggested revisions in style and substance. I appreciated Andrew Wright's positive response to some of the early chapters, while Juliet McMaster and James Kincaid offered many useful suggestions as the project neared completion. My daughters, Rachel and Sophia Nardin, gave me a great deal of encouragement.

Earlier versions of the sections on *Rachel Ray* and *Barchester Towers* were published as "Comic Convention in Trollope's *Rachel Ray*," *Papers on Language and Literature*, 22 (1986), 39–50, and "Conservative Comedy and the Women of *Barchester Towers*," *Studies in the Novel*, 18 (1986), 381–394. Parts of the concluding chapter appeared as "Tragedy, Farce, and Comedy in Trollope's *He Knew He Was Right*," *Genre*, 15 (1982), 303–314.

Introduction

In 1850 an obscure writer named Anthony Trollope published his third work of fiction, *La Vendée,* a serious historical novel about the royalist uprising that followed the French Revolution. When a revolutionary army attacks the chateau where he has taken refuge, the novel's hero, Henri de Larochejacquelin, rushes to rescue his sleeping fiancée, Marie de Lescure. Entering her chamber "without much ceremony," Henri raises the healthy young woman from the bed, "as though she were an infant," folding her in a cloak that he has thoughtfully caught up on his way to the room. "We haven't one instant to throw away. Remember who has you in his arms," he tells Marie soothingly, while "with his right hand [he] arraign[s] the cloak around her person . . . Carrying her out into the passage, [he] hurrie[s] to the window," and readies himself to jump (II, 8).

The leap from the second story window, the narrator remarks, "was one which few young men might much hesitate to take with empty arms, [but] it was perilous with such a burden as Henri had to carry." As Henri climbs the sill, a revolutionary soldier rushes up behind him and grabs Marie's cloak, pulling it "from off her neck and shoulders. . . . Her pale face, and white neck and bosom were exposed: her eyes were fast closed, as though she expected instant death, but both her arms were tightly fastened round her lover." Though somewhat hampered by his "burden," Henri manages to kill the attacker by driving "the butt-end of the pistol which he held right through his skull." Hotly pursued by a German soldier, Henri races through the garden still carrying Marie, accompanied by the narrator's frantic encouragement: "Run now, Henri, run your best, for the load you carry is heavy, and the German is strong and light of foot . . . run faster with that precious trembling burden of your's." Henri outruns his pursuer and deposits Marie, now completely "senseless," in the waiting escape-wagon, considerately turning his back "that he might not gaze on the fair bosom, which was all exposed, and the naked limbs, which her dishevelled night dress did not suffice to cover" (II, 8).

The assumptions about men and women that underlie this scene have failed the test of time. It seems more ludicrous than thrilling to the contemporary reader of serious fiction—though the reader of popular romances might be less inclined to scoff. Only if one believes that women are delicate creatures, incapable of facing danger courageously, can one regard Henri's decision to carry Marie—instead of telling her to run with him—as the decision of a sane man. But the fact that Marie actually does faint when she learns she is in danger proves that in the fictional world of *La Vendée* Henri's assumptions about female frailty are valid, his escape plan rational. Men, the passage implies, are heroic and ready-witted, bound to protect their trembling women and always prepared to do their duty.

This view of men as powerful and active, women as passive and fearful, offers pornographic possibilities, and the passage exploits them with little self-consciousness. Henri may turn away chivalrously from the spectacle of his nearly naked Marie overwhelmed by her fears of male violence, but readers are encouraged to examine her closely and to appreciate what they see. The narrator seems unaware that when women are seen by men as helpless objects, they can as easily become objects of sadistic exploitation as of chivalrous protection.

Twenty-five years later, in 1875, Trollope, now one of England's most successful writers, published *The Way We Live Now*, a panoramic novel about the commercialization of English society. One of its subplots concerns Winifred Hurtle, an American widow whose English fiancé, Paul Montague, has decided to jilt her because he has heard disturbing rumors about her past. Mrs. Hurtle admits to Paul that these rumors are by no means without foundation. Reaching womanhood in the western wilds of the United States, Mrs.

Hurtle repeatedly found herself in danger from violent men. She once shot a rapist in the head and had defended herself against her drunken husband with firearms.

The reader, like Paul, is at first inclined to suspect that a woman who has so often resorted to violence must be naturally violent, but *The Way We Live Now* makes it clear that Mrs. Hurtle is a person of "genuine kindness" (47), possessing "all a woman's natural desire to sacrifice herself" (51). When forced to decide between violent self-assertion and passive victimization, she chose the former alternative, although she had no desire to hurt anyone. But Paul judges Mrs. Hurtle by ordinary standards and finds her unfit to be his wife because she has lost the innocence that, for the Victorians, characterizes the feminine woman. Could such a woman possibly become the submissive wife he desires? Paul wonders. "What man would wish to marry her?" he asks himself, revealing that his response to her is both conventional and egotistical. "She had seen so much of drunkenness, had become so handy with pistols . . . that any ordinary man might well hesitate before he assumed to be her master" (47).

So Mrs. Hurtle finds herself cast off by this ordinary man not for her faults, but for the misfortunes she has experienced, not for her weaknesses, but for the strength she has been forced to acquire. In her youth Mrs. Hurtle had to choose between feminine acquiescence in her own exploitation and unfeminine resistance to it; now she must re-enact that hopeless choice in her response to Paul's mistreatment. She writes Paul two letters that encapsulate the possibilities life has offered her. In the first letter Mrs. Hurtle, accepting the justice of the conventional standards according to which Paul has found her unfit for marriage, exonerates him with the prescribed feminine self-abnegation. "You are right and I am wrong. Our marriage would not have been fitting. I do not blame you. . . . God bless you, and make you happy" (47).

Mrs. Hurtle cannot send this letter, however, because she does not really believe that her painful experiences ought to prevent her from becoming a decent man's wife. She cannot accept the double standard that judges women so much more harshly than men. Paul's treatment of Mrs. Hurtle is just another in a long series of wrongs which men have done her, wrongs which it has been the necessity of her life to resist. So she writes Paul a second letter telling him, "You shall suffer retribution. I desire you to come to me . . . and you will find me with a horsewhip in my hand. I will whip you till I have not a breath in my body" (51). But Mrs. Hurtle can no more mail this letter than she could its predecessor, for its defiance of convention will cost her whatever she still possesses of Paul's esteem—a woman's father or brother, not the woman herself, should horsewhip the man who has wronged her. The two letters represent the two sides of Mrs. Hurtle's lifelong dilemma: either she can maintain her feminine softness and allow men to abuse her, or she can resist and suffer condemnation for having "unsexed" herself. "Shall a woman be flayed alive because it is unfeminine in her to fight for her own skin? . . . Why,—why should I be such a victim?" (51) she wonders. Unable to send either letter, Mrs. Hurtle realizes that she has been reduced to silence by the impossible alternatives her world offers to women: "Go, and let there be no other word spoken," she tells Paul hopelessly, when he comes to say good-bye (51).

In *The Way We Live Now* the objectified woman is seen clearly as a target of sexual violence—and no longer does a heroic protagonist automatically appear to rescue her. Further, Mrs. Hurtle's experiences suggest that when life forces a woman to deviate from the ideal of sheltered, passive femininity, society punishes her savagely for her deviation. Mrs. Hurtle's story shows that although active resistance to victimization dooms a woman no less certainly than acquiescence, some women are too self-respecting to give in without a fight. The image of Mrs. Hurtle shooting a rapist with *her* pistol is light-years away from that of Marie de Lescure fainting in her disheveled nightie, as Henri bludgeons an attacker with *his*. And when Mrs. Hurtle tells herself that, given the way she will be judged, "it would have been better for her to have turned the muzzle against her own bosom" (47), she articulates a sophisticated understanding of the dilemmas created for women by men's idealization of them. Nothing in *La Vendée* could have prepared Trollope's readers to expect such an analysis from his pen.

During the twenty-five years that separated *La Vendée* from *The Way We Live Now,* Trollope's ideas about masculinity and femininity underwent a dramatic change—but this change has not received much attention from his critics. It is generally acknowledged that Trollope's early novels exalt the innocent ingenue in a typically Victorian manner.[1] A few critics have also remarked that Trollope's originally conservative view of women grew more liberal as the years passed.[2] And a larger number have argued that several of the novels Trollope published between the late 1860s and the 1880s demonstrate a sustained interest in the plight of women under the rule of Victorian custom.[3] But no one has yet looked closely at the novels Trollope wrote in the first half of his career to see how, when, and why the change occurred.

Among those who think that Trollope's later novels express sympathy with dissatisfied women, however, there does seem to be a consensus that the shift did not occur before the mid-1860s. And there seems to be agreement, as well, that unlike the later novels, the novels written between the mid-1850s and the mid-1860s are only intermittently concerned with the position of women. The fact that few critics have chosen to discuss the treatment of women in Trollope's early novels is proof that such agreement exists. The importance of the woman question in Trollope's early novels has probably been overlooked because the later novels demonstrate their sympathy toward unhappy women so much more openly. Critics who have discussed the later novels differ about the limits of this sympathy, because all of Trollope's novels contain elements that resist a feminist reading—but in the later novels, at least, there seems little doubt that Trollope is interested in women and sympathetic with their grievances. This deep interest and open sympathy, however, did not appear out of nowhere.

In this study, I propose to argue that Trollope ceased to organize his novels around conventional Victorian notions of male and female nature and began to subvert those notions earlier than most critics have realized: the shift from acceptance to dissidence was, in fact, completed between the writing of *Barchester Towers* in 1855 and that of *The Belton Estate* in 1865. I shall also argue that the position of women was a more central concern in the novels Trollope wrote during these years than earlier criticism has acknowledged.

In this decade, Trollope's growing concern with women's problems led him to experiment with a number of formal techniques whereby he could conceal an unorthodox subtext beneath the conventional surface of novels written to please a conventional public. Nearly all the techniques that Trollope uses so energetically in the later novels were pioneered in the early 1860s. The dissatisfied women of the later novels are more dissatisfied, the independent ones more independent, and the novels themselves more openly on the side of such women. But in the ideas they develop and the techniques they use, the later novels add little that is really new.

Because Trollope was such a prolific writer, any study of his novels must, however regrettably, be limited in one way or another. In this study, I propose to look in some detail at the issue of woman's place in twelve of the fourteen novels that Trollope wrote between 1855 and 1865.[4] I have chosen this period as the focus of my study primarily because Trollope ceased to affirm conventional Victorian notions about women and began to subvert them during these years. So important a change deserves detailed discussion. But I have also chosen to look closely at these early novels because few critics have yet paid much attention to their treatment of women—and I believe that this oversight has impaired our understanding of the novels themselves. If we look at the way Trollope's early novels treat the issue of woman's place, we can often find solutions to interpretive problems that have hitherto puzzled their critics. The subtle interplay of formal elements through which Trollope hints at unorthodox ideas about women is one of the most fascinating aspects of his early novels. And because that interplay is so subtle, one must go into some detail in order to reveal it.

Since the "feminist" inclinations of the novels Trollope wrote after 1865 are widely recognized, it is more feasible to discuss the feminist elements of these novels in isolation from their context than to do this with the early novels. Therefore, the concluding chapter looks selectively at the treatment of women in Trollope's later novels, tracing its features, both thematic and formal, back to their origins in his early fiction.

1 The Woman Question in Trollope's Life, Times, and Art

This chapter will offer a historical, biographical, and formal context for the analyses of Trollope's fiction that follow. To this end I shall describe the Victorian theory of the proper relationship between the sexes—a theory that deeply influenced Trollope himself, as well as his narrators and his characters. I will suggest some reasons why Trollope, around 1860, began to suspect that the theory gave an inadequate account of reality and to feel increased sympathy with the plight of dissatisfied women. I will also try to account for the ambivalent attitudes to women revealed both by Trollope's own remarks and by nearly all his novels. When so many of Trollope's pronouncements in letters, nonfiction, and autobiographical writing, as well as the frequent comments of his narrators, were hostile to the women's movement, how can a critic claim him as an early sympathizer with its grievances?

Part of the answer lies in Trollope's relationship with his audience, one that made him reluctant to reveal subversive views about emotionally charged social issues. In considering Trollope's attitudes toward women, we must also remember that ambivalence and complexity characterize his moral vision and the fictional structures in which that vision is embodied. I shall briefly discuss these two aspects of his art in the concluding section of this chapter. Conceptual tensions and expanded sympathies, not tidy resolutions and simplistic moral judgments, are to be expected of Trollope. We should not register surprise when we do encounter them, but rather when we do not.

Different Natures, Separate Spheres

Among the Victorian middle classes for whom Trollope wrote, there was a consensus that men and women are naturally different from one another and that the differences between them justify the existing pattern of social relations in England. Not everyone endorsed this ideal of womanhood and manhood in its entirety, of course. The ideal existed in various versions, was by no means free of internal contradictions, and came increasingly under attack as the century progressed. But its hold on the collective imagination was tremendous. None of the major Victorian novelists—except perhaps Dickens—endorsed the standard middle-class view of the sexes without reservation. Yet none of them—except perhaps Emily Brontë—was entirely immune to its appeal.

Victorian writers who addressed themselves to a middle-class audience had to come to terms with a theory of gender which held that males and females are as different from one another mentally as they are physically. And because their differences were ordained either by God or by nature, they cannot be eradicated by social reform. Physically, women are weak, incapable of sustained labor; morally, they are purer and more self-sacrificing than men. In addition, women are intensely affectionate and naturally pious. Rarely are they troubled by religious doubt. Sexually, of course, a good woman is innocent and not easily excitable. Because she is an emotional creature, as well as a virtuous one, a good woman's character displays "the passionate gentleness of an infinitely variable . . . modesty of service."[1] She has the talents she needs to care for others, but not those needed to fulfill ambitious longings. And she possesses the instinctive wisdom about personal relations that her role as selfless servant demands: "that intuitive right judgment which is safe at first thought."[2]

Second thoughts, however, are not her strong point. In both logical reasoning and the worldly action founded upon it, men are as greatly women's superiors as they are in physical strength and in their capacity to perform sustained labor. Man is "eminently the doer, the creator, the discoverer, the defender. His intellect is for speculation and invention; his energy for adventure, for war, and for conquest."[3] Because their intellects are speculative, men are frequently assailed by religious doubts. Emotionally, they seek the fulfillment of their own desires. Ambition drives them—the desire for love and the need to serve are only secondary motives. Sexually men are "the coarser sex," driven by "ready, strong, and spontaneous" passions.[4]

Because of their contrasting natures, women and men should perform different social roles. A well-run society must assign separate spheres of action to males and females. Woman's sphere is the home and man's sphere is everything else. But woman's mission at home is as vital to society as man's in the outer world: "Let each fulfill their separate sphere of usefulness, and there need be no detraction of worth on either part."[5] At home the daughter, wife, or mother can teach her menfolk by the example of her selfless piety—counteracting the corrupting effects of their daily lives in the competitive worlds of school and business. To do this, she must make home so attractive that the males of her family will feel it to be a haven from the harsh world outside. "This is the true nature of home—it is the place of Peace; the shelter not only from all injury, but from all terror, doubt, and division."[6] Women should make their homes appealing by their accomplishments as amateur musicians and artists, and by their skill in housekeeping. The good daughter "looks attentively after the holes in her father's gloves. She is a clever adept in preparing gruel . . . and the thousand little household delicacies of a sick room."[7]

But the comforts of home are not enough to keep men happy there. Women must also give their men companionship, learning enough about the subjects men find interesting to be intelligent listeners but not enough to challenge male authority. Women should never make their homes unpleasant, and so lose their influence over men, by outspoken criticism or disagreement. They should allow the example of their self-forgetfulness to argue for the moral values they wish to teach, backing up example only by an occasional word of gentle counsel. In most cases a man will respond to this treatment, coming to worship the angel in his house, protecting her weakness and emulating her virtues. Where the man does not respond as prescribed, the woman must nonetheless try to reclaim him by feminine methods: her "highest duty is so often to suffer and be still."[8] Open rebellion violates the God-given laws which ordain that the husband is to rule the family.

The ideal for men was individualistic and permissive, but the ideal for women was unitary and prescriptive. Whether as daughters or wives, all women were if possible to perform the same function within the home: domestic manager, agreeable companion, and moral example to men. Women should cease being sheltered, contented daughters, only to become sheltered, contented wives: "The woman who is considered the most fortunate in life has never been independent, having been transferred from parental care and authority to that of a husband."[9] A girl's education should prepare her to become a wife and mother; her husband would not "be a happier man in his mind if he were mated with a 'being' who, instead of mending his clothes and getting his dinner cooked, had a taste for a literary career upon the subject of political economy."[10] The proper education should protect a girl's ignorance of sin, especially sexual sin. Unlike a boy, she would not benefit from the moral testing that experience brings. Once educated, a girl should help her mother at home until the time comes for her to make the one significant choice of her life, the selection of a husband.

In directing how a girl should make this vital choice, however, the ideal revealed some troubling internal contradictions. Women are pure and sexually unexcitable, yet they are supposed to live for love alone. What sort of response, then, should a girl feel toward an attractive suitor, and when should she feel it? It was often suggested that a good girl could not love a man who had not yet declared his intentions.[11] To love before the proposal would imply an interest in romance or a sexual excitability that was incompatible with girlish innocence. But if a girl was not to love a man until after he proposed, how could she decide upon his proposal? How was the love to begin? And when, if she was naturally pure, should she start to feel sexual interest in him? For many Victorians, the answer to this last question was never; for others, the wedding night was the appropriate time.

Further, there were tensions between the standard view of women as emotional creatures to whom love alone matters and the more practical view that, as "married life is a woman's profession,"[12] she must choose a suitable husband rather than an appealing one. Girls owe it to their femininity to refrain from aggressive husband hunting and to refuse any man they do not love, yet as dutiful daughters they owe it to their families not to marry imprudently.

Once a girl got engaged new problems arose. Now she was authorized to love her fiancé, and she had to prove her womanliness by devoting herself to him wholeheartedly. Yet they were not, in fact, married; if the match were broken off, it would be quite unfeminine of her to thrust love from her heart and speedily begin to search for a replacement. Having allowed herself to feel emotions inappropriate to a young girl, how could she again play that role before an audience aware of her unsuitability for it? Wasn't she now an experienced woman? Courtship required careful management, for "many a girl has been ruined in consequence of a very slight deviation from propriety."[13] Yet girls who were too careful in their treatment of accepted lovers compromised their emotional sincerity, and with it their femininity.

And what of the unfortunate woman who had no husband or father to maintain her in a situation of protected subservience? Women who have no homes in which they can minister to men are "superfluous women," an unfortunate by-product of an otherwise ideal system. The Victorians found it upsetting that these women were often inadequately educated and able to find only the most ill-paid labor. But many felt that the price of remedying this problem by opening male jobs and professions to women was simply too high. The preferred solution was that England should provide homes for all its women, in the colonies if necessary—and not that it should offer alternative possibilities to those who had no homes. Women who must work should continue to do so in quasi-domestic occupations such as teaching, needlework, domestic service, and nursing.

This theory of male and female nature had great emotional power—and great staying power as well. Though we may suspect that few Victorians swallowed it whole, we must also conclude that fewer still found it nauseating. It remained the "official" middle-class view of gender, and its power was acknowledged by the tactics its critics adopted. At mid-century, as women began to press for the franchise and for access to higher education and entry into the professions, they frequently couched their pleas for change in conservative terms. "Many of those who accepted the need for women to obtain some form of higher education," one historian contends, "still believed in [the old doctrine of] separate spheres for men and women. . . . Their reasoning seems to have been that the two spheres were, and should remain, distinct, but that women, within their own sphere, should be trained to competence."[14] Reformers often argued—though not always with complete sincerity—that a particular reform would promote the ideal of womanhood more effectively than existing arrangements. Thus early supporters of medical education for women contended that feminine purity demanded this reform—for a modest woman should not have to discuss her gynecological symptoms with a male doctor. That frontal attacks upon the ideal were not the rule, even among reformers, attests to its influence on the Victorian mind.

The Women's Movement

The ideal I have just described was enshrined in an intricate set of laws and customs. At the beginning of the Victorian era, English law did not systematically recognize women as separate persons. Theories of female dependence and inferiority found expression in laws identifying the interests of women with those of their fathers or husbands. In domestic law the consequences of these theories were pervasive and dramatic. And because a woman's interests were identified with those of the male who headed her family, most Victorians felt that she did not need direct political representation.

Married women surrendered control over their lives with striking finality. "A man and wife are one person in law; the wife loses all her rights as a single woman."[15] Her husband became the owner of everything she possessed and could even confiscate the income from property that had been legally settled on her before marriage. He could claim anything she might earn. He could restrain and chastise her physically, provided his punishments did not threaten her life. She could make a will only with his permission, and she could not enter into binding contracts except as his agent.

Before 1857 an individual could be divorced only by special Act of Parliament. Parliament granted divorces on grounds of infidelity to husbands who could afford the expensive legal process involved, but women could not divorce their husbands for adultery alone. It was extremely difficult for women to obtain even a legal separation. "If the wife sue for separation for cruelty, it must be 'cruelty that endangers life or limb,' and if she has once forgiven, or, in legal phrase, '*condoned*' his offenses, she cannot plead them."[16] Should there be a separation "the law takes no cognizance of which is to blame,"[17] but supports the husband's right to the wife's property and gives him custody of the children. The mother retained only a limited power over infants.

By law and custom single women had greater rights than married women, but during the early Victorian era, they did not, of course, have the same opportunities as men. Most middle-class girls received a sketchy education—stressing decorum, accomplishments, and piety—from women who, in many cases, were not much better educated than their pupils. The universities were closed to women, as were the professions for which they prepared young men. Women could not enter medicine, the law, or the ministry. It would be a mistake to admit single women to the professions in the hope of thus providing for them, because "the very act of thrusting men out of employment would be the way to send them in greater numbers to the colonies . . . creating a still greater disproportion in our female population at home."[18]

Shortly before the middle of the nineteenth century, precisely at the moment when the ideal of female subordination reached its fullest flowering, dissatisfaction with women's legal and social status began to grow. Aided by sympathetic men—of whom John Stuart Mill was the most effective—women began to agitate for changes in the laws and customs defining their position in Victorian society.

The movement pursued a variety of related aims: to gain for women a measure of legal equality with men; to improve women's educational opportunities; and to increase the range of jobs and professions open to them. As the movement achieved limited success in all these areas, it gained momentum. Although most of its supporters did not engage in the frontal assaults upon conventional notions of gender which made Mill and Harriet Taylor so notorious, they criticized the inequities arising from those notions, articulated their dissatisfaction with their position in society, and altered the terms of the debate concerning woman's mission.

In 1854, the feminist Barbara Bodichon published a pamphlet, *Married Women and the Law*, describing the legal position of English wives in shocking terms. Her associates gathered twenty-six thousand signatures on a petition asking Parliament to guarantee the right of married women to control their own property. Although the Married Women's Property Bill of 1857 was defeated, the petition supporting it represented the first large-scale effort at feminist political action in England. The Divorce Act, which Parliament actually did pass in 1857, provided separated, divorced, or deserted women with some property rights. During the sixties, bills proposing some sort of women's parliamentary suffrage received considerable support in the House of Commons. In 1870 a Married Woman's Property Act was finally enacted, though the House of Lords, fearful that financially independent women would not prove obedient wives, curtailed its provisions. All of the legislation proposing changes in the status of women was widely discussed; none of the reforms enacted was followed by the disasters opponents had predicted.

The movement to improve women's educational opportunities was very successful. One early supporter claimed in 1882 that "perhaps no movement of equal importance and involving such far-reaching results ever developed so rapidly."[19] In an attempt to improve the education available to prospective governesses, Queen's College was founded in 1848—the first English institution to offer professional training to women. Six months later Bedford College tried to realize the more comprehensive aim of educating any woman who desired to pursue a rigorous course of study. During the fifties graduates of these two colleges established schools for girls modeled on the public schools attended by middle-class boys. In 1869 an experimental institution, later called Girton College, was established. There women, for the first time in British history, took the same college courses as men. The remainder of the century saw women gradually winning the right to earn university degrees. In no case did women fail the educational challenges offered to them, nor did their health suffer, as many had predicted.

After the census of 1851 revealed a "superfluous woman problem" of major proportions, several essays and pamphlets forced the reading public to acknowledge that the options open to unprotected females were tragically limited. For middle-class women the ill-paid professions of schoolteaching and governessing were the only possibilities, while women of the lower orders worked as domestic servants, needlewomen, and factory hands, for wages that averaged about half what men earned. As people realized how many Englishwomen were living in poverty, a movement to open new occupations to them gained momentum. In the early fifties they were tried as telegraph operators and were discovered to do the work well, for lower wages than men would accept. The Society for Promoting the Employment of Women, founded in 1859, hoped to introduce female workers into trades that had previously been closed to them. The society's efforts were rewarded with considerable success by the 1880s.[20]

Women also breached the barriers that had kept them from qualifying as physicians when in 1865 Elizabeth Garrett, after a long struggle, was licensed by the Apothecaries' Society, "the one medical licensing body in Great Britain which found itself precluded by its charter from refusing to examine women [for licensing] on the ground of sex."[21] Other women were quick to follow, so that by 1880 it was possible for a woman to obtain both a medical education and licensing in Britain. Progress for women in law and the ministry was, however, considerably less rapid.

Between the 1850s and the 1880s, then, the issue of women's rights was widely discussed, a variety of reforms proposed, and a few significant alterations effected. Often the dissatisfaction leading to reform stemmed less from a rejection of the ideal of male-female relations than from a sense that, in practice, things were not working quite the way they should. Ideally the husband should rule his wife firmly, but kindly—their interests should be identical. But if men abused their wives, then these women had to have some legal recourse. Ideally the woman should be supported by the man, but if a population of single women existed, they had to have education and jobs. As women organized for reform and achieved new levels of educational and professional competence, the conventional view of feminine selflessness and debility could not be maintained without alteration. The circumstances of women's lives changed—not radically, but enough to show that women were stronger and more practical than had been believed. The terms of the debate about woman's sphere gradually shifted as women proved that they could perform feats long supposed to be beyond their capacities.

"As the writer of the leading article picks up his ideas of politics among those which he finds floating around the world . . . so does the novelist his ideas of conduct," Trollope once wrote. "He collects the floating ideas around him as to what is right and wrong in conduct, and reproduces them with his own coloring."[22] During the period covered by this study, questions about the adequacy of conventional Victorian notions concerning men and women did not merely float in the English air—more and more they came to fill it. In his first three novels, *The Macdermots of Ballycloran* (1847), *The Kellys and the O'Kellys* (1848), and *La Vendée* (1850), Trollope accepted conventional views about women but was not sufficiently interested in the issue to make it thematically central to any of them.

Immediately after completing *La Vendée*, Trollope wrote *The Noble Jilt*, a play about the impact of the French Revolution on Belgian politics, which, like the novel, should probably be seen as a response to the 1848 revolutions.[23] But it is also Trollope's first attempt to characterize a female malcontent, and as such probably represents his earliest reaction to the nascent women's movement. Margaret De Wynter, the play's revolutionary heroine, rebels against both marriage and monarchy. Despite the fact that her "revolt" lasts less than a week and is resoundingly defeated, the manager who read the piece for Trollope thought it would offend the public. He argued that even an idealistic jilt who quickly repents "meets but little sympathy" from an audience hostile to rebellious women (*Autobiography*, 5).

By making the issue of woman's place a central focus of *The Noble Jilt*, Trollope produced a total failure; he therefore avoided this theme in his next novel, *The Warden* (1855). But when he began to write *Barchester Towers* in 1855, he knew that the ideal of separate spheres was still under attack by women's rights advocates, and he moved to defend it more persuasively than he had done in *The Noble Jilt*. Nor did he ever again lose interest in the issue. During the decade from 1855 to 1865, Trollope's views—like the general climate of opinion—were gradually liberalized by the successes of the women's movement. In his growing sensitivity to women's problems, as well as in his refusal to reject the Victorian ideal of womanhood completely, Trollope was indeed a product of his times. But he gave his own coloring to every treatment of women's problems which came from his pen, and as the years passed he became deeply interested in the sufferings of dissatisfied women.

Trollope's Relationships with Women

Growing sympathy does not necessarily mean complete sympathy, and the ideas about woman's nature that emerge from Trollope's novels reveal a degree of unresolved ambivalence. His own public pronouncements and the pronouncements of his narrators are often hostile to the feminist aspirations of his contemporaries and his characters. But he returns repeatedly to the frustration of ambitious women trapped by the very views of feminine nature he sometimes defends. One source of Trollope's ambivalence toward women is certainly to be found in his personal experiences with them. And during the early 1860s, Trollope's interactions with women altered in a way that probably made him more receptive to unorthodox views about their nature and place in society.

In spite of his declared reluctance to "speak of the little details of [his] private life" in his autobiography, Trollope devotes many of its pages to his relationship with his remarkable mother, Frances Trollope (*Autobiography*, 1). Obviously she was an important influence on him. It would have been impossible for Mrs. Trollope's son to accept, without modification, the view that genteel women are incapable of sustained practical effort and dependent on male protection. It was Trollope's father, not his mother, who lacked practical good sense. "The touch of his hand," Trollope noted sadly, "seemed to create failure" (*Autobiography*, 2). As the years passed, Mrs. Trollope realized that "unless she could . . . succeed in making money, there was no money for any of the family" (*Autobiography*, 2). After an unsuccessful commercial venture in the United States, she turned to authorship as a means of earning the money she urgently needed. When her first book, *Domestic Manners of the Americans*, became a best seller, Mrs. Trollope saw that she could now support her husband and children.

So she began to write steadily at the age of fifty, producing dozens of books before she laid down her pen at seventy-six. At first she wrote by night, while nursing her dying husband and their two dying children during the day. In public she was a conventional lady absorbed in angelic ministrations to others. But in her bedroom she was a hack writer desperately producing whatever would sell. "The industry was a thing apart, kept to herself," her son remembered. "It was not necessary that anyone who lived with her should see it" (*Autobiography*, 2). Trollope thought his mother possessed a "power of dividing herself into two parts" that he had never seen equaled (*Autobiography*, 2).

Trollope knew that his mother's capacity for work was unusual, but he believed that in intellect and temperament she was a rather ordinary woman. She had the feminine qualities of generosity and imagination, and she lacked masculine clear-headedness. "Of reasoning from causes, I think she knew nothing," her son remarked. He conventionally located the source of this problem in her femininity: "Whatever she saw she judged, as most women do, from her own standing point" (*Autobiography*, 2). Trollope noted with masculine disdain that "in her attempts to describe morals, manners, and even facts, [she] was unable to avoid the pitfalls of exaggeration" (*Autobiography*, 2).

Trollope learned from his parents that a strong woman married to a weak man cannot practice wifely submission if she wants her family to survive. Through his mother he learned to look beneath the conventional surface a woman presents to the world for some hidden, unfeminine talent or desire. Her character taught him to qualify, but not wholly to reject, contemporary views of women— for in many ways his remarkable mother was just a woman after all. Perhaps the foundation for the sympathetic ambivalence toward ambitious women that Trollope's novels often display is to be found in these childhood experiences.

In *An Autobiography* Trollope tells his readers a great deal more about his mother than about his wife. But the few details he does reveal suggest that Rose Trollope was a domestic woman, who helped her husband in a variety of ways—from raising his sons to copying his manuscripts—but occupied a limited place in his busy life. She was there for those rare times when the writing, the editing, the work at the post office, the hunting, and the literary socializing were all completed. If in Trollope's view of his mother conventional and subversive ideas about women were held in tension, a similar argument might be made concerning his wife. Trollope married the ideal Victorian helpmeet: pure, subordinate, intelligent enough to be helpful, and no threat to her husband's superiority. But the absence of references to Rose in *An Autobiography* suggests that this marriage was not as central to Trollope as marriage to a more interesting woman might have been. Some of his letters imply that Rose was a woman of depressive tendencies, which her inactive life probably exacerbated. "Keep up your heart & be as happy as you can" (*Letters*, 651), Trollope wrote on one occasion when he had left Rose to her own devices. "Rose writes in most lachrymose spirits" (*Letters*, 173), he told a friend during another separation.

If Trollope was a bit bored with Rose, it would be only natural that he should find more unconventional women attractive —and this is exactly what happened. In a series of short stories about his experiences as an editor, Trollope makes humorous capital of his penchant for falling in love with aspiring authoresses. The auto- biographical character, Dr. Wortle, in the 1881 novel, *Dr. Wortle's School*, is attracted by Mrs. Peacocke, a free-thinking American big- amist. In 1860, Trollope met a young American woman, Kate Field, with whom he was to carry on a platonic love affair for the remainder of his life. Even in old age he could "always strike a spark by thinking of her" (*Autobiography*, 17), and at one point his interest in her reached a level that, he admitted, "teased [his] wife" (*Letters*, 439). Kate was the quintessential new woman: writer, lecturer, actress, and advocate of women's rights. Her independence attracted Trollope as much as her beauty. Indeed, he liked American women in general and sometimes compared them favorably with their quieter English sisters. They "have in all respects come up to my ideas of what . . . women should be: energetic, having opinions of their own, quick in speech, with some dash of sarcasm at their command . . . each with a personality of . . . her own" (*Autobiography*, 17).

In his own marriage, Trollope realized the Victorian ideal: a match between an authoritarian but responsible husband and a home-loving wife. It was precisely the relationship that his own parents had failed to establish, and through it Trollope was perhaps trying to redeem his father's failure, to prove that the ideal was possible. The Trollopes ran their marriage as a marriage was supposed to be run, and it seems to have been happy enough. But as the years passed, Trollope discovered that he hankered—not seriously perhaps, but persistently—after a different sort of woman. Trollope's experience of marriage helped to sustain the ambivalent feelings about woman's place that his relationship with his mother had generated. His admiration for Kate Field, however, suggests one reason why his novels began to grow more sympathetic to rebellious women shortly after he met her.

During the sixties, Trollope's relationships with women writers helped still further to temper his initially conservative views about women's ability to work. After the immensely successful serialization of *Framley Parsonage* in *The Cornhill* in 1860, his social circle widened as he became a well-known figure in literary London. Over the next few years, even before he began editing *St. Paul's Magazine* in 1867, Trollope got to know many women writers, both socially and as colleagues. He was friendly with George Eliot and Annie Thackeray. Trollope also developed an amicable relationship with Emily Faithfull—one of the feminist "Ladies of Langham Place," who founded the Society for the Promotion of Employment for Women—and contributed to her journal, *Victoria Regia*.[24]

By 1868 he had come to see authorship as "the profession in which women can work at par along side of men" (*Letters,* 430). And he recognized that women were as likely as men to be talented writers. An editor must tell nearly every aspirant he deals with that she should "darn her stockings or that he should prune his fruit trees," the narrator of an 1869 story claimed. But "it is equally so with the works of one sex as with those of the other" (*An Editor's Tales,* p. 113). Fiction writing, of course, was the most inoffensive profession available to the feminine woman: it could be pursued at home and did not require specialized training. But even if he was unwilling to see their success as having wider implications, Trollope's acquaintance with women writers must have changed his opinion of female capabilities, and as this acquaintance increased, ambitious women began to assume greater prominence in his novels.

Trollope and His Public

Trollope's pronouncements about women display both continuing ambivalence and growing comprehension of the problems that the prescriptive ideal of femininity created for many individuals. Throughout Trollope's life the ideal of separate spheres continued to possess a certain emotional allure for him, as it did for many of his contemporaries. "Chivalry has been very active in raising women from the hard and hardening tasks of the world; and through this action they have become soft, tender, and virtuous," he wrote approvingly in the travel book *North America* in 1862 (18). The necessity for separate spheres "comes direct from nature,—or, in other words, from the wisdom of an all-wise and all-good Creator," he claimed a few years later.[25]

Trollope also seems to have consistently endorsed a version of biological determinism. So long as women bear babies, sensible division of labor will keep them at home. So long as women know that most of them are needed at home, they will be reluctant to train for demanding jobs. "It is very well for a young man to bind himself for four years, and to think of marrying four years after that apprenticeship be over. But such a prospectus will not do for a girl. While the sun shines, the hay must be made, and her sun shines earlier in the day than that of him who is to be her husband," he notes euphemistically (*North America*, 18). It would not be efficient to create opportunities that will appeal to only a few exceptional women. And society must be run on principles of efficiency, formulating its rules to suit the majority: "If we admit that the laws of life among us, such as they are, are good for the many, we should hardly be warranted, either by wisdom or justice, in altering them for the proposed advantage of a few."[26]

Further, because men are physically stronger than women, they can never be displaced as the rulers of society, even if such displacement is desirable on other grounds. "You cannot, by Act of Congress or Parliament, make the woman's arm as strong as the man's," Trollope wrote in 1868 to a friend who feared that a proposed bill giving women greater rights within marriage would put an end to male supremacy as embodied in the existing "family arrangement." And therefore, he concludes, "the necessity of the supremacy of man is as certain to me as the eternity of the soul" (*Letters*, 821). Trollope was in fact arguing in favor of the bill, but doing so on the conservative ground that its passage did not seriously threaten existing, biologically determined power relationships between the sexes.

But though he never rejected biological determinism, conventional generalizations about woman's nature grow less frequent in Trollope's writing as the years progress. He did not renounce the standard Victorian position completely, but he became more willing to acknowledge that the doctrine was causing problems for many women. "It is a woman's right to be a woman, and her duty to utilise [a man's] earnings and minister to his comfort," he claimed in his conservative lecture "Higher Education of Women" in 1868, but he was quick to admit that for "thousands of women" this prescription does not work. "In this great matter of the arrangement of men and women all does not run smoothly. There are some accidents,—some ill-cooked joints,—some imperfect fruit."[27] The tone may be jocular, but the admission is significant nonetheless.

Though he argued for the ideal, Trollope supported reforms to protect women from abuse by husbands who failed to live up to it. "Even in England there has grown up a feeling that the old law of the land gives a married man too much power over the joint pecuniary resources of him and his wife. . . . Why should a married woman be able to possess nothing?" he wrote nearly a decade before the passage of the first Married Women's Property Act (*North America*, 18). In *The Belton Estate* (1865), he ridicules the male-supremacist Mrs. Winterfield for her vocal disapproval of the 1857 legislation that provided protection for separated and divorced women. She hopes Parliament will soon rescind this "godless" act, and "restore the matrimonial bonds of England to their old rigidity" (8).

Trollope was attracted by conventional views of feminine self-lessness, but not by the double standard of moral judgment based upon them. Women should not, he argued with ever increasing force, be judged more harshly than men on the grounds that men are naturally sinful, women naturally pure. "Fathers & mothers will forgive anything in a son, debauchery, gambling, lying—even the worst dishonesty & fraud—but the 'fallen' daughter is too often regarded as an outcast" (*Letters*, 524). He came to reject the notion that womanly purity is best protected by ignorance of sexual matters. Defending his right to deal with adultery in novels intended for family reading, Trollope wrote, "Thinking as I do that ignorance is not innocence I do not avoid . . . the mention of things which are to me more shocking in their facts than in their names" (*Letters*, 316). Underlying this is a subversive view of female sexuality. This potent force should be directed intelligently, but instead society denies its existence then punishes its expression.

Trollope gradually grew more emphatic in his sympathy with the ambitions of women who were not contented with the female role. He might believe that biology would keep most women in domestic occupations, but when a woman wanted to find—or had to find—other employment, he came to wish her well, as an in-dividual, if not as a social phenomenon. "Who is the man of the world who exclaimed that 'a lecturing woman is a disgrace to her sex?'" (*Letters*, 708), he asked Kate Field angrily, implying that no sensible man would take such an outrageous position. He encour-aged the young novelist Rhoda Broughton, whose daring works had been called immoral, to persevere in her profession. He considered the charge that she had written novels "not indeed becoming any woman" to be unfounded (*Letters*, 434). He went to observe the newly hired telegraph girls and was "gratified at the success of this branch of female employment" (*Letters*, 706). Indeed he seemed positively pleased to report that the telegraph boys "were as unsatisfactory as the girls were the reverse" (*Letters*, 718). Finally, Trollope made a startling remark in a letter he wrote to Field in 1870: the radical feminist Wallachia Petrie, a figure of fun in his recent novel, *He Knew He Was Right,* "did not entertain a single opinion on public matters which you could repudiate . . . she was only absurd in her mode of expressing them" (*Letters*, 509).

But the sympathy that emerges from Trollope's private remarks about women is often countered by a more conservative public stance. The subversive elements of his vision emerge in letters to friends or to readers who criticized the treatment of women in his novels. But when he lectured on the woman question, or discussed it in his journalism and travel books, he doubtless felt under some pressure to hew to the standard line, for the topic was a very emotional one. Only when directly accused of advocating subversive views about women in his fiction would he acknowledge and defend those views to strangers.

Another source of inconsistency is Trollope's inclination to be conservative in general and liberal in particular. His most sweeping statements about woman's nature might well annoy the modern feminist. But his support of particular reforms and his sympathy for the plight of individual women trapped by the restrictions of the Victorian ideal tell another story. This approach was not only typical of the time, as I noted earlier, but it is also exactly what we should expect from a man who described himself as "an advanced, but still a conservative, Liberal" advocating cautious change within the context of respect for tradition (*Autobiography*, 16). His endorsement of biological determinism suggests that Trollope did not believe radical changes in the position of women to be a real possibility. Amelioration was the most they could hope for—gradual reform of glaring injustices was all they could realistically ask. This approach harmonized well with his insistence that social customs usually have some justification—and that even when they do not, we tamper with them at our peril. Rational schemes to reconstruct society demonstrate a kind of arrogant stupidity—and radical feminists offer such a scheme. The hostility to feminists that Trollope sometimes expresses should be seen in the context of his hostility to all those, from John Bold to President Neverbend, who devise abstract plans for rectifying the mistakes of the past.

It is no accident, then, that Trollope's first feminist character, Margaret De Wynter of *The Noble Jilt*, rebels against both the traditional position of women and traditional political arrangements. She is a Belgian supporter of the French Revolution, who hopes to join the revolt against Austrian rule and "give every nerve . . . to freedom and to France; drown thought in action, forget [her] sex and be a stirring rebel" (II. ii). She learns what a dangerous game she has played in rejecting tradition when the revolutionary for whom she jilted her law-abiding lover announces that marriage is "an obsolete sacerdotal ceremony" (II. i) and proposes to make her his mistress. Her lover promises to forgive "the mad ambition" that made her a rebel (V. iii), and Margaret accedes to her aunt's advice that she "never play the jilt again. . . . 'Tis better for [women] twice to submit than once to rebel" (V. iii). Her feminist rebellion is just one aspect of her "crack-brain[ed]" (V. iii) rejection of the past. Later on Trollope grew more sympathetic to feminists. If the doctrinaire ones never ceased to annoy him, this was less because they were feminist than because they were doctrinaire.

After about 1860, as Trollope began to question conventional views, a tension developed between what he wanted to say about women and what he thought his public wanted to hear. And just as Trollope's public and private remarks about women tend to differ in emphasis, so too his novels are often characterized by their divided treatment of issues concerning women. Their more public aspects—the narrator's generalizations, the generic conventions they follow or pretend to follow, the familiar character types they employ—often seem to affirm conventional views of femininity and masculinity. On the other hand, they frequently contain a subtext that subverts their "public" stance. In a few of the earlier novels, Trollope's changing and conflicting views about women created thematic confusion. But in the novels that follow *Framley Parsonage* (1861), he is pretty much in control of this duality, manipulating its elements so that conservative readers will not be offended by the book's subversive aspects and may be led to liberalize their views. By the time he wrote *The Belton Estate,* Trollope's reservations about the ideal of femininity had risen very close indeed to the surface of his fiction.

Trollope's remarks in *An Autobiography* about his art and his relationship with his audience suggest that a complex set of artistic imperatives and commercial pressures helped to shape the dualistic or deceptive form his novels often employ to deal with the issue of woman's place. Debunking the idea of art for art's sake, Trollope stressed his view of the artist as a craftsman who creates his wares in order to sell them. His favorite analogy is between an artist and a shoemaker. He began writing novels, Trollope claimed, to earn a reputation and to supplement his income, and he never changed his view that novel writing was a business, governed by laws of supply and demand.

But tensions concerning Trollope's view of his art gradually become apparent in *An Autobiography*. As is so frequently the case with Trollope, things are more complex than they seem. In the first place, Trollope was a storyteller long before he became a novelist. As an unpopular young boy, he amused himself by creating long mental narratives in which he played a heroic role. Thus his training as a teller of tales came in inventing stories that appealed to his own imagination and were not conceived with any other audience in mind.[28] When he wrote his stories down, Trollope did not begin with a tightly organized plot, but rather with an intriguing character. Yet he was well aware that this was not the method of composition most likely to produce commercial success: "A good plot—which, to my own feeling, is the most insignificant part of a tale,—is that which will most raise it or most condemn it in the public judgment" (*Autobiography,* 7). Trollope lived intimately with the characters he created, letting their personalities slowly develop in his mind—sometimes, as with Glencora and Plantagenet Palliser, over several decades. Trollope was, at least in part, a writer who drew his fiction from the depths of his imagination, who had to write in his own way, whether or not that way was the one best calculated to please his public. Like other writers, he had to compromise between his desire to sell and his need to obey the laws of his own imagination—no mere shoemaker after all.

"I have ever thought of myself as a preacher of sermons," Trollope claimed, "and my pulpit as one which I could make both salutary and agreeable to my audience. I do believe that no girl has risen from the reading of my pages less modest than she was before" (*Autobiography*, 8). Given the censorship exercised by the editors of periodicals and the proprietors of circulating libraries, a novelist could not write successfully for a middle-class audience in Victorian England unless he or she taught "the modest girl" the approved moral values in a recognizable form. Trollope wished to do so, yet his subtle conceptions of character and morality—the very intricacies that set his imagination to work—made the teaching of simple moral lessons difficult for him. One does not want to exaggerate this tension: many of Trollope's readers were prepared to sympathize with imperfect characters and to understand the difficulty of making moral judgments. But the tension was certainly there. David Skilton's study of the contemporary response to Trollope's novels demonstrates that Trollope was frequently in hot—or at least uncomfortably warm—water over his unconventional handling of controversial issues, and the water got hotter as the years progressed.[29]

Trollope's discussion of *The Warden* in *An Autobiography* describes the pressure he often felt to simplify his complex vision of reality. He began the novel intending to expose "two opposite evils. . . . The first evil was the possession by the Church of certain funds and endowments which had been intended for charitable purposes, but which had been allowed to become incomes for idle Church dignitaries. . . . The second evil was its very opposite . . . the undeserved severity of the newspapers towards the recipients of such incomes" (*Autobiography*, 5). But later he came to think that a novelist only irritates his readers by asking them to look sympathetically at both sides of a difficult issue. He should either, he quipped, have "described a bloated parson, with a red nose and all other iniquities, openly neglecting every duty required from him," or a "hard-working, ill-paid minister of God's word . . . subjected . . . to the rancorous venom of some daily Jupiter," and not straddled the fence as he had done (*Autobiography, 5*).

The tension Trollope felt between his desire to give the public what it wanted and his desire to write the fiction that appealed to his imagination caused problems where his female characters were concerned. Trollope knew that the average novel reader responded most favorably to the love plot derived from the model of stage comedy: the story of two attractive young people, separated by external obstacles or their own failings, who manage to marry at the close of the work, after the evils that kept them apart have been vanquished. "There must be love in a novel," he remarked again and again. His admiration for *Pride and Prejudice* shows that he had nothing against romantic comedy in itself. But the comic love story—with its unseasoned protagonists and predetermined plot line—did not appeal deeply to Trollope's imagination, and from the start he chafed against the necessity of writing such stories.

An Autobiography shows us that Trollope strove to include at least one love story in every novel but was rarely happy with the results. Not until *The Three Clerks* did he think he had produced a "well-described love-scene" (*Autobiography, 6*). He often locates the love plot as the worst part of a particular novel, calling one ingenue "weak and vapid" (*Autobiography, 20*) and remarking that another "has passed utterly out of my mind" (*Autobiography, 19*). Once, tramping through Glasgow with a group of postmen, trying to decide if their routes should be altered, Trollope listened to the grumbling men and wondered "how it would be with them if they had to go home afterwards and write a love-scene" (*Autobiography, 7*).

Since marriage is the joyous event that concludes romantic comedy, it is not surprising that Trollope's disinclination to include such a plot in every novel grew as he became more concerned about the powerless position of the Victorian wife. He knew that "it is admitted that a novel can hardly be made interesting" (*Autobiography, 12*) without a satisfying love story; he knew that the success of *Framley Parsonage* was largely due to the vitality of the conventional comic romance between Lord Lufton and Lucy Robarts. But during the sixties, as his growing fame assured him that his novels pleased the public, he became more daring. Never did he go so far as to reject romantic comedy, but he began to undermine it more and more openly through the manner of his treatment.

Part of Trollope's resistance to romantic comedy is explained by his interest in women who are more developed than the typical comic heroine, an innocent young girl waiting for love. In his own judgment, Glencora Palliser was among his three greatest creations: significantly, she never appears as the heroine of a romantic comedy. She interests Trollope because neither character nor fate permits her to play the ingenue's predictable role. When we meet Glencora in *Can You Forgive Her?*, she has just failed to marry the man she loves and is trying to adjust to the marriage her family forced upon her. As the years pass, Trollope portrays Glencora's acceptance of her unromantic marriage and her attempts to widen her restricted life. In *The Duke's Children* he follows Glencora beyond the grave— tracing the influence of her memory on her husband and children.

One reason Trollope finds Glencora fascinating is that she does get older, for he was convinced that people grow more interesting as they age. Trollope's own childhood was devastating, and his talents developed late in life. Only after he went to Ireland at twenty-six did he begin to earn a reputation as a good public servant; he was nearly forty, and had been married a decade, before he achieved success as a writer. Trollope knew that character continues to develop long past marriage, the point where romantic comedy ends. And since he wrote his best novels as a middle-aged man, it is not surprising that he found the problems of young lovers less interesting than those of the middle-aged. In *An Autobiography* he makes no hostile remarks about the aging lovers who appear in his novels, though he often sneers at his weak young heroes and vapid ingenues.

But Trollope's belief that experience develops character was at odds with the fictional treatment of women his public expected. According to the most extreme version of the "separate spheres" theory, a good woman moves from a protected girlhood to protected connubial bliss. She has to age, but she should not change radically or learn too much about life. When Eleanor Bold offers to discourse in public about "dresses, babies, and legs of mutton" but refuses to undertake any other topic, the reader realizes how limited her life has been and will continue to be (*Barchester Towers,* 24). Because the conventions of romantic comedy, like the conventions of Victorian society, prescribe marriage as the happy ending for women, when Trollope took a feminine heroine like Eleanor Bold or Mary Thorne along the standard comic route, he closed off any possibility of further action for her. Insulated from experience, she became a bore to her creator. Yet her story was the one in which his readers delighted.

Trollope thought that the spunky Lucy Robarts was "perhaps the most natural English girl that [he] ever drew." But he quickly adds this revealing qualification: that is, "of those who have been good girls" (*Autobiography,* 8). He prefers, if not the bad girls, at least the contrary ones, women whose lives do not follow the pattern prescribed both by romantic comedy and by Victorian convention, women who encounter life's darker possibilities. Lily Dale "could not extricate herself sufficiently from . . . her first great misfortune" in love to make a comic match with the second suitor for her hand, and so Trollope judges her an interesting character (*Autobiography,* 10). Glencora, a would-be adulteress, is his favorite. The women who fascinate Trollope diverge from the ideal of homebound innocence, unsullied by experience of temptation or contact with sin.

Trollope's interest in women who did not embody the ideal grew as the years passed. He knew that his role as "preacher of sermons" (*Autobiography,* 8) demanded that he idealize the modest young girl, but his imagination was less and less able to do much with her. Explaining his refusal to begin serial publication of unfinished novels, Trollope gave an example of the kind of difficulty the practice could create: "When some young lady at the end of a story cannot be made to be quite perfect in her conduct, that vivid description of angelic purity with which you laid down the first lines of her portrait should be slightly toned down" (*Autobiography,* 8). This reveals how Trollope's interest in flawed, human women would unconsciously thwart his conscious intention to idealize his heroines.

Nor was this process of subversion always unconscious. A decade after the failure of *The Noble Jilt,* Trollope's confidence in his ability to please the public was high. He began to vary the comic plots that he had conscientiously included in every novel of the intervening period and to develop his female characters along unusual lines. When, in the early sixties, he reused the plot of *The Noble Jilt* as the main plot of *Can You Forgive Her?*, he treated Alice Vavasor more sympathetically than he had treated her prototype, making her the heroine even though he knew that her character would not sell the book. Alice's portrayal is "carried through with considerable strength, but . . . [it] is not attractive," he noted (*Autobiography*, 10). Strong women may have been unattractive to the Victorians, but Trollope no longer refrained from using one of them as his heroine on that account. In *The Vicar of Bullhampton*, he set out somewhat fearfully "with the object of exciting not only pity but sympathy for a fallen woman." He was nervous enough about asking readers to acknowledge a common humanity with a fallen working-class girl to write a preface that justified his choice of subject. And Trollope did not dare "venture to make [Carry Brattle] the heroine of [his] story," though he wished to do so (*Autobiography*, 18). Indeed he felt constrained to add a conventional love plot that he found desperately dull. By the time he wrote *An Autobiography* he had forgotten everything "the [romantic] heroine does and says—except that she tumbles into a ditch" (18).

Trollope's relationship with his female characters was very complicated; in portraying women he had to deal with conflicting pressures not unlike those from which women writers suffered so severely. The authors of *The Madwoman in the Attic*—a study of submerged feminist themes in the work of nineteenth-century women novelists—argue that the woman writer suffers from "the anxiety of authorship," a "radical fear that she cannot create" in a world that views the female artist as an unappealing aberration.[30] Fearful of disapproval, she will conceal her unorthodox views behind a conventional facade—if, indeed, she manages to write at all. But male Victorian novelists also experienced anxiety when they endeavored to question traditional notions about women without sacrificing their popularity. Thinking of himself primarily as a commercial writer and conflicted in his own view of women, Trollope did not always resist pressure from his public to idealize the pure young girl and the sheltered wife. But as an artist who drew his stories from the depths of his imagination and who found independent women more and more fascinating as time passed, he would not always submit. As his views of women became less conventional, his willingness to experiment with the form of his novels increased. The balance of his fiction shifted, and he began to treat the ingenue and the comic love plot, as well as the ambitious, experienced, or sexual female, in more subversive ways. But even at his most subversive, he always remembered to consider his audience.

Form and Feminism in Trollope's Novels

It is not surprising that many critics have considered Trollope's novels (the early ones, in particular—but sometimes the later ones as well) highly conservative in their view of women. One simply cannot miss the caustic pronouncements many a Trollope narrator makes about dissatisfied women: "What should a woman do with her life? There had arisen . . . a flock of learned ladies asking that question, to whom it seems that the proper answer has never yet occurred. Fall in love, marry the man, have two children, and live happily ever afterwards" (*Can You Forgive Her?*, 11). Nor is it difficult to find examples of feminist characters, like the Baroness Banmann and Wallachia Petrie, who are used for comic relief. And, of course, likable ingenues, who are treated warmly by the narrator, abound. It is easy to conclude that these striking surface features settle the question: Trollope is an advocate for traditional views of woman's place. Patricia Thompson states a position shared by many other critics when she argues that "the Victorians must have felt that their ideal of wifely submission was in its finest hour" as they read Trollope's novels.[31]

Recent criticism, however, has suggested that the meaning of Trollope's novels is to be sought in the complex interplay of their various elements.[32] Those who have analyzed the tensions between formal elements in Trollope's novels often see his position on the woman question in a new way—though they have used this approach primarily to illuminate the later novels. For example, Juliet McMaster has argued that in spite of the hostility to feminism that the narrators of the Palliser novels often express, Trollope's "deep sensitivity to the women in his novels . . . and his constant reference to the social structure that debarred them from men's activity, make his novels . . . prominent documents in the women's cause."[33] The authors of *Corrupt Relations*—a study of the way Dickens, Thackeray, Trollope, and Collins covertly attack "the Victorian sexual system"—suggest that in many of Trollope's novels, especially the later ones, "symbolic patterns quietly emerge and alter the very substance of the [antifeminist] surface narrative."[34] Some recent criticism that is not concerned with woman's place illuminates the issue by its general analysis of Trollope's attitude toward rebels against convention. When Robin Gilmour argues that Trollope respects "the norms that hold society together" but is nonetheless "drawn again and again to the creation of [sympathetic] characters who flout and transgress these norms," he makes a point that can be applied to Trollope's treatment of rebellious women.[35]

Critics who have discussed the Trollope narrator suggest some reasons why readers should look suspiciously on his conventional pronouncements about women. "Trollope's most serious and pressing claim to be recognized as a major artist rests principally with his subtle and organic use of the dramatized narrator," James Kincaid claims.[36] No mere spokesman for the author, this narrator is a master of rhetorical devices that lead his readers, emotionally and intellectually, along infrequently traveled paths. The narrator of *Barchester Towers,* says Robert Polhemus, "poses as conventional himself, and then shows [through the story he tells] how conventions either need reform or are shifting."[37] Kincaid argues that "one important use of the narrator is to nudge us, against our conscious knowledge and probably against our will, into accepting a most extraordinary value system. . . . We are forced to relax into heightened insight" by a narrator whose conventional tone wins our confidence, and who uses that confidence to move us toward acceptance of unconventional views.[38]

When the Trollope narrator pursues this particular strategy, he often begins by espousing an antifeminist position, and only later suggests reasons why his readers ought to feel greater sympathy for the rebellious women whose aspirations they originally scorned.

But, as the following chapters will demonstrate, Trollope in fact uses several narrative strategies—of which the initially reassuring, subsequently subversive narrator is only one—to evoke empathy toward women for whom the ideal never became a reality. Peter Garrett identifies one such strategy when he argues that in *Can You Forgive Her?* the narrator's "tone of personal opinion . . . [and his] emphasis on particular cases rather than general principles restrict . . . the authority of his commentary"[39]—thus encouraging readers to think for themselves about the feminist grievances with which the novel is concerned.

But the tension between the narrator's stance and the implications of the tale he tells is by no means the only one that Trollope's novels exploit in their treatment of women. Garrett suggests that Victorian multi-plot novels develop a variety of "unresolved tensions between structural principles which, like different forms of consciousness, offer divergent perspectives on the world."[40] Trollope had at his command a dazzling array of formal devices that could be played off against one another, either to develop his ideas about women in a subtly qualified manner, or to conceal the subversive nature of his treatment from a conventional public, or to persuade readers to liberalize their attitudes. The balance that emerges from the interaction of formal elements in even the most unified of these novels is by no means easy to locate. One aspect of a novel tells us that Victorian women suffer acutely from the restrictions of their lives, another that these women have no real cause for complaint. The critic sometimes feels, with a certain desperation, that the glass could be called half full or half empty more or less at will. In addition, Trollope seems on a few occasions to have lost control of the interrelationship between the formal elements in a novel because of his own ambivalence about its female characters, creating an even more vexing sort of critical problem.

Trollope's novels often evoke a tension between character and action. When Trollope said that he valued character more highly than plot, James Kincaid argues, he was not merely expressing his distaste for complicated, sensational plotting. Rather he was rejecting the Aristotelian view that "a pattern of meaning can be inferred from a pattern of action." For Trollope "the sense of being is more and more separate from action."[41] He realizes that society does not grant everyone equal power to express character through action, and he knows that people do not always act "in character." Women, clearly, are one group whose ability to express themselves in action is highly circumscribed. They have little power to impose their wills on others and are restricted in expressing their feelings by the narrow limits of acceptably feminine response. Tensions between character and action will, therefore, be important in judging Trollope's female characters. Their failure to achieve their ends does not necessarily reflect discredit upon them. That they settle for marriage does not prove their deepest longings have been fulfilled.

A second formal tension in Trollope is between main plot and subplots, or between one subplot and another. But as we search for the patterns of meaning arising from the interplay of thematically related subplots, problems develop. Minor plots, Kincaid claims, often portray "an action that runs counter to, or even burlesques, the main plot, thus disrupting its easy symmetry and complicating our responses."[42] When "subplots carry on a burlesque of the wish-fulfillment romance that is controlling the main plot, or . . . solve with ridiculous ease the agonizing problems occupying the main characters," it is not always easy to decide just what these tensions add up to.[43] As Garrett remarks, the various narrative strands in Victorian multi-plot novels are analogically related to one another, but "the inherent plasticity and reversibility of analogies" makes these relationships susceptible to a variety of plausible interpretations.[44]

Kincaid argues that the only formal element in Trollope's novels which operates straightforwardly, according to traditional rules, is the main plot, typically a romantic comedy ending in blissful marriage: "Opening the form through a manipulation of the elements in the main plot is . . . rare in Trollope." In Kincaid's opinion, Trollope "opens" the main plot in just one way: "He shows a marked tendency to resist one of the major traditional requirements of romantic comedy, namely the full-hearted satisfaction women feel in anticipating marriage. The victory is also seen as a trap."[45] Kincaid is correct in asserting that Trollope's reservations about Victorian marriage as a happy ending for women subvert the form of his comic love plots by denying the reader the joy that comedy ought to yield. But the following pages will demonstrate that Kincaid has overlooked other tensions that emerge from Trollope's handling of romantic comedy, for Trollope frequently undermines conventional notions about women by varying traditional comic patterns. The tensions surrounding Trollope's unorthodox use of romantic comedy are among the most important formal tensions his novels exploit to create a feminist subtext.

In the chapters that follow, I shall trace the patterns that emerge from the interaction of formal elements in Trollope's novels. Is there a tension between the narrator's pronouncements and the events his tale relates? Is the narrator self-contradictory in his approaches to character and theme? Does his language seem either excessively flowery or suspiciously flat? What is the relationship between the characters' aspirations and their achievements? Between one subplot and another? Between the traditions of romantic comedy and the way Trollope handles the characters and action of his comic plots? Between the ideal of womanhood and the experiences of the novel's women? Given the complexity of these considerations, it is unlikely that Trollope's readers will ever agree about the patterning in any given novel. But I hope these readings will demonstrate that in most of his early novels, Trollope's treatment of women was both serious and subtle.

2 *Affirming the Ideal*

Conservative Comedy in *Barchester Towers*

The women's rights movement was gathering steam in the 1850s, unsettling many a Victorian male. By the time Trollope began *Barchester Towers*, he wanted to assay again the theme of female rebellion that had failed so signally in *The Noble Jilt*—and he developed some new strategies for handling it. The play's heroine was a revolutionary feminist, and Trollope's attempt to evoke sympathy with her idealism, while showing it to be mistaken, proved unsuccessful. Like *The Noble Jilt, Barchester Towers* links female discontent to the spirit of reform and uses a discontented woman as its heroine. But Eleanor Bold's rebellion against the restrictions of her life is not nearly so violent as Margaret De Wynter's. She could hardly offend the reader, as Margaret offended the manager who read *The Noble Jilt* for Trollope. In *Barchester Towers* the enthusiastic rebels against conventional limitations are the comic minor characters, Mrs. Proudie and Madeline Neroni, at whom the reader can laugh from a position of comfortable detachment. By splitting the rebellious heroine of *The Noble Jilt* into a slightly rebellious heroine and two very rebellious grotesques, Trollope can raise the issue of feminism without using an unpalatable protagonist like the one who caused the failure of his play.

The symbolic patterns about women's capabilities that emerge from *Barchester Towers* do not seriously undermine the conventional views that its narrator espouses.[1] Conventions concerning a woman's proper place are indeed under attack by several female characters. But the patterning of events in *Barchester Towers* suggests that return to an earlier mode of relations between the sexes, not reform of that mode, is desirable. The tensions between formal elements, so important to the treatment of women in the novels that follow, are hardly exploited here.

Trollope never wrote a story more closely resembling classic stage comedy than the subplot of *Barchester Towers* concerning the love affair between Eleanor and Mr. Arabin. Inhibitions, misunderstandings, and the interference of aging relatives and unwanted suitors prolong the romance in a farcical manner that Trollope rarely employs in other novels. It is, as the narrator remarks, a "comedy of errors" (15). But although the basic conflict in this subplot is the disagreement between Eleanor and her elders about whom she should associate with and ultimately marry, Trollope is not here using the time-honored comic plot in which innocent young lovers are kept apart by corrupt guardians and by the values of an old order in need of reform. Instead it is Eleanor's own moral values that must be corrected before she and Arabin can come together. And her values are mistaken because they are excessively, stupidly progressive.

Barchester Towers embodies its most positive values in the elderly Mr. Harding, who loves the past, respects the wisdom of tradition, and accepts human imperfection as inevitable—a man who has learned from experience that we must be tolerant, since we can never be perfect. The other members of the "high and dry" church party in Barchester share Mr. Harding's affection for tradition but lack the gift for self-doubt that prevents his conservatism from becoming complacency. The novel's villains—and *Barchester Towers* comes closer than most Trollope novels to having actual villains—are power-loving reformers who want to cart away the "rubbish of centuries" (as the worst of them, Mr. Slope, likes to call the wisdom of the past), replacing it with panaceas designed by themselves. When Slope preaches a sermon attacking cathedral services from the pulpit of Barchester Cathedral itself, Mr. Harding knows that this attack on ancient custom and those who love it is simply wrong. The maintenance of civility is more important than the promulgation of any private view of truth, however progressive. "Courtesy should have kept him silent, even if neither charity nor modesty could do so" (8), Mr. Harding tells his daughter when she argues that Slope felt duty bound to express his convictions.

Customs inherited from the remote past are not always rational or just. In *Barchester Towers,* as in dozens of other novels, Trollope shows the inequity of many customs and gently mocks the tendency of prosperous Englishmen to view injustices—in church patronage or parliamentary representation, for example—as charmingly picturesque. Nonetheless, the greatest censure in *Barchester Towers* falls on the overconfidence of those who would tamper with the past, rather than on the complacency of those who love it. And Mr. Harding, who is willing to sacrifice to his sense of justice any personal advantage he might gain from the quirky traditions of the Anglican church, proves that a good man can love the past without complacency. This being so, it is not surprising that Trollope cannot incorporate into *Barchester Towers* a comic plot in which the corrupt values of the past, espoused by the older generation, block the joyous conclusion.

In the main plot of *Barchester Towers,* which deals with the struggle between the ascendant forces of the new bishop, Dr. Proudie, and the declining forces of the old-fashioned "high and dry" churchman, Archdeacon Grantly, the meddlesome arrogance of the former is, for the most part, defeated and exposed. And Eleanor's comic love plot mirrors the main plot, for it tells of a woman whose head is turned when she acquires power, who meddles with matters not suited to her sex, realizes that she has overreached herself, and finds happiness by submitting to traditional restrictions upon women's freedom of action. In this conservative novel, the treatment of women is also conservative: *Barchester Towers'* comedy of errors begins when a woman tries to think for herself.[2]

Eleanor Bold has proved a problematic character to many readers of *Barchester Towers.* The narrator's tone in speaking of her is generally most indulgent. She is "My Eleanor" (15), or else "Poor Eleanor" (14). She receives praise for her feminine qualities: her mildness, her quiet beauty, and her devotion to her first husband. The narrator and several other characters speak of her quick, yet modest intelligence. It is hard to reconcile this chorus of adulation, however, with the impression Eleanor's misguided or needlessly aggressive deeds and words make on the reader. Hugh Walpole thought she was "Trollope's most tiresome heroine,"[3] and many readers have agreed with him. It is hard also to reconcile the narrator's tender remarks about Eleanor with the contemptuous criticism of her conduct that he occasionally voices.[4]

James Kincaid suggests that Eleanor resembles Amelia Sedley in *Vanity Fair* and that through her character Trollope, like Thackeray, is trying to undermine the very notion of the "angel in the house"— the sweet and devoted wife and mother, whose sweetness, more closely examined, proves to be weakness, and whose maternal devotion reveals itself as a kind of twisted narcissism.[5] This is true of Amelia, but there may be another way of explaining the tensions that characterize Trollope's portrayal of Eleanor. Instead of undermining the notion of the angel, Eleanor's story implies that the angel role is the appropriate one even for an intelligent woman. She makes her mistake in assuming that she has the capacity to be something more than an angel. Eleanor's often-praised intelligence is a feminine intelligence, adequate to domestic life but unequal to charting an independent line of conduct in the world of ecclesiastical politics. Her attempt to transcend the angel role connects her with the overreachers of the main plot, Mr. Slope and Mrs. Proudie— the latter of whom is also eager to leave woman's traditional sphere. The narrator may find Eleanor's "baby worship" (16) tiresome, but his affection for her turns to disapproval only when she tries to act independently in the world at large.

When *Barchester Towers* opens, Eleanor has just been left a widow with a large income at her own disposal. Up to this point, she has been a sweet and submissive angel. When she lived at home she "declared that whatever her father did should in her eyes be right" (2); after she married a highly imperfect man, she loved his very faults "as the parasite plant will follow even the defects of the trunk which it embraces" (2). Eleanor is well able to play the conventional female role of clinging ivy, and according to the narrator she does so charmingly.[6] But independence goes to her head, and she begins to think she can become an oak.

Mr. Harding, never comfortable in the exercise of authority, convinces himself that widowhood has emancipated Eleanor from his control. Thus, at the start of *Barchester Towers,* Eleanor is for the first time in her life subject to no male authority. Intoxicated with freedom, she resents the one man who still presumes to offer guidance: her brother-in-law, Archdeacon Grantly. The archdeacon is an overbearing man and Eleanor has "never accustomed herself to be very abject before him" (18). But it is only after her husband's death that Eleanor begins to rebel openly against Dr. Grantly's authority.

Her desire to resist the archdeacon leaves Eleanor wide open to Mr. Slope, who is adept at manipulating excitable women: "He knows how to say a soft word in the proper place. . . . Could Mr. Slope have adapted his manners to men as well as to women . . . he might have risen to great things" (8). Slope's fulsome praise does not annoy the morally tone-deaf Eleanor. As the battle over ecclesiastical power takes shape, Eleanor aligns herself with Slope and goes so far as to encourage Mr. Harding to add a Sabbath-day school to Hiram's hospital—ignoring both the fact that these repressive schools are anathema to the high church party, and the fact that appending one of them to a home for the aged is a peculiar idea. Like the novel's other reformers, Eleanor chooses the side of "progress" largely because it offers wider scope for her own energies.

Eleanor is unwilling to surrender her basically positive opinion of Slope, though all her friends agree in their judgment of him and though his twistings and turnings are clearly dishonest. So she persuades herself that her friends are motivated by a partisan zeal that prevents them from acknowledging the virtues underlying Slope's oily manner. "I never saw anything like you clergymen," she tells Mr. Arabin sententiously, "you wage your wars about trifles so bitterly" (21). Only she herself, Eleanor implies, stands above party and tries to see the virtues of both sides. Eleanor's sin is spiritual pride, and in order to maintain her pride, she systematically represses her misgivings about Slope. The sense of superiority to Dr. Grantly and the scope for independent action that her championship of Slope gives her are too precious to relinquish. "You think Mr. Slope is a messenger direct from Satan. I think he is an industrious, well-meaning clergyman. It's a pity that we differ as we do" (29), she tells the archdeacon smugly.[7]

Eleanor is wrong not only about Slope's character but also about his motives for seeking her out. *Barchester Towers* has scarcely opened before Eleanor acquires two suitors, Mr. Slope and Bertie Stanhope, who want her only for her money. Neither Slope nor Bertie's sister Charlotte, who takes upon herself the task of active wooing which Bertie is too lackadaisical to pursue, is at all a subtle suitor, yet Eleanor fails to realize what they are after. Eleanor is an obvious target for fortune hunters, and her blindness to this is not entirely due to feminine delicacy or devotion to her late husband—as the narrator sympathetically suggests—but also to a startling lack of worldly wisdom. The once sheltered young wife thinks she is equipped to defy her elders, but she is quite mistaken.

Eleanor, indeed, is so confused about the issues she wishes to judge for herself that she flirts simultaneously with the low church sabbatarianism of the Proudie party and the infidelity of the Stanhope family without any sense that she is being inconsistent. Dr. Stanhope, a well-connected pluralist, has for years lived a luxurious life on the shores of Lake Como. Through Dr. Stanhope, Trollope explores the dangers of accepting a tradition solely because one benefits from it. All the novel's high churchmen, except Mr. Harding, incur some guilt on this point, but only Dr. Stanhope uses the church with unadulterated cynicism. Because they have seen their father exploit the positions that time-honored customs of church patronage conferred upon him, Dr. Stanhope's children have become skeptics who grant no moral authority to traditional customs or beliefs. Charlotte is an infidel, while Bertie moves easily from Judaism to Catholicism and then back to Anglicanism. Madeline Stanhope Neroni scoffs at women who unthinkingly obey the dictates of custom: "She is just one of those English nonentities who would tie her head up in a bag for three months every summer, if her mother and grandmother had tied up their heads before her. It would never occur to her to think whether there was any use in submitting to such a nuisance" (15), she remarks of Eleanor.

In her flirtation with Slope, Eleanor aligned herself with those who would reform tradition; in her flirtation with the Stanhopes, she aligns herself, more dangerously, with those who dismiss it— rejecting her own friends to indulge an ill-considered inclination toward modern thought. Confusion about gender plagues the cyn-

ical Stanhopes—with their effeminate son and powerful daughters—just as it does the reformist Proudies. The Stanhopes dismiss
conventional ideas about the sexes in the same cavalier way they
dismiss other conventions.

The domineering manner in which the archdeacon advises her
against Mr. Slope irritates Eleanor, but she has less excuse for
disregarding the tactful hints of her sister-in-law, Mary Bold, that
the Stanhopes are unfit companions. The feminine Mary "had positively discouraged the friendship of the Stanhopes as far as her
usual gentle mode of speaking had permitted. Eleanor had only
laughed at her, however, when she . . . suggested that Charlotte
Stanhope never went to church" (44).

Eleanor's blindness to the motives of those who court her ends
when she receives insulting proposals from Bertie and Slope: Bertie
tells Eleanor he hopes she will say no, and Slope, taking her acceptance for granted, embraces her. Eleanor slaps his face—an act
that, the narrator remarks, logically concludes the course of unfeminine self-assertion she has pursued. "It were to be wished devoutly
that she had not struck Mr. Slope. . . .Had she been brought up
by any sterner mentor than that fond father, had she lived longer
under the rule of a husband, she might, perhaps, have saved herself
from this great fault. . . . She was too keen in the feeling of independence, a feeling dangerous for a young woman" (40). The
point here is complex: Slope deserves to be slapped, so the narrator's
horror at Eleanor's conduct is not entirely sincere. But Eleanor has
willfully exposed herself to insult, and so the reproof is partly serious. Eleanor's attempt to leave the safe enclosures of tradition for
the high road of progress ends in a mess: "There was no one to
whom she could turn for comfort" (44).

This angel who tried to leave the house must return home to
achieve the happy marriage that will conclude her comic subplot.
For Eleanor's arrogance was the main obstacle to her union with
Arabin from the very start. Her championship of Slope discouraged
the modest Arabin from pursuing her. Her huffy dignity retarded
the rapprochement between them.[8] Further, Eleanor's dislike of the
condescending tone in which Mr. Arabin speaks to women slows
the development of her affection for him.

Like Eleanor, Mr. Arabin, a celibate follower of the Oxford movement who narrowly escaped "going over" to Rome, must moderate his view of woman's place before the two can marry. He must learn that a wife can be as important to a clergyman as to any other man, must stop seeing women "in the same light that one sees them regarded by many Romish priests" (20). His doing so signals his return to the Anglican traditions from which he had strayed under Newman's influence—and so the view of women at which Arabin ultimately arrives is a highly conventional one. He is now prepared to grant them their "proper" place. Eleanor, he says, "would well grace any man's house" (38) and he wants her to grace his. But the comic conclusion comes about less because Arabin realizes that he needs an angel in his house than because Eleanor finally decides to sacrifice her pride in order to win him. He was ready to accept her long before her manner gave him any encouragement.

Trollope's desire to make this point unambiguously seems the only explanation of the scene in which Madeline Neroni decides to advise Eleanor about her relationship with Arabin. Madeline's jealousy of Eleanor—"that vapid swarthy creature in the widow's cap, who looked as though her clothes had been stuck on her back with a pitchfork" (15)—hardly prepares us for the interest she takes in Eleanor's fate. But the incident is important because it contrasts with earlier scenes in which her elders told Eleanor to be more attentive to convention. Previously, Eleanor resisted all suggestions that her rebellious behavior might get her into trouble. Now Madeline tells Eleanor that unless she beats a hasty retreat, she will lose Arabin—and Eleanor listens.

Eleanor does not like Madeline any better than Madeline likes her, and she finds the interview between them very humiliating. Madeline says that though Arabin is indeed in love with Eleanor, he is "simple as a child in these matters," a man with whom a woman cannot coquette to save her self-respect. Eleanor, realizing that she must "stoop to conquer" (45), is for the first time willing to bend because she finally sees that more than dignity or autonomy, she needs the right man to love and obey: "A glimmering of a thought came to her also,—that Mr. Arabin was too precious to be lost" (45). Eleanor finds that though there has been much in the interview "to vex her proud spirit . . . there was, nevertheless, an under-stratum of joy. . . which buoyed her up wondrously" (45). Further, "she fully resolved to follow the advice given her" (45).

And at her next interview with Arabin, she does. In marked contrast to her earlier manner, Eleanor is now almost abject. Previously, to the narrator's dismay, Eleanor had been too proud to show Arabin how much she cared, but now she cannot conceal her tears, as she looks "slowly, gently, almost piteously up into his face" (48). Arabin takes the hint and the two become engaged. Eleanor's attempt to expand her sphere of action has failed, so she is ready for a comic conclusion that is premised on her return to the traditional woman's role. After the engagement, Eleanor sees that she "idolized, almost worshipped" (48) Arabin as she once had her father, and this is the purpose for which her essentially imitative intelligence is suited. "When the ivy has found its tower . . . we know how the parasite plants grow and prosper. They were not created to stretch forth their branches alone, and endure without protection the summer's sun and the winter's storm. . . . But when they have found their firm supporters, how wonderful is their beauty" (48).

And that's that—the pattern of Eleanor's story reinforces the conventional terms in which, all along, the narrator has analyzed it; there seems no reason to read its conclusion ironically. Just as, in the main plot of *Barchester Towers*, arrogant attempts to meddle with the wisdom of the past deservedly fail, though that wisdom is not perfect, so too, in the comic subplot, traditional options for women, though restrictive, are affirmed as appropriate enough. Eleanor proves herself unsuited to action outside the home. This comedy involves a return to old-fashioned values, and not, as is so often the case with comedy, their reform.

The handling of the novel's other female characters confirms the view of women that the comic subplot implies. For *Barchester Towers* exhibits little of the sympathy with women's extra-angelic ambitions we find in so many of Trollope's novels. The narrator's tone is more consistently misogynistic than is usually the case, and there is a lot of rib-digging, antifeminist humor. Henpecked husbands like Bishop

Proudie are trembling, contemptible creatures, while Mrs. Proudie should be categorized as a man "because of her great strength of mind" (33). Women are typically petty and hostile to each other. They possess an organ by which they "instinctively, as it were, know and feel how other women are regarded by men" (38). With this sort of humor, the narrator castigates the female characters who transgress traditional limits in their pursuit of power. He reserves a respectful tone for those women who exercise influence in the approved manner. And here, as with Eleanor's romantic comedy, the patterns that emerge from the text support the narrator's views.

Dissatisfaction with her proper place separates Mrs. Proudie—the farcical termagant who meddles far more boldly than Eleanor Bold with ecclesiastical matters and who exercises within marriage the sort of power that Eleanor could not claim even as a widow—from Susan Grantly, *Barchester Towers'* ideal wife. Bishop Proudie is incapable of independent action, so it does not really matter whether he is ruled by his wife, by Mr. Slope, or by the government. Thus Mrs. Proudie's lust for power does little harm, but this should not blind us to the selfish way she uses her influence. Ignoring Mr. Harding's just claim to the Wardenship of Hiram's Hospital, Mrs. Proudie "gives" the position to Mr. Quiverful because he will be a submissive vassal. Although the Quiverfuls are truly pitiable, that has little to do with Mrs. Proudie's championship of them.

The Quiverfuls resemble the Proudies and reinforce the point made through Mrs. Proudie about the personal way in which women use power. Mr. Quiverful is not a strong man, but he *can* see beyond his own interests. Even in his desperate poverty, Quiverful wants "to be right with his own conscience" (24). Mrs. Quiverful's conscience, however, has buckled under the pressure of want: "She recked nothing of the imaginary rights of others" (24). Like Mrs. Proudie, with whom she shares tremendous vitality, Mrs. Quiverful cannot see beyond the personal. When she and Mrs. Proudie prevent Mr. Harding's return to the hospital, they commit an act of injustice. We sympathize with Mrs. Quiverful's dire predicament and thwarted energies, but neither she nor Mrs. Proudie is fitter than Eleanor to exercise power outside the domestic sphere.

Susan Grantly, on the other hand, exercises power in acceptably feminine ways. Although Archdeacon Grantly is not an easy man to live with, Susan has made their marriage a success, giving to Plumstead Rectory an attractive "air of home" (20). She never challenges her husband openly. Her manner in private disagreement is "mild [and] seducing" (29), and she lets her husband take the credit for her ideas whenever possible. Archdeacon Grantly often domineers, but he values his wife sincerely. When he learns that Arabin is engaged to Eleanor, he tells him tearfully that "if she does her duty by you as her sister does by me, you'll be a happy man" (50). As a married woman, Susan is the example Eleanor must follow, while Mrs. Proudie represents a comic vision of the danger that menaces her if she continues her mistaken ways.[9]

The single—or, in the case of the deserted Madeline Neroni, effectively single—women in *Barchester Towers* form a similar pattern of example and warning. The "good" spinster is Monica Thorne, who espouses the novel's conservative values in their most comically extreme form. Miss Thorne and her brother pride themselves on their Saxon lineage. Miss Thorne longs for the return of the era preceding the Norman conquest and speaks of Addison and Steele "as though they were still living" (22). The Christian religion, the narrator quips, "was the most modern [reform] of any to which she had as yet acceded" (22).

Initially Miss Thorne appears no less grotesque than Mrs. Proudie, but as the novel progresses, feminine kindness emerges as her most prominent trait. A scene that is crucial in humanizing Miss Thorne shows her preparing for a fête champêtre where she hopes her guests will ride at the quintain. But when she asks her brother to test the quintain for her, he cuts "her to the heart" by refusing to attack "such a rattletrap as that" (35). She quickly recovers from her disappointment, however, by reminding herself of another aspect of her conservative creed: female subservience. "It had ever been one of the rules by which Miss Thorne had regulated her conduct through life, to say nothing that could provoke her brother. . . . The head of the family should never be upbraided in his own house" (35). Miss Thorne's self-suppression wins the same response that Susan Grantly's does. Seeing "the tear in her eye," her brother apologizes remorsefully.[10]

Miss Thorne "had once declared, in one of her warmer moments, 'that now-a-days the gentlemen were all women, and the ladies all men' " (35). Two other single women in *Barchester Towers*—Madeline Neroni and Charlotte Stanhope—validate Miss Thorne's fears. They also appear, initially, to undercut the novel's conservative view of the sexes, for Madeline's jokes about men and marriage are very disturbing.[11] But in the end Trollope affirms convention by using Madeline and Charlotte to parody two mistaken versions of the "angel in the house" figure in order to suggest that submissive tenderness is the one trait that brings a woman happiness.

Madeline represents the ornamental aspect of the angel figure, who should, in some versions at least, be beautiful and useless, existing solely to amuse and charm men. Certainly Madeline, witty and beautiful, but so badly crippled as to be completely unfitted for all practical purposes, is an angel in this sense. That Madeline charms by flaunting her sexuality perhaps emphasizes the incompatibility Trollope sees between the sexual allure that *really* makes the ornamental angel attractive to men, and the tenderness that a reasonable man should desire in his wife.

Madeline, however, might have become a better sort of angel had she not been prevented by a combination of bad conduct and bad luck. In her youth, her unrestrained sexuality got her into trouble and she was left a cripple, deserted by her ne'er-do-well husband. Madeline finds amusement in exposing male hypocrisy, for she truly possesses the critical insight to which Eleanor mistakenly laid claim. But Madeline is simply "the fruit of the Dead Sea, so sweet and delicious to the eye, so bitter and nauseous to the taste" (27). Apart from occasionally exposing pretense or offering advice, she can do nothing constructive with her intelligence, for there is no sphere apart from marriage to which she can apply it in a sustained way. Nurtured in the dark experience brought by rebellion and disaster, Madeline's intelligence is a mixed blessing at best—for all her vitality, she is very unhappy.

Miss Thorne has the final word on Madeline's fitness for marriage: "She is a woman all men would like to look at; but few I imagine would be glad to take her to their hearths, even were she unmarried and not afflicted as she is" (48). Though Madeline dismisses marriage as "tyranny on one side and deceit on the other" (15), the grapes are clearly sour. In advising Eleanor to marry Arabin, Madeline exclaims, in an "impassioned way" quite unlike her usual delivery, "what would I not give to be loved in such a way by such a man" (45). Unlike dissatisfied women in Trollope's later novels, Madeline would be an angel if she could; the advice she gives Eleanor is so conventional that it might have come from Archdeacon Grantly. When a brilliant and passionate rebel advises a hesitant rebel to renounce rebellion, her words have extraordinary weight. Nor is it only in arranging Eleanor's match that Madeline aids the forces of tradition in Barchester. She protects the ultraconservative Mr. Thorne against Slope's mockery and inadvertently, but effectively, humiliates Mrs. Proudie by ripping off her train. Surprisingly, Madeline fights on the side of the high church party—a tacit acknowledgment that she regrets her own rebellion against convention.

Charlotte Stanhope parodies a second aspect of the angel figure: the practical homemaker who is a "clever adept in making gruel" and arranging the tea trays. Never a beauty, Charlotte at thirty-five has left the ornamental side of angelhood to her sister and "in no way affected the graces of youth" (9). But she runs the household. "She gave the orders, paid the bills, hired and dismissed the domestics, made the tea, carved the meat, and managed everything" (9). Charlotte, however, is no closer to being a real angel than Madeline, for she caters to the comforts of her family with the selfish object of gaining power over them. The true angel makes her comfortable home a school of good moral conduct that she teaches by example. But Charlotte "had aided her father in his indifference to his professional duties. . . . She had encouraged her mother in idleness in order that she herself might be mistress and manager of the Stanhope household" (9).

Because of her heartlessness, her mental independence, and her wish for power, and despite her unquestionable talent for the practical feminine arts, the narrator finds Charlotte sexually unclassifiable. "She was a fine young woman; and had she been a man, would have been a very fine young man" (9). She returns to Italy, where presumably she belongs. There, under her heartless management, the Stanhope family fortunes will continue to decline. Danger to the family really does result when, to quote the words of Miss Thorne, the young women become just like the young men.

Madeline, Charlotte, Eleanor, and Mrs. Proudie are unhappy with their allotted role as "angels in the house," but *Barchester Towers* treats their desires for change far less sympathetically than Trollope's later works were often to treat the dissatisfactions of intelligent women, doomed to live restricted, powerless lives. It is hard to see any of them as victims of systematic repression, and the ones who most long for power are least able to use it intelligently; in these respects *Barchester Towers* differs from many of the later novels. For all her vitality, Mrs. Proudie is little more than a comic butt; Charlotte and Madeline prove that talent will not help a woman find happiness if she lacks tenderness of heart; Eleanor comes to realize that her attempts to evade male authority were completely misguided. Eleanor retreats and for her the comic conclusion is therefore possible. But these other modern women are excluded from the conservative rejoicing that marks the novel's close.

Sexual Balance in *The Three Clerks*

To a far greater extent than *Barchester Towers*, *The Three Clerks* (1857) expresses Trollope's fear that Christian morality may be disappearing from Victorian England. Unrestrained competition has become the way to commercial success, and with the introduction of competitive examinations, the new values invade even the civil service. Like other Victorians, Trollope wondered how a society that viewed success as the measure of merit could be prevented from degenerating into a jungle. And most of his contemporaries would also have agreed that the remedy he suggests in *The Three Clerks* offered society its only hope: if the world of commerce crushes men's moral sensibilities, those sensibilities must be revived by the example of the domestic angel. *The Three Clerks,* James Kincaid rightly argues, is "ethically and morally puristic; it . . . reaches toward very drastic action and extreme solutions; . . . it is didactic."[12] And its simplistic treatment of women is the corollary of its simplistic approach to morality—for it insists on the dire consequences that will follow if they fail to play their role as exemplars of virtue.

In *The Warden* Trollope had parodied Dickens' tendency to oversimplify moral issues, but here he experiments with several Dickensian techniques.[13] The narrative voice is often highly emotional and highly partisan,[14] the topical attack on civil service examinations is quite unmodulated, the villain is a figure of pure evil, and the female characters have a stereotypical quality that even Trollope's early works generally avoid. To impress readers with a good woman's power to reclaim an erring man, Trollope strives for a Dickensian pathos that he usually scorns. Like its predecessor *Barchester Towers* and its successors *Doctor Thorne* and *The Bertrams, The Three Clerks* defends traditional values against contemporary threats. But where the other three novels identify women's dissatisfaction with their prescribed role as one of several threatening modern developments, *The Three Clerks,* having identified feminine selflessness as the solution to the problems of modernity, includes no rebellious women among its characters. All its women are contented to spend their lives ministering to men—and the novel judges them by their success in performing this mission.

Though its approach to the issues it raises is by no means subtle, *The Three Clerks* is an elaborately structured novel. Three young men, Alaric Tudor, Harry Norman, and Charley Tudor, marry three sisters, Gertrude, Linda, and Katie Woodward—but only after Alaric has jilted Linda, and Gertrude refused Harry. The heroines differ from one another in terms of the balance between qualities conventionally identified as "masculine" and "feminine" that marks each one's personality. The calculating, ambitious Gertrude is insufficiently feminine, while Linda's femininity is carried to such an extreme that it becomes weakness. Only Katie achieves the ideal degree of femininity. Each hero is the male counterpart of his future wife: Alaric is too masculine; Harry is too feminine; Charley eventually finds the strength appropriate to his sex. The couples are symmetrically arranged on this continuum, but within each couple the woman's moral character is better than the man's—in keeping with the usual Victorian view of the sexes. The contrasting careers of the three pairs suggest that a balance between the masculine and feminine principles is desirable both within the individual personality and within the family. The marriage of an ideally feminine woman and an ideally masculine man can become a positive force in the deteriorating modern world.[15]

The favorite child of the widowed Mrs. Woodward, Gertrude is more beautiful and intelligent than her younger sister Linda. She has an "air of command," is "hardly so soft as so young a girl should be," detests fools, and is often unkind enough "to declare who the fools were whom she detested" (3). But unlike many of Trollope's powerful women, Gertrude has no ambition beyond marriage to the man she loves—the threat to tradition in *The Three Clerks* comes from the competitive spirit and not from feminism. The women in this novel want only to be good wives, but some of them understand the concept better than Gertrude does. Gertrude's deficient femininity is expressed through the predominance in her character of masculine traits like ambition, academic cleverness, and insensitivity to personal relations. She admires the masculine qualities of strength, drive, and even ruthlessness. "I think every man is bound to do the best he can for himself," she tells her mother, "that is, honestly; there is something spoony in one man allowing another to get before him, as long as he can manage to be first himself" (12).

Gertrude thinks that she has found the strength for which she is searching in Alaric Tudor. The son of a widowed father, Alaric has not benefited from a mother's feminizing influence; his personality therefore exhibits, in a disturbingly exaggerated way, many qualities the Victorians saw as characteristically male. Alaric is obsessed with success and convinces himself that no "man ever rose to greatness . . . who thought it necessary to pick his steps" according to a strict moral code (7). Aesthetically insensitive, Alaric cannot "feel an interest in works of art. . . . He panted rather for the great than for the beautiful" (7). Insensitive to feelings, Alaric, when he realizes that he has lost Mrs. Woodward's affection, determines "not to trouble his mind" (12) about so minor a matter. Insensitive to piety, Alaric writes official reports on Sunday mornings. With women he is aggressive and irreverent. "Why not put your arms round a goddess?" he asks jokingly (3).

There is a failure of the feminine principle in Gertrude and Alaric's marriage. Alaric shows himself determined to make the women he loves see life from his vantage point, determined not to let them alter the way he thinks about moral issues. When Mrs. Woodward criticizes his unscrupulous conduct, Alaric tells himself that "success would ultimately bring her round" (12). Alaric's resolution to resist uplifting female influences is, of course, extremely ominous. The male-supremacist Alaric is a very autocratic husband, but because Gertrude shares his dubious ambitions, she could not act as an effective counterpoise to them even if he were willing to listen to her. She urges Alaric to pursue success—stoically refusing to complain when he begins to spend the evenings at his club making useful connections. Because of her own worldliness, Gertrude cannot make her home the source of healing moral influence. She encourages Alaric's ambition until humanizing domesticity ceases to affect his life: "The gambols even of his own baby were unattractive to him" (36).

"Easy, very easy, is the slope of hell" (29), says *The Three Clerks*'s preachy narrator of the course on which Alaric has embarked. Sure enough Alaric slithers down a slippery moral slope, beginning his career of dishonesty by accepting a bribe and concluding it by embezzling a fortune. Only after Alaric is arrested does the balance in the Tudor marriage begin to shift. Though both Tudors were too enamored of success, Gertrude retained some of her moral scruples while Alaric surrendered his completely. Now, in adversity, Gertrude stands by her husband, acknowledging that he has sinned and striving to redirect his ambition. The humiliated Alaric is finally ready to respond to a woman's uplifting example. On the morning of his trial, Gertrude brings him their baby, and as Alaric kisses the child, the reader knows that he has come under feminine influence and will reform.

But though Gertrude's moral suasion brings Alaric back to the paths of virtue, the narrator constantly assures us that she is not the novel's ideal woman. Ironically, it is the opportunity for action offered to her by Alaric's disgrace that enables Gertrude to show what she is made of. When the morally flawed husband she chose because of her own deficient moral sense can no longer protect her, she gets a chance to develop that would have been denied her if she had married a better man. Forced to diverge from the ideal of sheltered femininity, Gertrude can demonstrate a devotion to her husband which the narrator, revealing a tension within the ideal, judges admirably feminine.

But even in her devotion, she is too strong, too independent to please him. The narrator regrets her willingness to throw off "all traces of juvenility" as she takes control of her family's fate (43). Caught between his conventional admiration for womanly devotion and his equally conventional belief that an innocent, juvenile woman is more admirable than one who has encountered evil and expressed her devotion in decisive action, the narrator cannot resolve his feelings about Gertrude. After Gertrude's troubles have matured her, he thinks that Linda has become "the more lovely of the two, and certainly the more feminine." But, on the other hand, he feels constrained to admit that if "devotion be feminine, and truth to one selected life's companion . . . then Gertrude was not deficient in feminine character" (43). The narrator grows to respect Gertrude's strength, but he never loses his sense that such strength in a woman is unfortunate, if not unnatural—and he continually reminds the reader that Gertrude's dark experience has cost her more than it is worth.

Gertrude remains to the end an unappealing character, willfully determined to blame English society for Alaric's crimes. "She was determined to hate all the antecedents of his life, as though those antecedents, and not the laxity of his own principles, had brought about his ruin" (43). Gertrude's basic integrity redeems Alaric, but she cannot give him the moral sensitivity she herself lacks. At the end of the novel, their marriage remains unbalanced, a grotesque inversion of the oak-and-vine ideal, in which neither husband nor wife is playing the appropriate role: "She had entwined herself with him in sunny weather; and when the storm came, she did her best to shelter the battered stem to which she had trusted herself" (47).

Almost a parody of the domestic angel, Linda Woodward is characterized by her piety, her submissiveness, her indiscriminate affections, and her inability to think for herself. "Prone to lean on the nearest support that came to her hand" (14), she is "quite content to be told . . . what she ought to do, and how she ought to think" (5). Though Linda has grown up in Gertrude's shadow, she feels an affection for her sister that is almost untinged with jealousy. When her own lover proposes to Gertrude, Linda is able to repress her anger completely, sacrificing her feelings to her sister's happiness. Mrs. Woodward tells Linda that she must resolve to "listen to her sister's joy, to enter into all her future plans . . . and to do this without once giving vent to a reproach" (14). A tall order for a broken-hearted girl, but the submissive Linda does "all that circumstances and her mother required of her" (14)—after she recovers from her fainting fit. A true Christian, she forgives Alaric for the harm he has done her. Self-sacrificing femininity could go no further, and the narrator is pleased that Linda can "overcome herself, and put her own heart . . . into the background, when the hopes and happiness of another required it" (14).

But there is a problem with Linda's femininity. "Made of that stuff which can bend to the north wind" (16), Linda sacrifices herself through feminine weakness, not through feminine strength. She does not surrender Alaric to Gertrude because her love for her sister is passionately generous, but rather because her love for Alaric is lukewarm. She is simply not "susceptible of being torn to tatters by an unhappy passion," the narrator remarks (16). And she obeys the teachings of her religion with unreflective passivity: "She had had her grief, and had been told to meet it like a Christian; she had been obedient to the telling" (16). Without someone to tell her how a Christian should meet grief, Linda might well have failed to figure it out for herself. Such a limp woman cannot perform her highest duty: to set an example of sensitive moral conduct for her husband. Because she carries to an absurd extreme the submissiveness that distinguishes the "feminine" girl, Linda is paradoxically unable to win the reader's real admiration.

Eventually Linda marries Harry Norman, the feminine man who is her male counterpart. Like Linda, Harry is a second child whose interests have been subordinated to those of the older sibling, and perhaps this subordination is the source of his womanly qualities. Harry repudiates the prevailing values of the age, telling Alaric not to "allow yourself to believe that the end justifies the means, because you see that men around you act as though they believed so" (7). Like a woman, Harry is more concerned with morality than with practical action. He is feminine too in his "interest in works of art" (7) and in the piety whose strength is proved by his "never omitt[ing] divine worship" (11). Sensitive to the feelings of others, Harry values friendship highly. And he is intensely emotional. After Gertrude rejects him, he sobs miserably, "like a young girl" (12). Passivity in love comes more naturally to Harry than aggression. When he proposes to Gertrude, his "confusion was so great, that he could hardly see the girl whom he now hoped to gain as his wife" (12).

Though conscientious, Harry is almost as deficient in courage and intellect as Linda. His superficially principled behavior, like hers, often springs from weakness. Thus, Harry decides to drop out of the examination for promotion in his office, not because he disapproves of competitive examinations, as Trollope did, but through fear of failure. "Put utterly out of conceit with himself by what he deemed the insufficiency of his answers" (11), Harry childishly quits. Nor is Harry's moral sophistication superior to Linda's. Where Linda never does wrong because she follows orders to the letter, Harry, being a man, is incapable of such self-abnegation and unconsciously bends the teachings of Christianity into conformity with his feelings. Harry cannot forgive a real injury: his anger at Alaric for marrying Gertrude never subsides. When he becomes engaged to Linda, he stipulates that she may never see her brother-in-law, arguing that "there are injuries which a man cannot forgive" (15). Like Linda's, Harry's is a kind of rote goodness, grounded in habit and timidity, rather than in a sophisticated commitment to the moral tradition he endorses. But Linda is the more consistent of the two, proving again that in *The Three Clerks* woman's goodness exceeds man's.

If Gertrude and Alaric's marriage demonstrates a deficiency of the feminine principle, Linda and Harry's relationship exhibits a deficiency of the masculine. Harry lacks the courage to fight for his rights and the critical acumen needed to defend his viewpoint effectively; Linda can only rubber-stamp his decisions. Because neither possesses masculine strength of intellect and will, they make a pathetic, directionless couple. The best Harry and Linda can hope for is safety. Harry inherits his father's estate and embraces rural retirement. Living by tradition clearly will suit him, while "at Normansgrove, with . . . her husband always by to give her courage, Linda would find the very place for which she was suited" (46). They are too weak to be a force for good in the complex, corrupt London world. An excess of the feminine principle is preferable to an excess of the masculine, but not ideal.

The novel's ideal man and woman turn out to be Katie Woodward and Charley Tudor. In the book's early sections, they appear less impressive than the other two pairs, for Katie is a mere child and Charley has gotten off to a bad start in life. When they mature, however, both find the qualities of insight, feeling and decency appropriate to their respective sexes. As individuals and as a couple they achieve perfect balance.

The narrator never allows the slightest ambiguity to undermine his admiration for Katie. He dwells repeatedly on her "young sweet angel face" and the "almost divine" nature of her touch (20). Her character is a golden mean between the excessive femininity of one sister and the deficient femininity of the other: "To her belongs neither the soft easiness of her sister Linda, nor the sterner dignity of Gertrude. But she has a character of her own, which contains, perhaps, higher qualities than those given to either of her sisters" (16). More pliant than Gertrude, Katie tempers virtue with an intelligence and tenacity denied to Linda. But the ways in which Katie demonstrates these qualities may surprise readers familiar with some of Trollope's later novels.

At sixteen, Katie falls into the Thames and is rescued by Charley, an old family friend. The affection she has always felt for him quickly turns to passionate love. But Katie demonstrates her purity by remaining "entirely unconscious of the state of her own feelings" (28). A week after the accident, not having quite recovered from the shock (though Charley was able to go bathing the following morning), Katie overtires herself and becomes a semi-invalid. Katie finally realizes that she is in love with Charley, but quietly accepts her mother's caveat that the dissipated Charley cannot be considered as a prospective spouse. Though she tries heroically to conquer her feelings, the effort almost kills her. Convinced that she is dying, Katie calls Charley to her bedside and implores him to reform for her sake: "Dearest, dearest Charley, good-bye; perhaps we shall know each other in heaven" (42). Charley does reform, and Katie recovers. The narrator stresses the conventionally ideal nature of their relationship when he remarks that "it would seem as though it were ordained that [Charley's] moral life and [Katie's] physical life were to gain strength together" (45). They marry.

In creating Katie, Trollope unwittingly falls into a Victorian version of the very trap that writers of the novel of sensibility encountered in the eighteenth century, as they vied with one another to create heroines who excelled in the quality the genre valued most highly: strength of feeling. Trollope hopes to show that Katie is a perfect woman, capable of absolute devotion and intuitively intelligent in her grasp of complex moral issues, which she decides for herself. "She had never spoken of her love; . . . for her mother's sake she had determined to suffer and be silent," the narrator says approvingly of one such independent, but conventional, moral decision (37).

But here a problem arises: Katie's principled submission to her mother, her acceptance of the limits tradition places on her freedom of action, leaves her with no useful way to demonstrate her devotion to Charley. Unlike Gertrude, Katie does not make the errors that would expose her to sin and, ironically, to opportunities for significant action. As an ideally restrained girl, Katie is suspended in a limbo of passivity from which she cannot escape. Trollope can prove the strength of her love only by dramatizing the suffering it causes her. We know that Katie loves Charley because—like the heroine of a novel of sensibility—she goes first into hysterics and then into a decline. But unlike her predecessors, who cry because they are so sensitive, Katie must cry because the conception of femininity on which her character is premised forbids her to act.

In his desire to embody the perfect balance of feeling and principle, strength and tenderness, in a perfect woman, Trollope par-
alyzes Katie and renders her absurd. Unlike the later heroines, none
of whom is capable of such self-abnegation, she lives for love, cannot
recover from its loss, but does not become angry with those who
forbid her to fulfill her desires. Katie's strength makes her even
more self-abnegating than the passive Linda, who suffered less
severely in renouncing her less powerful desires. The ideal woman
of *The Three Clerks* turns out to be a nonperson who lives for others
and expects no reward for doing so.

At times the narrator seems uneasily aware that Katie's complicated exemplary function is destroying her credibility. He imagines
a skeptical reader objecting that Katie is "still a child, and yet arguing
to herself about spendthrift debtors and self-sacrifice! All this bombast at sixteen and a-half. No, my gentle reader. . . . The bombast
is mine. It is my fault if I cannot put into fitting language the
thoughts which God put into her young heart" (30). He fears that
he is failing to characterize Katie convincingly, yet he remains passionately committed to the ideal she represents, for in *The Three
Clerks* feminine influence offers the only hope of moral regeneration.

Katie is a better influence on her lover than either the too-mas-
culine Gertrude or the too-feminine Linda was upon hers. As a
young boy, Charley is placed in an office where no one does any
work. He takes to drink and becomes entangled with a barmaid.
Again and again, the narrator remarks that lack of good female
influence is at fault. Charley is snatched from the burning by Katie,
whose eyes "had so often peered at him out of heaven, teaching
him to think of higher things" (20). He reforms himself by strenuous
moral effort, becoming a mature man who tempers ambition with
feeling for others. Once married, Katie and Charley balance masculine strength and feminine tenderness. They remain in London,
where Katie provides the stable home in which Charley writes
humorous novels attacking the foibles of the age, novels that may
contribute to social progress. More domesticated than Alaric, more
active in the world than Harry, Charley becomes the ideal husband
through the help of a wife who teaches by example. Wanting no

more than to reform him, Katie becomes the ideal wife, whose influence stretches beyond her home although—or perhaps because—she does not actively seek such influence.

The three main plots of *The Three Clerks,* then, affirm the prevalent Victorian view that women are naturally more virtuous than men and that they find both their truest satisfaction and their greatest utility when they exercise those qualities within marriage. To a certain extent, however, the elaborate and conventional conceptual scheme on which the novel is premised breaks down, revealing internal contradictions. And this breakdown manifests itself in the narrator's ambivalent feelings about his female characters. As I noted earlier, his response to the strength and maturity Gertrude gains is mixed—she almost escapes from his control. And though he praises "happy, happy Linda" (43) for her conventional femininity, she clearly bores him, and he frequently forgets about her altogether. Winding up Linda's subplot, he makes no attempt to involve the reader, remarking flatly that her prudent romance is "not of a nature to give much scope to a novelist. . . . The engagement was duly ratified by all the parties concerned" (31). Katie makes the narrator uneasy as he comes to sense that she can express her feminine strength only by willing her will out of existence. *The Three Clerks* tries to ignore these problems, but they finally do pull it slightly out of shape, suggesting a certain uneasiness with the view of woman's place which most of its formal elements affirm.

Trollope more successfully avoids ambiguity in his treatment of the novel's comic characters, Lactimel and Ugolina Neverbend, and its villain, Undecimus Scott. The Neverbend sisters meddle with matters for which women are not intellectually suited: utilitarian "Lactimel would have clothed and fed the hungry and naked," while transcendental Ugolina "would have brought mankind back to their original nakedness" (25). But like the other women here, the sisters do not rebel against woman's traditional role. They take up "doctrines" only in the hope of attracting men as age destroys their beauty, for they are "painfully anxious . . . to maintain their places but yet a little longer in that delicious world of love, sighs, and dancing partners, from which it must be so hard for a maiden . . .

to tear herself forever away" (25). Even these grotesque women prove that it is woman's nature to live for love.

Unlike most of Trollope's novels, *The Three Clerks* has an honest-to-god villain who demonstrates the full horror of masculine ambition untempered by feminine goodness. Since women in this novel elevate and reform, it is appropriate that the unscrupulous Undecimus Scott, who coldy tempts Alaric to ruin, should be a man from whose life female influences have been excluded. Undy's father, the Earl of Gaberlunzie, advises his eleven sons to sell their names in loveless marriages. Undy marries for money and then chooses to live apart from his wife— spending his nights in a rented room and dining at his club. The narrator expresses his contempt for Undy in Dickensian cadences: "With what a savage joy, with what exultation of heart, with what alacrity of eager soul, with what aptitude of mind to do the deed, would I hang my friend, Undy Scott . . . if I could but get at his throat for such a purpose! Hang him! ay, as high as Haman!" (44). Undy is a warning of the moral destruction that threatens men who reject female influence, a warning of what Alaric might have become without Gertrude, or Charley without Katie. To save a single man from so terrible a fate is, in *The Three Clerks,* sufficient reward for any woman.

Marriage and Mobility in *Doctor Thorne*

As many critics have noted, *Doctor Thorne* (1858) dramatizes the pressure that the social changes accompanying industrialization placed upon rural England. The novel is set in East Barsetshire, a "purely agricultural" bastion of Tory conservatism, "agricultural in its produce, agricultural in its poor, and agricultural in its pleasures" (1). But though the narrator claims that "England is not yet a commercial country" (1), so many invaders from the world of commerce appear in the Barset of *Doctor Thorne* that it is no exaggeration to call the novel "one of the broadest studies of the parvenu in Victorian literature."[16] The pastoral county of Barset is once again threatened, but here the threat does not come, as in *Barchester Towers,* from the forces of reform. It comes instead from the temptations of wealth and power in a mobile society, temptations that undermine the commitment of its natural defenders to the values of the pastoral world.

In their discussions of class conflict and social mobility in *Doctor Thorne,* however, critics have not remarked the extent to which Trollope focuses his attention on the way social mobility affects marriage.[17] The novel opens with an analysis of two marriages that were ruined by the divisive effects of ambition; it closes by showing how the heirs of these two families unite a divided world when they enter a marriage based upon traditional English values. In the process, Trollope makes yet another conservative estimate of the role a woman should play in society. One might argue, indeed, that the comedy in *Doctor Thorne* is even more conservative than the comedy in *Barchester Towers.* Eleanor and Arabin, tempted by modernity, must return to traditions from which they have strayed, but which are still alive and well among their fellow townsmen. The romantic hero and heroine of *Doctor Thorne,* however, have a more difficult task. Before they can achieve the comic conclusion, they must recover a moral tradition that most of the older generation has lost or betrayed.

The novel opens with a retrospective that shows how the Gresham family got into the financial difficulties that threaten to overwhelm it. When the Tory Squire Francis Gresham married Lady Arabella De Courcy, daughter of the great Whig family, they were a wealthy couple, admired by their tenants "in spite of a little hauteur." Twenty years later his estate was heavily mortgaged, and "none of [the tenants] were proud of him" (1). The unity—and even the viability—of the estate has been destroyed, and the Gresham marriage is the cause.

Squire Gresham made a socially ambitious match, and Lady Arabella was aware that she had married beneath her. Not a very intelligent or practical woman, Lady Arabella demanded that her husband attempt to place himself on a footing of equality with the De Courcys by emulating them in everything. Within two years of his marriage, the Squire's tenants noticed that "he was somewhat less familiar with them than of yore, that he had put on somewhat too much of the De Courcy airs" (1). Lady Arabella decides "to live as she had been accustomed to do" (1), and soon the Greshams are in debt. But the most destructive of Lady Arabella's efforts to turn her husband into a De Courcy comes when she pressures him to take the Whig side in politics.

Lady Arabella is one of those modern women who want to be something more than domestic goddesses: "She was one who would fain be doing something if she only knew how" (1). The plight of such women receives great, if not unmixed, sympathy in Trollope's later work, where he frequently shows them to be both intelligent and responsible. But in this early novel Lady Arabella's ambition proves as ludicrous as Mrs. Proudie's lust for power did in *Barchester Towers*. Lady Arabella is stupid in the way she goes about trying to gain political influence—unlike such politically ambitious women as Alice Vavasor or Lady Laura Standish in the Palliser novels. They hope to marry men whose views coincide with their own and to help them gain power—with money in Alice's case, with social influence in Lady Laura's. Though these plans fail, they are not illogical.

But Lady Arabella's plan for her husband is doomed by its very nature. As the daughter of a Whig family married to a Tory member who lives in a conservative district, she foolishly decides to "turn her respectable young Tory husband into a second-rate Whig bantling" (1). In her pride of rank she fails to see that her husband can stay in politics only if he pleases his constituents by remaining a committed Tory. Working on Squire Gresham's ambition to be accepted by the Whig aristocracy, she turns him into "such a member—so lukewarm, so indifferent, so prone to associate with the enemies of the good cause" (1) that he soon disgusts the voters and loses his seat.

At this point, Squire Gresham learns his lesson and would be happy to spend his remaining years as Master of Fox Hounds, a necessary, though expensive, job that he is capable of performing well—indeed, he knows "every hound by name" (1). But Lady Arabella will "allow nothing near him or around him to be well" (1); she persistently pushes for showy expenditure, while opposing her husband's involvement in hunting. This power struggle ends in a draw: "Lady Arabella, though it could hardly be said of her that she was under her husband's rule, certainly was not entitled to boast that she had him under hers" (1). Unable to agree, they decide to tolerate one another's extravagance. Through failure to give up their own desires, as well as through ambition and pride, the Greshams approach disaster. A marriage in which husband and wife wield equal power, but will not make sacrifices for the family welfare, is even less satisfactory than a marriage in which a selfish husband rules. The Greshams would be better off if the Squire dominated his wife, but this he cannot do because of the power her rank gives her. Thus the modern promise of speedy, dramatic upward mobility and the equally modern phenomenon of female ambition undermine the traditional distribution of power that might have saved the Greshams from ruin.

When the novel opens, the Gresham estate can be saved only if the heir, young Frank Gresham, can be convinced that "he has no alternative. In his position he must marry money" (4). Because of his parents' failure, Frank cannot both do his duty to the estate and remain true to the girl he loves, penniless, baseborn Mary Thorne. Through a most un-Trollopian coincidence—doubtless attributable to the fact that *Doctor Thorne*'s plot was suggested to Trollope by his brother, Tom—the creditor who is about to seize the Gresham estate is Mary's uncle, the self-made magnate, Sir Roger Scatcherd.

Years earlier, disaster struck the newly married stonemason Roger Scatcherd, when his sister was raped by a neighboring "gentleman," Henry Thorne—brother of the virtuous Doctor Thorne. Henry thought he could get away with violence toward a working-class girl, but Scatcherd upset Henry's calculations by murdering him. Scatcherd later works his way to fortune and a baronetcy, but as a rich man from a working-class background, he finds in alcohol the only consolation for his social displacement. The cruelty of the upper classes and the social system that leaves a worker who earns a fortune nothing to do but die and pass it on to more genteel heirs combine to ruin this talented man.

Trollope carefully parallels the Gresham and Scatcherd marriages with one another. Squire Gresham hoped by means of his marriage to leap from the squirearchy into the aristocracy; Lady Arabella, her husband's social superior, could not accept her subordinate role as a wife. Similarly, class-related stresses ruin Sir Roger's marriage. The honest, sober young worker, with a wife from his own class, should have been happy and respectable. But the difficulties of his rapid rise in the world strain his promising marriage. As he starts to rely on drink, his uneducated wife becomes an embarrassing appendage. He can be called "Sir Roger" in something other than a spirit of complete mockery, but she is just a joke as "Lady Scatcherd." He can no longer respect her, for his success has changed his values, desires, and ambitions.

Sir Roger is a "masterful man . . . accustomed to rule his wife and household as despotically as he did his gangs of workmen" (12). A wife like Lady Scatcherd, temperamentally inclined to worship her husband "as it behoved her to do" (10), could never have tried to dominate such a man the way Lady Arabella tried to rule her husband. But she might have retained some influence, had their marriage remained the economic partnership of a working-class couple. As it is, she knows he is drinking himself to death but can do nothing: "Sir Roger was his own master, and if kill himself he would, kill himself he must" (22). Despite his contemptuous treatment of her, his death leaves her heartbroken, a true wife who has nothing to do but uselessly fold and refold the linen that her household no longer needs. If the Gresham marriage foundered because the wife claimed too much power, the Scatcherd marriage fails because the husband denies his wife her legitimate influence. The love between these spouses could not survive the psychological strains to which a flexible, but powerful, class system subjected it.

These marital failures, however, are not really as symmetrical as their pairing would seem to imply. The Gresham marriage is unbalanced because the wife challenges the husband's authority, though she cannot overthrow it. The Scatcherd marriage is unbalanced because the wife has no influence at all. In *Doctor Thorne*, then, a wife's legitimate role is not to wield power but to exercise influence freely granted her by an authoritative husband who can see that she deserves it precisely because she does not demand it. Trollope affirms the ideal of wifely subordination by suggesting that it is just as disastrous for a wife to claim equal power as it is for the husband to disregard her completely.

Frank Gresham must suffer for his father's ambition, and so, in a far more serious sense, must Sir Roger's pathetically named son, Louis Phillipe, pay the price of his father's rapid rise in the world. Like other self-made Englishmen, Sir Roger wanted his heir to become a gentleman, and so sent him to Eton and Cambridge. This prescription for achieving gentility was often effective, but in Louis Scatcherd's case the whole process is too accelerated for safety. At Eton, Louis learns that boys "are at least as exclusive as men" (24) and starts drinking to deal with the social pressure to which his anomalous status subjects him. Louis reaps "the fruits of the worst education which England was able to give him" (24) and dies of delirium tremens.

Through the Scatcherds and the older generation of Greshams, Trollope demonstrates that the quick and easy social mobility characterizing Victorian England can place considerable strain on family relationships. But clearly he is not condemning all mobility. When members of the upper classes like Squire Gresham grow selfish and effete, an infusion of new blood from society's lower ranks is needed. The effects of this "blood restoration"[18] are salutary for society as a whole, though the process, unfortunately, may bleed individuals like Roger Scatcherd to death. And the straightforward romantic comedy that is the main plot of *Doctor Thorne* shows the positive side of social mobility by suggesting that an unequal marriage can be unequal in constructive ways. Through the marriage of Frank Gresham and Mary Thorne—the surviving heirs to the unsatisfactory Gresham and Scatcherd marriages—Trollope demonstrates that a successful marriage can cross class lines if it is contracted in a spirit of respect for what is best in the English moral tradition. Gradual social mobility is beneficial and traditionally English; rapid changes in class are harmful and modern.

In contrast to Louis Scatcherd, Mary Thorne, the illegitimate daughter of Roger Scatcherd's sister and Henry Thorne, demonstrates the way an individual should rise from one class to another. Cared for from birth by her gentlemanly uncle, properly educated, befriended by the Gresham family, Mary gradually and naturally becomes a lady in both feelings and manners. She makes the social and moral transition which Louis Scatcherd could not achieve during his few years at Eton, but she is still baseborn. Can she then be a suitable wife for a gentleman like Frank Gresham?

Mary originally believes that a woman in her position is not a fit wife for a man in Frank's, but she comes to assert the primacy of love as a basis for marriage. Doctor Thorne, the only member of the older generation who has not surrendered to modern values, is a great believer in the importance of blood, and he has passed this belief on to Mary. Mary rejects Frank's first proposal partly because he is just a boy but also because "she would give no one a right to accuse her of assisting to ruin the young heir" (23). But her views change under the pressure of her growing love for Frank. She begins to wonder "what, after all, was this blood of which she had taught herself to think so much? Would she have been more honest, more fit to grace an honest man's hearthstone, had she been the legitimate descendant of a score of legitimate duchesses?" (29).

So Mary accepts Frank's second proposal, having decided that her love for him obligates her to take him if their marriage is necessary to his happiness. But she determines to leave Frank free to break the engagement should he decide it is unwise. In this way Mary rejects her earlier views on the value of blood, while still allowing that a man's conception of duty might go beyond the affirmation of personal affection upon which she, as a woman, takes her stand. But offering to free Frank is a different thing from terminating the engagement herself. When Mary decides that gentility of feeling is more important than blood, she rejects the only aspect of the well-born Doctor Thorne's value system that is self-interested and out of harmony with sound English tradition, for the English aristocracy has traditionally been an open one, welcoming outsiders who can prove that they have learned its manners and embraced its values.

But it is not easy for either the reader of *Doctor Thorne* or for most of its characters to say that Mary and Frank ought to maintain their engagement in the face of so much evidence that their marriage will complete his family's ruin. Ought Frank to become a tenant on the remnant of his father's estate for love of a baseborn girl? Surprisingly, the answer to this question proves to be yes. Unlike the romances in such novels as *Barchester Towers* or *Framley Par-*

sonage, the romance between Frank and Mary is not prolonged by misunderstandings or even by family opposition, which they ultimately defy. Having taken their stand, they wait a year simply to prove that their love is strong enough to bear suspense, and then they assert their right to marry. Although every prudential consideration urges Frank to give up the engagement, he chooses love and remains, for one of Trollope's childish young heroes, surprisingly firm. Mary asks him, "Is not this imprudent? Is it not wrong?" And he answers her stoutly, "I say it is not wrong; certainly not wrong if we love each other" (36).

And to this commitment he remains true, until the very moment when, about to become a working farmer, he learns that, though Mary will never have blood, she now possesses untold wealth. Because Mary and Frank have maintained their feeling for one another against the pressures that threatened to crush it "by the very weight of metal" (41), they are still united and hence able to benefit from Mary's good fortune. Where his father allowed modern ambitions to take precedence over traditional duties, Frank, though he marries a baseborn girl, acts like a true Tory gentleman—placing personal integrity before gain of any sort. Respect for blood is not the most important of traditional English values, he and Mary both realize. Sincerity and decency come first. Thus Frank and Mary rediscover a moral tradition that has been lost by his parents—and distorted even by Doctor Thorne himself—and the comic conclusion is premised on this rediscovery.

Frank and Mary's marriage is ideally conservative in being free from any modern mercenary taint, and it is ideal as well in Mary's conservative refusal to use the leverage that her money might have given her to claim equality of power with her husband. Social mobility, which tends to unbalance the traditional power relations of marriage, is no threat when a wife is committed to traditional views of woman's place. And unlike many intelligent women in Trollope's later novels, Mary never resents her powerless position as a female. Asked to wait alone in the drawing room while Doctor Thorne and the Gresham men arrange her future, Mary "obediently did as she was bid; and there she sat, for the next three hours, wondering, wondering, wondering" (46). She does not protest, or

even regret, her exclusion. Mary proves her commitment to a conservative view of woman's place when she freely gives "all that had
ever appertained" (47) to the Greshamsbury estate back to Frank,
refusing to tie it up legally on her own behalf. "She would only
trouble herself to see that [Frank] was empowered to do as he did
think fit" (47). And because she is so deserving, Mary need not
fear that her husband will deny her a wife's legitimate influence.
Thus Frank and Mary's marriage redeems the failures of the older
generation.

Marriage, in *Doctor Thorne,* is central both to the unity of society
and to personal happiness. The Gresham estate is regenerated not
just by Mary's money but also by the guidance she and Frank, as
a perfect couple, will bring to it. Trollope never implies here, as
he does in so many later novels, that Victorian marriage offers a
wife insufficient scope for action. Lady Arabella is dissatisfied with
domesticity, but her dissatisfaction is completely unjustified. The
institution of marriage, at its best, is the moral center of the novel,
the force that cures—just as it was in *The Three Clerks.* In a materialistic, unstable world, the good marriage may be hard to achieve,
but that is the fault of materialism and instability, not of marriage
itself.

And for a well-disposed woman, marriage is a surer prescription
for happiness here than it will ever be again, healing disease literally
as well as figuratively. When Mary asks the doctor how two of his
female patients are getting along, he replies that the wealthy widow
is "really as bad as ennui and solitude can make her," while the
poor wife "is getting better, because she has ten children to look
after, and twins to suckle" (36). The only thing to do with a likeable
female character whose fate has not been decided when the story
ends is to promise her marriage: "Patience also, of course, got a
husband—or will do so. Dear Patience! it would be a thousand
pities that so good a wife should be lost to the world" (47).

But the way Trollope arranges the conservative comic conclusion
of *Doctor Thorne* is suspiciously facile. Mary and Frank win through
by refusing to allow conceptions of duty which are tainted by the
ambitious ethos of Victorian England to destroy their love. Then,
quite illogically, Trollope rewards them with a fortune that would

satisfy the most rabidly ambitious couple. Mary, offered the possibility of power in marriage by her commercial fortune, refuses it, though her lawyer's "scanty hairs . . . almost stood on end as he thought of the outrageous manner in which the heiress prepared to sacrifice herself" (47) for her penniless husband. We know, however, that Frank will not deny Mary the power that she voluntarily sacrifices. And so this couple magically takes the best of the new world and incorporates it into their ultratraditional arrangement. The ideal of disinterested love and feminine subordination is affirmed, but in the novel's dark world Frank and Mary's remarkable luck appears anomalous. It is no wonder that critics of *Doctor Thorne* have been disturbed by the fairy-tale way in which it takes troubling social problems like commercialization and female powerlessness and effortlessly solves them on the personal level.[19]

The Bertrams, or Rebellion Repressed

Women who are ambitious to leave their proper sphere or meddle with matters for which they are not intellectually suited are by no means rare in the three novels we have just discussed. But most of these rebels are minor comic characters like Mrs. Proudie and Lady Arabella. The only heroine who joins them is Eleanor Bold, and her rebellion is tentative and childishly misguided. Though she is the heroine of *Barchester Towers,* no one takes her very seriously. The major women characters in *The Three Clerks* and *Doctor Thorne* are content with woman's traditional role, even if, as in the case of Gertrude Woodward, the corrupting effects of materialism prevent them from playing it well. In *The Bertrams* (1859), however—for the first time since *The Noble Jilt*—the heroine herself is a powerful rebel, able to articulate her discontent with women's limited opportunities. As we have seen, Trollope was unable to make such a heroine simultaneously likeable and threatening in *The Noble Jilt*; *The Bertrams'* heroine is equally problematic, though for different reasons.

Those few critics who have discussed *The Bertrams* agree that it is an incoherent failure. In a typical appraisal, Kincaid calls it "the least controlled of Trollope's dark comedies. What appears at the beginning to be the main plot is submerged so deeply and for so long that it has to be hauled to the surface with much unpleasant straining at the end; the startling religious theme seems to be connected only loosely to the love stories."[20] Polhemus locates two additional problems: "illogical subplots" and "discrepancies in tone."[21] The critics are certainly correct that *The Bertrams* is a mess. The book's narrator seems uncertain of what is important and what peripheral to the tale he is telling. Two significant plots are dropped for long stretches, while self-contained subplots interrupt the main story line almost in the manner of Fielding's inset stories. The central plot seems to wander from its intended course and then to be yanked violently back at the eleventh hour. And this wreaks havoc with the consistency of the central characters.

But the failure of *The Bertrams* is both explicable and interesting and can be attributed to Trollope's growing sympathy for the plight of independent women. I shall argue that in beginning *The Bertrams* Trollope had a coherent, conservative plan for developing his characters, plot, and themes. The opening chapters of the novel introduce the reader to characters who are carefully contrasted with one another in terms of their relationship to several key themes. The character parallels thus established imply that the book will concern itself with how an increasingly competitive and materialistic social climate injures the moral character of both men and women. The novel's hero, George Bertram, seems slated to show how a childhood devoted to academic competition could destroy both a man's capacity for sustained work and his commitment to traditional standards of conduct. And the novel's heroine, Caroline Waddington, seems intended to demonstrate the evils of the modern woman's ambition to become something more than a loving wife to the first man who took her fancy. If George and Caroline's romance runs into trouble, these early chapters suggest, the guilt will be equally divided between them. The experiences of two contrasting characters, Arthur Wilkinson and Adela Gauntlet, will demonstrate the benefits of principled self-denial. Such a tale is exactly what one might have expected from the man who had just written *The Three Clerks* and *Doctor Thorne*.

But as the novel progressed, Trollope was unable to follow this plan because his sympathy for Caroline grew, while his interest in Adela and Arthur declined. The middle sections of the novel seem less a critique of Caroline's independence than a critique of the conventions that destroy her freedom. The narrator never acknowledges what is happening, and Trollope himself, apparently, was somewhat horrified at the direction his story had taken. So he tacked onto it an ending, which emphatically reasserts his original intention, an ending strikingly inappropriate to the story that has actually been told. Trollope's growing conflicts about women's ambitions never manifested themselves more clearly than in *The Bertrams*. Plot and characterization evoke great sympathy for the independent heroine, yet the narrator treats her with almost complete hostility. Subversive elements are far more important here than they were in Trollope's previous three novels. But the feminist subtext has forced an entrance in spite of Trollope's intentions to the contrary, and he has not yet devised the formal techniques for controlling it that were to emerge in the novels following *Framley Parsonage*. Consequently it rips the narrative apart.

The Bertrams begins with a diatribe against the stress English society places on competition. "Success is the god that we delight to worship" (I, 1), the narrator protests, and success is often meted out according to a proficiency in taking examinations that has little connection with the ability to do valuable work. The novel's two heroes are characterized through their relation to this system of artificial competition. Brilliant and lazy, George can gain the highest rewards by applying himself intermittently to his studies. But Arthur, though he works steadily, fails to earn a first. Both young men are attracted to new movements within the church but, characteristically, the undisciplined George supports the voluntary principle and disestablishment, while the self-denying Arthur prefers the rigors of the Oxford movement. The way in which the young men's experiences with the competitive system influence their religious development seems planned as an important theme in the novel.

Just as Arthur and George are characterized by their relationship to the competitive system, so are the women they love characterized by the degree to which they have been infected with the vice of ambition—including the unfeminine ambition to make a noise in the world. Adela, who incarnates feminine self-denial, is one of the most passive heroines Trollope ever created. She wants nothing but Arthur's love, the narrator remarks with little irony, and "would have been contented to live on potato-parings could he have been contented to live with her on potatoes" (I, 4). Her faith teaches her to endure suffering without resentment; she is fond of reminding her friends that there is always "more cause for thankfulness than for complaint" (I, 4).

Caroline, on the other hand, is the first of Trollope's ambitious young women who see marriage as a profession and who hope, by selecting the right man, to achieve both worldly success and scope for significant action. Annoyed that women have no other option than marriage, she protests irritably that "it is useless for a woman to think of her future; she can do so little towards planning it" (I, 10). But since marriage is a woman's only opportunity to influence her future, Caroline does not intend to be ruled by emotion either in choosing a husband or in dealing with him afterwards. "It was impossible," the narrator thinks, that Caroline "should ever grow into a piece of domestic furniture, contented to adapt itself to such uses as a marital tyrant might think fit to require of it" (I, 9)—to become, in short, an ordinary Victorian wife. Though she has no ambition beyond marriage, Caroline's resolution to cling to the coattails of a man likely to achieve wealth and fame—love is "only a third necessity" for her (I, 11)—violates the ideal of femininity and shocks the narrator.

In fact, the narrator finds Caroline's personality disturbingly masculine in several ways. He spends an entire paragraph struggling with the ambivalent emotions her beautiful eyes arouse in him: "What of her eyes? Well, her eyes were bright. . . . They were clever eyes too—nay, honest eyes also, which is better. But they were not softly feminine eyes. . . . bold eyes . . . daring eyes . . . courageous, expressive, never shrinking, sometimes also suspicious. They were fit rather for a man than for so beautiful a girl" (I, 9). Caroline's disturbing eyes are the outward sign of her "stubborn, enduring, manly will" (I, 9) and her masculine traits of mind. There is "something in her style of thought hardly suitable to the softness of girlhood. She could speak of sacred things with a mocking spirit" (I, 9)—and she often does.

At the outset, then, *The Bertrams* symmetrically contrasts its four young lovers in terms of their relationships to a society that worships success and correspondingly devalues personal relations and religious commitment. Unlike *The Three Clerks*—which it resembles thematically—*The Bertrams* suggests that women have been morally endangered by the spirit of competition and now want to live as if they were men. It appears to promise further development of these ideas, but this promise is only partly fulfilled.

At his father's death, Arthur forgets all about the Oxford movement and becomes a parish clergyman with no specially marked views. His problem is not with celibacy, as one might have expected, but rather with marriage. Forced to support his mother and sisters, Arthur decides that he cannot marry Adela, for he fails to see that poverty would not deter this selfless woman from accepting him. Arthur's failure of insight results partly from the worldliness fostered by years of academic competition, but far more directly from innate emotional obtuseness. The question of Arthur's religious development is dropped; the personal problems that prevent him from finding happiness seem only tangentially related to the issue of competition. The idea that Adela's religious commitment helps support her through years of suffering is more consistently developed, but on the whole Trollope loses interest in Arthur and Adela, who disappear from the middle portion of the novel to reappear only at its close.

Where the Arthur-Adela plot merely dwindles, the George-Caroline plot must be said to derail. Uncertain if he can accept ordination, because of his devotion to the voluntary principle, George goes to Jerusalem to test his vocation. Approaching the sacred city, he expects his heart "to melt into ecstatic pathos" (I, 6). But instead, exhausted from a day on horseback, he makes his entrance "swearing vehemently at his floundering jade, and giving up to all the fiends of Tartarus the accursed saddle which had been specially contrived with the view of lacerating the nether Christian man" (I, 6). Piety fails to conquer a sore bottom, but an inspiring visit to the Mount of Olives prevents George from losing his faith. The voluntary principle loses its importance to George, as the many warring sects in Jerusalem show him the unpleasant consequences of schism. Suddenly the church seems "to him to be the only profession in any way desirable" (I, 7).

But George finds himself unable to retain his sense of vocation when he meets Caroline. Immediately smitten, George takes her up on the Mount to propose that she become the mistress of the humble parsonage he plans to inhabit. In a scene closely paralleling the episode in Jane Austen's *Mansfield Park* where Mary Crawford pressures Edmund Bertram to abandon the church, the worldly, irreligious Caroline undermines George's conviction that he has chosen a noble profession. Like Mary, Caroline despises the average clergyman: "They are generally fond of eating, very cautious about their money, untidy in their own houses, and apt to go to sleep after dinner" (I, 10). Both temptresses hint that the teachings of Christianity fail to improve the character of those who disseminate them. Mary recommends the army and navy for having "everything in [their] favor; heroism, danger, bustle, fashion,"[22] and Caroline offers similar advice: "Earn [your bread] then in such a manner that the eyes of the world shall be upon you" (I, 10). Thus far, at least, Trollope successfully associates Caroline's ambitions with a disturbing cynicism about religion and with an ominous literary precursor.

In the Regency England of *Mansfield Park*, however, sound moral traditions ultimately triumph. Sir Thomas Bertram, tainted by the age's growing materialism, nonetheless raises his son Edmund to take the idea of duty seriously. But thirty years later the rot has spread—George Bertram's early Victorian childhood did not give him the firm principles that save Edmund. Unlike Edmund, George is the son of an amoral bon vivant; his uncle is a heartless miser; his guardian, Mr. Wilkinson, devoted himself to managing his son Arthur's quest for academic prizes. George's world has taught him that success alone is important and that success is measured by how often one gets the prizes for which one competes. Since Caroline is the prize George desires, the habits of a lifetime spent jumping through other people's hoops make it natural for him to decide that he will do whatever is necessary to win her. George feels "an intense desire for success when once he has committed himself to his offer" (I, 10) to marry Caroline, and his spiritual aspirations evaporate with ludicrous speed.

Up to this point Trollope has developed his ideas about competition, female ambition, and religious doubt according to plan. But George and Caroline's story now veers off course as Trollope's unacknowledged sympathy for Caroline begins to affect the way he develops her character. George decides to become a barrister, and Caroline, forgetting her resolution that she will marry only a man who is both wealthy and talented, accepts him. Good at acquiring any kind of knowledge for a purpose, George begins his studies with great success and presses Caroline to marry him immediately. Caroline, who understands the instability of George's character, worries that he is "not sufficiently collected, not sufficiently thoughtful, and perhaps almost too enthusiastic" (I, 11). She also knows that he has never experienced the slightest financial hardship. Because she feels sure that George cannot live contentedly with her on a small income, and not because she fears poverty for herself, Caroline refuses to break "the one great resolve of her life, that she would not be a poor man's wife" (I, 15). Though she knows that long engagements are hard on women, she insists for George's sake that he complete his studies before they marry.

Caroline's essentially altruistic decision is not, in fact, motivated by the ambition that the narrator originally stressed as the central feature of her character, but rather by a sound understanding of her lover's defects. By showing how damaging the atmosphere of competition in which he was raised has been to George's stability, Trollope has provided a justification for Caroline's refusal to trust him immediately. The competition theme intensifies and the antifeminist theme dies away when Caroline's decision to postpone the marriage offends the spoiled George, whose life has convinced him that endeavor should receive an instant reward. In begging him to accept the postponement, Caroline, no longer the coolly ambitious woman of the novel's opening section, takes George's arm and "almost press[es] it to her bosom" (I, 15), but this gesture of affection is lost on her angry lover.

Convinced that Caroline does not care for him and used to working only with an immediate aim, George abandons his legal studies. "Why should he work? Why sit there filling his brain with cobwebs. . . . He had had an object, but that was gone" (I, 17). He plunges into a course of sexual dissipation of which the narrator speaks rather openly. "He went down to Richmond with Twistleton, and Madden, and Hopgood, and Fortescue. Heaven knows what they did when they got back to town that night—or, rather, perhaps heaven's enemy. And why not? Caroline did not care whether or no he amused himself as other men do" (I, 17). George punishes Caroline by telling her exactly how he is spending his time.

Instead of studying, George writes a series of subversive religious pamphlets, and Caroline rightly sees this abrupt change in his religious views as further "proof of his unsteadiness" (I, 18). Though many of George's arguments have genuine force, his skepticism results not from conviction but simply from pique. He wants to show Caroline that her refusal to trust him has undermined his commitment to decency in thought as well as conduct, and he vents his anger at her by snubbing God. Caroline's response shows her characterization diverging further from its initial premises, for she reacts to George's apostasy with great distress—not, as one might have expected from her earlier skepticism, with indifference or pleasure.

If Caroline's decision to postpone her marriage needed justification, George's reaction surely provides it. But the narrator, failing to see the issue in this light, imposes an antifeminist interpretation on a situation that does not support it. George plunges into "a life of dissipation" (I, 18), and the narrator blames Caroline's unfeminine prudence for his weakness and irritability: "Miss Waddington had been very prudent, but there might perhaps have been a prudence yet more desirable" (I, 17). Nor does the narrator dissent when George tells Caroline that "all the changes in himself for the worse . . . were owing to her obstinacy" (I, 18). Instead, he mildly commends George for not becoming completely "filthy and vicious, callous and bestial" (I, 18), though Caroline's behavior has been so provoking. George makes a confidante of Caroline's friend Adela, complaining repeatedly that Caroline "has no heart" (I, 17), and the narrator does not fault him for disloyalty.

But when Caroline, wounded by her lover's cruelty, tells her sorrows to George's friend Henry Harcourt, the narrator—who has commented extensively on many matters only tangentially related to his story—condemns her and ignores the similarity between her conduct and George's. Yet if this sort of confidence is blamable, surely George is more blamable than Caroline. He seeks out Adela to accuse Caroline unfairly of heartlessness, whereas Henry schemes to ingratiate himself with the legitimately worried Caroline. After Henry maliciously lets George know of his intimacy with Caroline, George, conveniently forgetting his own intimacy with Adela, writes Caroline an insulting letter. Deeply stung, Caroline shows Henry the letter, and when George learns of this, he breaks their engagement, telling her quite falsely that he has "no friend to whom I allow the privilege of going between me and my heart's love" (I, 20).

Once again, however, the narrator does not acknowledge that a double standard is being applied here, and he agrees with George that Caroline committed a "great fault" (I, 18) in showing the letter. Indeed, he justifies George by an appeal to the very customs whose unfairness has just been demonstrated: "We—speaking for the educated male sex in England—do not like to think that anyone should tamper with the ladies whom we love" (I, 19). He mocks Caroline's unwillingness to abase herself when George attacks her, claiming she sees herself as a Juno "mindful of her pedestal, still remembering that there she stood a mark for the admiration of gods and men" (I, 20). Rejected by George, Caroline marries Henry—not to advance herself, but because she hopes to be of use as his wife—and the narrator stresses her growing realization that a resolution to do one's duty is not sufficient basis for marriage. George also regrets his actions, but the narrator never concludes that his was the greater guilt.

Caroline wins her freedom when the cold and domineering Henry—from whom she separates herself after a long struggle to make him a loyal wife—commits suicide. Henry's dishonesty has offended his political associates; he is deeply in debt; preferring death to disgrace, he shoots himself. His marital troubles had little, if anything, to do with his ruin, but the narrator, true to form, decides that Henry's tragic destruction is really Caroline's fault. Even such deserved disgrace as Henry's, he claims, should be lightened by the sympathy of a loving wife: "But there was no loving heart here. All alone he had to endure the crushing weight of his misfortunes" (II, 378, 24). Though the narrator blames Caroline both for Henry's death and for George's troubles, he offers little evidence to support either interpretation.

Caroline's story, then, does not turn out to be the promised tale of a girl corrupted by her thirst for independence. It emerges instead as the story of a prudent but loving woman. She is not destroyed by ambition but by the strange social law that requires her to subjugate herself to a lover whose judgment she rightly suspects. But the narrator's comments on this story sound for the most part as if it were proceeding as planned. And his inappropriate conclusions concerning the issues of male-female relations that the main plot raises are reinforced by its juxtaposition with the Adela-Arthur subplot, which surfaces toward the close of the novel.

Just as Caroline is clearly George's superior in character, so too is Adela superior to Arthur in terms of self-knowledge and strength of purpose. After timidly deciding that he cannot ask Adela to be his wife, Arthur tells her of his decision in a tactless manner and then spends several years miserably moping. But when Arthur rejects her, Adela, unlike George, does not become angry with her lover for what she sees as his mistaken prudence. Adela embraces the standard view of the sexes, forgiving faults of instability in men while she judges them harshly in women. When she reads Caroline's touching letter explaining her rupture with George, she feels no sympathy with her friend: "She condemned Caroline altogether" (II, 1). But she is quick to assure George that "she acquitted him . . . the greater fault was not with him" (II, 5). Although Adela sees a resemblance between Caroline's conduct and Arthur's, she blames only the former, and the narrator does not comment on her inconsistency.

The Bertrams ends with a chorus of praise for Adela. Even Caroline herself reaches the perplexing conclusion that Adela possesses "a truer, better, pride" than her own, in that Adela "could have brought [herself] to submit, to be guided, to be a secondary portion" (I, 19) of an "absolutely imperious" man who demands that his wife "serve him as his menial" (II, 1). The narrator predictably takes an even stronger line in praising Adela as the story closes. Though Arthur "was not worthy of her," Adela is "fully satisfied with her bargain—that she was so then and so continued—was a part of her worthiness. . . . She ever recognised him as her head and master" (II, 25). That Adela trusts herself to the guidance of an inferior man becomes the ultimate proof of her value as a woman. The story has shown that it would have been madness for Caroline to trust herself to the unstable George—but this is exactly what both characters and narrator decide that she should have done.

The details that conclude Adela's and Caroline's stories reinforce the narrator's peculiar estimate of their deserts. The reward of Adela's sacrifice comes not only from Arthur's realization "that God has given him an angel to watch at his side" (II, 25) but also in the gift of loving, healthy children. Caroline, on the other hand, suffers sterility as retribution for her sin against the ideal of feminine self-abnegation. This particular punishment was one that Victorian novelists often meted out to erring women. Though she is finally united with George, Caroline's married life is "childless, and very, very quiet" (II, 25). It seemed originally as if Caroline would be punished for sins of worldliness, impiety, and ambition, but she never commits these sins: the novel punishes her for claiming to be an autonomous human being.

About two-thirds of the way through the novel, Trollope, sensing that Caroline's story has gone off course, drops it as completely as he had earlier dropped Adela's. After painting himself into a corner with these two plots, Trollope had to decide what to do with the pages that remained to be filled. His solution was to insert three self-contained farcical subplots whose presence has mystified critics ever since. All three subplots deal with an independent woman like Caroline, and two of them compare her unfavorably with a feminine woman resembling Adela. The subplots, then, do have a function: in a different key, they restate the conservative views about women that the main plot had failed to develop consistently. Like the inappropriate conclusion, these subplots represent a desperate attempt to negate the feminist subtext and deliver the book to its original destination.

Long before the Caroline and Adela stories had gone awry, Trollope showed his uncertainty about what to do with the two characters when he used the space at his command to mirror them in parallel types of womanhood, rather than to develop them. The Muslim washerwomen in the Holy Land parody Adela's modesty, for they hold "in their teeth a dirty blue calico rag which passed over their heads . . . [and] concealed one side of the face and the chin. . . . They gave no sign of knowing that strangers were standing by them" (I, 9). A magnificent Jewish washerwoman, who appropriately stands out as a single figure, suggests the sinister side of Caroline's independence. "Her arms and neck were bare, as were also her feet; and it was clear that she put forth to her work as much strength as usually falls to the lot of a woman in any country. She was very fair to look at, but there was about her no feminine softness . . . no tenderness in the eye, no young shame at being gazed at" (I, 9).

This doubling continues in the subplots that fill the novel's last third. The character contrasts of the main plots are reflected, with comic distortion, in the story of Sir Lionel Bertram's simultaneous courtship of the independent Miss Todd and the timid Miss Baker. Like Caroline, Miss Todd knows more of life than a woman should. "*Au fait* at every bit of scandal" (II, 9), Miss Todd is well aware that her suitor keeps a mistress and is deeply in debt. Though Miss Todd is wealthy, Sir Lionel hesitates to propose to her because he knows that her husband will have to "struggle with every muscle of the manhood which was yet within him for that supremacy in purse and power which of law and right belongs to the man" (II, 9)—a reminder of the power struggle between George and Caroline. In spite of Miss Todd's many virtues, the narrator judges her as severely as he does Caroline for her sins against the ideal of feminine purity: "Miss Todd had been touching pitch for many years and was undoubtedly defiled" (II, 10).

Like Adela, Miss Baker is passive and pure. Miss Todd must enlighten the innocent Miss Baker in "a little conversation carried on . . . so entirely *sotto voce* that the reporter of this scene was unable to hear a word of it" (II, 10), concerning Sir Lionel's sexual misconduct. Miss Baker's sorrow at the loss of her lover is properly feminine, "a soft and gentle sorrow . . . neither loud, nor hysterical" (II, 10). Her passivity, like Adela's, earns the narrator's wholehearted approval.

A second self-contained subplot that also mirrors the main love plots concerns a shipboard flirtation between George and Arthur and two Anglo-Indian widows. The outspoken Mrs. Cox, with her "silvery, ringing laughter" (II, 17), is a sort of bargain-basement Caroline. The clinging Mrs. Price, whose "soft eyes" (II, 17) remind Arthur of Adela and who complains of faintness when dinner is delayed, falsely claims the kind of femininity Adela really possesses. But in the end, colonial women are not to be compared with ladies "who have lived in England, who have always had the comfort of well-arranged homes. They have been knocked about, ill-used, and forced to bear hardships as men bear them" (II, 17). When George and Arthur see this, they quickly retreat, understanding that not even the more feminine of these two experienced women will make a good wife.

The third subplot that Trollope implants in the last part of *The Bertrams* concerns the absurd delusion of Arthur's mother, Mrs. Wilkinson, that the patron of her son's living intended her to function as a sort of female vicar. When she and Arthur disagree about whether the parsonage belongs to him or to her, Mrs. Wilkinson goes to appeal her case to the patron, Lord Stapledean. After a hideously uncomfortable journey, she is reproved for her unwomanly aspirations by an angry Lord Stapledean: "Hold the living yourself! Why, are you not a woman, ma'am? . . . The woman's mad. . . . Stark mad" (II, 21). The most ludicrous parody of Caroline in the novel is humiliated in a final repudiation of feminine ambition.

Thus in the concluding section of *The Bertrams*, Trollope tries, by inserting several conservative subplots and by closing the main plot conservatively, to reverse the unexpected direction in which Caroline's story had developed. Caroline acknowledges crimes she has not committed, and in the process Trollope irreparably damages the consistency of her character. But the implicit sympathy with her strength, decency, and frustration exhibited by the middle portion of the novel is a harbinger of the new ideas about women that were shortly to appear in his work.

The Powerful Women of *Framley Parsonage*

Doctor Thorne's fairy-tale optimism undoubtedly explained its tremendous popularity. But *The Bertrams,* with its gloomy tone and unacknowledged feminist propensities "had quite an opposite fortune," failing to please even the author's best friends (*Autobiography,* 7). Immediately after the publication of *The Bertrams* in 1859, Trollope received an exciting commission to write the novel that would be serialized in the opening issues of Thackeray's *Cornhill Magazine.* Trollope knew this was a unique opportunity to increase his reputation and readership, and in planning his new novel, he did not forget the lessons that the contrasting fates of his two previous novels had suggested. He projected a work that would charm the public with its comic celebration of traditional English values—a celebration that not even *Doctor Thorne* could match.

In *Framley Parsonage* Trollope continues his investigation of a question first posed in *The Bertrams*: how can an intelligent woman control her environment in a world that reserves direct power for men? But he is careful to treat this potentially disruptive theme optimistically, to suggest that women can gain their legitimate ends without disturbing the status quo. He does not repeat the tactical error he made in both *The Noble Jilt* and *The Bertrams* of placing a formidable, discontented woman at the center of his work—and so creating problems of reader sympathy and identification. The central female characters in *Framley Parsonage,* Lady Lufton and Lucy Robarts, are by no means malcontents, though both have something to learn about how women should exercise power. Like Eleanor Bold—whose misguided ambitions are mild and easily surrendered—they overreach in the most forgivable manner. As Lady Lufton corrects her tendency to domineer, and Lucy corrects her tendency to defy convention, they fully retain the reader's affection.

In *Barchester Towers*, Eleanor must give up her ambition to exercise any influence beyond the boundaries of woman's narrow sphere. In *Framley Parsonage*, however, the female protagonists fulfill their desire for power and control. Unlike the heroines of *The Three Clerks* and *Doctor Thorne*, the women of *Framley Parsonage* experience longings that reach beyond marriage to the man they love: they have clear ideas about the kind of environment they would like, both within their homes and outside them. Unlike Eleanor, they do not have to renounce those desires and settle for love alone. By the time the novel closes, all its redeemable women have come to understand that they will achieve their goals if they teach by the example of their selflessness, rather than by precept. In this idyllic world, the women are influential because the men ultimately do respond to their goodness. By learning to exercise influence in feminine ways, these women finally succeed in arranging the world according to their desires—they earn the very reward that Victorian theory promised to the enduring, self-sacrificing woman.

Trollope acknowledges something here that his earlier novels tended to deny: many admirable women both want and deserve the power to control their lives. But he also suggests that though society does not grant women direct power, the indirect power it permits them to wield is so great that it ought to content them. In defending the pastoral world of East Barsetshire against a variety of menacing forces, the good women of *Framley Parsonage* find a cause that absorbs their energies and satisfies their need for achievement. The problem—so important in later Trollope novels—of what a good woman should do when a man misuses his power over her is raised only in the mildest of ways. In the Barset of *Framley Parsonage*, an enchanted island in space and time, the tension between being feminine and being human, a tragic tension in some of Trollope's later works, almost disappears.

Framley Parsonage is at once the most optimistic and the best unified of Trollope's early attempts to show that women should accept their traditional roles—a triumph of conservative comedy that delighted the public precisely because it suggested that women could gain their ends without threatening men. No wonder that in the years following its publication, as Trollope began to write novels that gave serious attention to the sufferings of dissatisfied women, he endeavored to hide the full extent of his sympathy from his readers, inventing and employing a wide variety of deceptive technical devices. He feared to alienate the public that had adored *Framley Parsonage,* and his fears were not without foundation.

Several of *Framley*'s many subplots are connected to the conflict between Lady Lufton, unwavering exemplar of Tory values, and the immoral duke of Omnium for the allegiance of the unsteady young heroes, Lord Lufton and Mark Robarts. Lady Lufton, widowed mother of two and foster-mother to many young friends, represents all that is best in matriarchy. Throughout the novel, she strives to make Framley into an orderly Tory parish directed by a resident landlord and a hard-working cleric. Initially, Lady Lufton is too fond of power, and before her ambitions for Framley can be realized, she must learn not to domineer. From the very start, however, she uses her power unselfishly, and even when she is wrong, her mistakes are generous ones. She wants to appoint a badly qualified mistress for the parish school, but only because "she is thinking more of her protegee than she does of the children" (1) and not because she is thinking of herself.

As her antagonist, the awe-inspiring Whig magnate, the duke of Omnium, is a grim parody of a patriarch. Lady Lufton is everyone's mother, but the duke is nobody's father. His only sexual relationship is a sterile affair with the married marchioness of Hartletop. Where Lady Lufton is passionate, if overbearing, in her efforts on behalf of various proteges, the duke ruins his without guilt. Where Lady Lufton actively manages her parish, the duke conducts all his vast concerns through an agent, while he devotes himself to pleasure.

The duke's friends attempt to lure Lord Lufton and Mark Robarts away from the safe, if not terribly thrilling, rural pleasures of East Barsetshire, into the exciting but dangerous worlds of West Barsetshire and London, while Lady Lufton tries to keep them at home. At issue is the future of Framley. Will it become the ideal parish Lady Lufton envisions or the neglected responsibility of an absentee landlord and a cynical clergyman? In the end Lady Lufton wins, but only because Lord Lufton and Mark respond to the example of generosity that she sets with increasing consistency—and only after she stops trying to control them. After failing to reform her reckless son by sensible advice that verges on nagging, Lady Lufton tries another tactic. When Lord Lufton gets involved financially with the wheeler-dealers of West Barsetshire, she discharges his debts, saying "hardly . . . a word to him as to that five thousand pounds" (13) she had paid on his behalf, tenderly protecting his masculine pride. Lord Lufton, touched, returns home for the winter.

Mother and son have a further disagreement when he selects Lucy Robarts as his bride—frustrating her scheme to marry him to a woman of her own choosing. Though Lady Lufton hates defeat, she loves her son so well that she agrees to accept Lucy, and her willingness to bend convinces all her friends that "she is the best woman that ever lived" (46). And as soon as she surrenders, Lady Lufton's relationship with her son improves. Everyone can see "how much he loved her for what she had done" (46) in agreeing to his marriage, and he decides to become the home-loving country magnate she wanted him to be all along. Thus Lady Lufton's increasing self-suppression in her dealings with Lord Lufton is rewarded with victory on the point she cares about most: his return to the duties of his position.

Originally Lady Lufton thinks that, as the patroness of Mark Robarts' living, she has a right to control him, and a lively power struggle develops between them, motivated more by Mark's unwillingness to be ruled by a woman than by real disagreement about how he should spend his time. Mark gives in to temptation not only because he is ambitious and avid for pleasure but also because he wants to show Lady Lufton who is boss: "He was not Lady Lufton's servant, nor even her dependent. So much he had repeated to himself on many occasions. . . . The fact of Lady Lufton having placed him in the living, could by no means make her the proper judge of his actions" (4). Lady Lufton's attempts to rule Mark backfire disastrously.

But when Mark's ambition results in his public disgrace, Lady Lufton charitably renounces her endeavors to assert her authority over him. She discusses the matter with him in the most feminine, considerate way imaginable; indeed, she "took away all the bitterness of the rebuke . . . she was so gentle to him" (46). No less conscientious than her son, Mark "could not but lean the more hardly on himself" (46) in response to her kindness. Soon he resolves to live out his life as a hardworking parish priest. Lady Lufton's experience validates the Victorian belief that the woman who defers to men controls them most effectively. She rescues Lord Lufton and Mark for the pastoral world, and her vision of Framley becomes a reality.[23]

Lady Lufton's feminine influence disarms her antagonist the duke with dreamlike ease. When the two foes collide accidentally at a party, Lady Lufton curtsies "with much feminine dignity" and "reprobate[s] the habitual iniquities of the duke" by the "haughty arrangement of her drapery" and the "gradual fall of her eye and the gradual pressure of her lips. . . . She spoke no word, and retreated, as modest virtue and feminine weakness must ever retreat, before barefaced vice and virile power; but nevertheless she was held by all the world to have had the best of the encounter" (29). Female virtue defeats male power by the use of body language alone—and the facility with which it does so suggests that in the world of *Framley Parsonage* a good woman has little to fear.

Lady Lufton and the duke are opposed to one another by every principle of their being. Two loving relationships in *Framley Parsonage,* however, resemble the interaction between these antagonists in that the woman triumphs over the man by feminine means. Through the relationship between Fanny and Mark Robarts, Trollope optimistically explores a situation that he treated more grimly in later novels: a woman married to her inferior in intelligence, strength, and decency. Fanny Robarts is no genius and Mark Robarts is not really a fool, but she is certainly the clearer thinking of the two. Like Lady Lufton, Fanny knows what shape she wants her world to take. She wants Mark to be a good parish priest and an attentive husband. But Fanny has to prove herself before her desire can be realized through Mark's acceptance of her values.

Mark rebels against Lady Lufton but avoids confronting her. He is a creative, if muddle-headed, rationalizer of his own restlessness, ambition, and cowardice. Again and again, Fanny sees that his weakness and confusion are leading Mark into bad courses, but she argues with him only in the most deferential manner. And she never denies him her love or support. Fanny, in fact, follows to the letter the Victorian prescription that a good wife should stand by her husband, submit to his authority even when she is sure he is mistaken, and try to redeem him with an occasional gentle word of counsel, accompanied by the eloquent example of her loving self-sacrifice. And in the end, Fanny's self-suppression, like Lady Lufton's, earns its reward.

When Mark decides to let Lady Lufton have her way about the appointment of the incompetent schoolmistress, so that he can have his way in taking a trip that interferes unwarrantably with his parish duties, Fanny knows his behavior is irresponsible. But after hinting that Mark is yielding on the wrong issue, Fanny "perceive[s] that, vexed as she [is], it would be better that she should say nothing further" (1), and she holds her tongue. When Lord Lufton proposes to his sister, Mark hopes Lucy will refuse the offer so as to save *him* from his patroness's further displeasure. Fanny does not reproach Mark for his outrageous egotism in asking Lucy to reject the man she loves in order to protect her brother from inconvenience. Instead, this loving wife tactfully suggests that she and Mark, "let their loyalty to Lady Lufton be ever so strong, could not justify it to their consciences to stand between Lucy and her lover" (31).

Fanny's affection is not diminished as Mark's recklessness brings debt and disgrace upon his family. When bailiffs arrive at the parsonage, Fanny rushes to assure Mark of her love. He tells her bitterly, "I wonder, Fanny, that you can bear to stay in the room with me" (44). "My own dear, dearest husband!" Fanny cries, "How can anything like this make a difference between you and me?" (44). When Mark most unclerically curses the friend for whom he has incurred debts, Fanny answers, "Vengeance is mine, saith the Lord." She speaks, however, as a woman ought, "not with solemn, preaching accent . . . but with the softest whisper into his ear" (44). And that soft whisper makes itself heard more distinctly than the loudest complaints. Mark resolves to give up signing bills and to resign the clerical appointment he obtained through the duke's influence. By her silent loyalty, Fanny becomes the dominant partner in her marriage.

With Mr. and Mrs. Crawley the pattern of a heroic woman married to a less heroic husband is repeated in a different key. The Robartses have faced the trial of premature prosperity, a trial that Trollope was always inclined to take seriously. When *Framley Parsonage* opens, Mark has already gained everything a man could wish for—a comfortable income, loving wife, the requisite two sons—and is suffering from acute ennui. The Crawleys, on the other hand, have had to face the greater trial of continued failure, living on the starvation wages of a perpetual curate in the unpleasant parish of Hogglestock. And Mr. Crawley has not borne up well under his fifteen years of undeserved suffering. Though he zealously discharges his duties, he resents more fortunate clerics. His touchy pride rejects all friendly attempts to ameliorate his family's suffering. Obsessed with his grievance against the church, Crawley sits for days, unable to work, "crying out that the world was too hard for him . . . that his God had deserted him" (14). Though he strives to remain an exemplary clergyman, Crawley's brand of Christianity, like Mark's, buckles under the pressures to which life subjects it.

But Mrs. Crawley rises to the occasion. "She was made of the sterner metal of the two, and could last on while he was prostrate" (14). Mrs. Crawley can experience injustice without being embittered by it and can understand the difference between true and false pride. Charity remains a virtue in her eyes, even though fate has forced her into the humiliating necessity of accepting it. When Fanny Robarts says that "of all my own acquaintance, Mrs. Crawley, I think, comes nearest to heroism" (22), no reader of *Framley Parsonage* would disagree.

The Crawleys show us the dark side of the pastoral world that *Framley Parsonage* celebrates; their subplot is the only part of the novel to suggest that this world stands in need of reform. The "time-honoured, gentlemanlike, English, and picturesque" arrangement (14) of clerical incomes, as the narrator remarks, creates five needy Mr. Crawleys for every prosperous Mark Robarts. But because *Framley Parsonage* is an idyll that affectionately memorializes what is best in English tradition, it does not explore the world of suffering and injustice the Crawleys inhabit. The Crawleys are on the edge of the story, just as their parish is on the border of East Barsetshire—a reminder of what has been excluded in order to create this warm and optimistic comedy.

And in terms of the power relations between them, the Crawleys also show us dark possibilities that the other subplots minimize, though these are not so fully explored as to undermine the novel's cheerful mood. Mr. Crawley is a doctrinaire advocate for male supremacy. When Lady Lufton asks him to help her convince Mark Robarts that a parson should not hunt, Crawley tells her harshly that her sex debars her from criticizing Mark: "It is not within a woman's province to give counsel to a clergyman on such a subject" (15). He rules his wife despotically, forbidding her to accept gifts that are necessary to maintain their children's health. Mrs. Crawley, desperate, deceives her husband and takes the aid she needs.

Nor, in the end, does Mrs. Crawley triumph over her husband as dramatically as Fanny Robarts triumphs over Mark. When Mrs. Crawley falls ill, Mr. Crawley continues for a while to refuse help. But when Lucy Robarts appears at his door prepared to nurse his wife, even Mr. Crawley can resist no longer. He values his wife more than his pride, and he acknowledges this tacitly by permitting Lucy to stay. But he never gives up his domineering ways or openly expresses his appreciation of Mrs. Crawley's character. She never gains the power to control her environment that Lady Lufton and Fanny both achieve. By gently reminding the reader that not every good woman can have their good fortune, Mrs. Crawley's experience qualifies the optimistic view of a good woman's influence that their stories imply. By darkening *Framley Parsonage* just a bit, the Crawleys make the pastoral world it depicts all the more convincing.

Framley Parsonage suggests that the word "heroism" is feminine in gender.[24] Most Victorians would have had no difficulty accepting the novel's implication that women are better able than men to endure suffering. They might have been surprised, however, that its women also act more practically and handle conflict more courageously than their husbands and sons, for these were "male"

virtues. But precisely because *Framley's* women are so self-abnegating, they can face an occasional conflict with the conviction that
they have nothing to hide or fear, though they state their views
with becoming modesty. The men, on the other hand, are plagued
by ambition, false pride, and an inability to deal with unpleasantness. They often hesitate to defend positions that they have espoused, at least in part, for selfish reasons.

The proper kind of heroism for a woman is the real issue in the
struggle that develops between Lord Lufton and his mother over
whether Lucy Robarts would make him a suitable wife,[25] and in
the struggle between Lucy and her conscience over whether she
should accept him. Lady Lufton must learn that Lucy does indeed
possess the kind of heroic strength that her son's wife ought to
have. For though the forceful Lady Lufton likes powerful women,
she thinks that there is only one kind of power appropriate for
young ladies. "The species of power in young ladies which Lady
Lufton most admired was the *vis inertiae* belonging to beautiful
and dignified reticence" (35). But the "species of power" to be found
in a reserved demeanor merely parodies the real power exercised
by the good women in this novel, who exert influence by their
quiet, submissive manner toward men. Beneath their passive surfaces, however, women like Mrs. Crawley and Fanny Robarts are
able to think for themselves. They choose quiescence out of strength,
not weakness, because they accept the theory of feminine subordination, and not because they cannot articulate their own thoughts.

By contrast, Griselda Grantly, the girl whom Lady Lufton prefers
as a bride for her son, possesses only the dignified demeanor; there
is no comprehension underneath. Griselda's silence does not indicate principled suppression of feeling, but a lack of anything
deeply felt to say. When her mother, with fear and trembling, tells
Griselda that her magnificent engagement to Lord Dumbello may
be broken off, Griselda calmly responds that, if there is to be no
marriage, she "had better give them orders not to go on with the
marking [of her wedding clothes]" (45). This would indeed be the
proper feminine response were the calm assumed and not completely genuine. Lady Lufton has mistaken the outward manifestation of feminine strength, quiescence, for the underlying reality.

Lucy Robarts, Griselda's foil, originally diverges from the novel's ideal of femininity because she lacks self-control. Lucy must learn the true nature of feminine heroism and Lady Lufton must realize that she has learned it. Lucy's dark coloring, "exquisitely rich and lovely" (10), provides a clue to her dangerously passionate and independent character. At the beginning of the novel, Lucy, proud of being "blessed with an intelligence keener than that of her brothers or sisters" (10), claims the right to defy convention in minor ways. She encourages Lord Lufton in his attempts to get to know her, "sure that in a little time she could feel a true friendship for him, and that she could do so without any risk of falling in love with him," even though she dimly realizes "that such a friendship would be open to all manner of remarks, and would hardly be compatible with the world's ordinary ways" (12). Soon Lucy finds that her confidence was misplaced, for she does indeed fall in love with Lord Lufton. When she hears that he is likely to marry Griselda she cannot contain her anger. In a startling exhibition of sexual jealousy, she lashes the pony she is driving, while "the tell-tale blood . . . suffuse[s] her face" (21). Lucy's deviation from *Framley Parsonage*'s ideal of feminine self-suppression suggests that she may be headed for disaster.

But no disaster materializes, for Lucy quickly learns the lesson of control. Realizing that her unconventional friendship with Lord Lufton has brought her to grief, Lucy quietly ends their intimacy. Lord Lufton demands an explanation of Lucy's reserve, telling her, "I have liked you so much . . . because you get out of the grooves . . . and go along by yourself, guiding your own footsteps; not carried hither and thither, just as your grandmother's old tramway may chance to take you" (16). Horrified by this accurate description of her defiant behavior, Lucy repudiates her past unconventionality: "Do you know I have a strong idea that my grandmother's old tramway will be the safest and the best after all? I have not left it very far, and I certainly mean to go back to it" (16).

And Lucy renounces her unconventional tendencies with a vengeance, refusing to accept Lord Lufton's proposal until Lady Lufton will accept her as a daughter-in-law. Lucy knows that she is not strictly bound to give up her lover merely because his mother dislikes her and that her decision might well be described as cowardly. But because she has just experienced the evils of self-assertion, she prefers to err on the side of safety. She will defer to Lady Lufton's rights in the prescribed feminine manner, Lucy decides, only partly motivated by a proud reluctance to go where she is not wanted. This act of self-suppression is followed by an equally heroic act of self-sacrifice, when Lucy risks her life to nurse Mrs. Crawley.

Thus Lucy moves toward the novel's ideal of femininity, proving once again that strength and restraint are not incompatible. And once again principled self-suppression wins power and happiness for the feminine woman: Lady Lufton comes to see that Lucy is "a good girl . . . ready-witted, too, prompt in action, gifted with a certain fire" (43), even though her manner never will have that commanding repose which Lady Lufton has always considered the outward sign of inner strength. Lady Lufton wanted a "pink and white giantess of fashion who would frighten the little people into their proprieties" (43) to support her son's dignity, but she learns that Lucy does have the strength she sought, though it manifests itself differently. Through her marriage, Lucy gains everything she ever wanted: wealth, status, scope for action as the lady of the manor, as well as a lovable husband with a pair of "fine, straight legs" (26).

Trollope only twice varies the pattern by which *Framley Parsonage* assigns the preservation of the pastoral world to its female characters. Griselda Grantly's quiet manner suggests that she is one of the novel's selfless women, but in fact she is as heartless as the duke of Omnium himself. Because she is not truly feminine, Griselda is no true denizen of Barsetshire. And it is therefore fitting that Griselda should marry the aptly named Lord Dumbello and that the duke should fail to establish the newly married couple in Barsetshire.

The duke's desire to obtain a Barsetshire home for Lord Dumbello is foiled by Miss Dunstable, the other woman who varies the novel's usual pattern of female decency reclaiming male weakness. The immensely rich Miss Dunstable is good at heart, but like Lord Lufton and Mark, she is in danger of being lured away from the pastoral world. She goes to London and appears to be growing ever more cynical. But Miss Dunstable is saved by a proposal from honest Doctor Thorne, the only man ever to offer her real affection. She gratefully accepts him, and the two settle in Barsetshire.

In the subplot involving Griselda an unworthy woman is expelled from Barsetshire, while in the Miss Dunstable subplot a good man returns an endangered woman to her proper place: the country. These subplots vary, but do not really undermine, the novel's dominant pattern in which heroic women draw their men back to the rural world of East Barsetshire. Lady Lufton makes a yearly trip to London, but she makes it unwillingly; the other women remain at home. Through their influence Lord Lufton and Mark Robarts return to their duties; through their kindness, Mr. Crawley's bitterness is at least somewhat softened. The triumph of sound English tradition, the triumph of the pastoral world, is, no less significantly, also the triumph of women—who by the end of the novel have turned their most ambitious dreams into sober realities.[26] But only in a world as gently comic, as delightfully idealized, as that of *Framley Parsonage,* can female strength, female desire for power, and a set of social arrangements requiring female submission coexist so happily.

3 *Subverting the Ideal*

Innocence and Experience in *Orley Farm*

The changing titles of Trollope's novels reveal his growing interest in women's experiences. The title of *Barchester Towers* draws the reader's attention to the church, an institution controlled by men. "The Three Clerks" and "Doctor Thorne" are men; "The Bertrams" is an all-male family. "Framley Parsonage" is the officially designated home of the Vicar of Framley—and only incidentally that of his wife. Male concerns are indeed central in these five novels, whose female characters, as we have seen, tend to be portrayed through their relationships with men and judged by their success in managing those relationships. The title of *Orley Farm* (1862), however, marks a change, referring as it does to the estate that an angry woman steals from her husband. The next four novels prove that this shift of interest from men to women was significant and lasting: "The Small House at Allington" is the home of a mother and her daughters; "Rachel Ray" is a woman; and the titles of *Can You Forgive Her?* and *Miss Mackenzie* announce the sex of their protagonists. As their titles suggest, these novels do more than identify the role women should play in a world dominated by men; they explore women's own experience of that world. Women's concerns become central, and their grievances obtain a sympathetic hearing.

The heroic women of *Framley Parsonage* are content to influence the world through their influence on their husbands and sons. Only with *Orley Farm* does Trollope begin to investigate the problems of a strong woman married to a man who does not respond to the moral suasion that works so well for *Framley*'s women. In marriage, the narrator of *Orley Farm* admits, the husband "has the power of the purse and the power of the law" (41) on his side, leaving the wife little to fall back on if tender influences fail. *Orley Farm* is the first of Trollope's novels to suggest that the mistreated wife is a more significant social problem than the henpecked husband—a change that may well result from the discussion of England's marriage laws that the women's movement had generated.

As he ponders the experiences of unhappily married women and comes to understand how suffering can change them, Trollope questions the notion that the most admirable women are those who have been most effectively sheltered from evil. *Orley Farm* suggests that women, like men, can grow morally through experiencing pain, responsibility, temptation—and even sin. This idea had forced its way into *The Three Clerks*, only to be speedily ejected. But here it becomes a central organizing principle. *Orley Farm* therefore demonstrates a much greater interest in older women than most Victorian novels, which tend to find such women boring if they are sheltered and happy or unappealing if they have lived too much. *Orley Farm* makes a two-pronged attack on the very notion of the angel in the house, for it suggests that many angelic wives fail to humanize their men, while others are stunted in their own moral development by the conditions of angelhood itself.[1]

Orley Farm's main plot contrasts two aging widows, Lady Mason and Mrs. Orme, each of whom was left after a short marriage to raise her only son. Lady Mason comes out of the business world, whose influence on an England where "all men are [now] more or less commercial" (6) the narrator deplores. Commerce at its most extreme can be seen in the novel's traveling salesmen; they become grotesque caricatures of the products in which they trade. The overweight Mr. Moulder sells groceries, while the angular Mr. Kantwise peddles metal furniture in "real Louey catorse" style (6). The commercial world, which deforms everyone it touches, trades in everything, including women: Lady Mason's bankrupt father sold her in marriage to his associate, Sir Joseph Mason, who is a full forty-five years older than his newly purchased bride.

Much later, Lady Mason explains why she agreed to marry Sir Joseph: "When they bade me marry the old man because he was rich, I obeyed them,—not caring for his riches, but knowing that it behoved me to relieve them of the burden of my support" (60).

Although Lady Mason was not deeply corrupted by her parents' materialism, she accepted their view that a female child, incapable of earning her own living, ought to relieve her family of the burden of caring for her at whatever cost to herself. Ironically, her belief that she is a worthless burden helps Lady Mason endure her unpleasant marriage with equanimity. Though Sir Joseph acted as "[her] master rather than [her] husband," Lady Mason nonetheless "served him truly" (79). She expected only that when her husband died she "should have the means to live" (60). Feeling she deserves nothing, Lady Mason at first is content with very little more than that.[2]

But Lady Mason is incapable of the permanent self-abnegation her husband demands. When she gives birth to a son, the apathy underlying her obedience disappears: "Till he lay in my arms I had loved nothing. . . . The world was all altered for me. What could I do for the only thing that I had ever called my own?" (60). Because she has been so thoroughly dispossessed, Lady Mason develops a twisted passion for this child who is her only possession. Scenes between Lady Mason and the grown Lucius suggest that Lady Mason's maternal fervor substitutes for the sexual love she has never known: "She then kissed him again and again, with warm, clinging kisses. She clung to him, holding him close to her" (63). Because Lady Mason feels valueless as a woman, she unconsciously seizes her chance to gain importance by asserting the value of her male child. Lady Mason simply cannot acquiesce in Sir Joseph's intention to bequeath all his land to his elder son, and she begs him to leave Orley Farm to Lucius: "Was he not his son as much as that other one. . . . Never once did I ask of him any favor for myself. . . . But I asked him to do this thing for his child" (60). Lady Mason understands that the customs governing inheritance do not oblige Sir Joseph, a mere tradesman, to leave his land intact to his eldest son, as a hereditary landowner should do. She argues quite conventionally for the equal rights of male children where a family estate is not at issue. Thus she makes a claim for Lucius without challenging the idea that males should control property.

Sir Joseph refuses, and Lady Mason, who has been willing to accept a bare maintenance for herself, must acquiesce in a similar negation of her son's rights. But this ultimate negation of her own worth, Lady Mason cannot accept—her legitimate son, at least, should be as the legitimate sons of other women. She tells her dying husband that he must leave Orley Farm to Lucius or she herself "would cause it to be done" (60) by forging a codicil to his will. The adult Lucius thinks forgery "one of the vilest crimes known to man" (73), because a forger steals another person's rights under the law. And that, of course, is the point of Lady Mason's forgery—to reclaim the power that patriarchal law has denied her. It is ironic that Lady Mason should only find the courage to disobey a legal system that grants women few rights on behalf of a male who has, in her opinion, been denied his rights within the system itself. To challenge it on her own behalf is more than she can contemplate. As we shall see, the dissatisfied women in Trollope's next few novels often rebel in this way—identifying some tenet of the system in the name of which they can assert themselves without surrendering their femininity or completely rejecting the conventional view of their place in society.

Lady Mason's secret defiance of a legal system administered by men in their own interest places her in a dangerous position. Sir Joseph's older son tries to upset his father's will, but fails. Twenty years later, when Lucius, who has inherited Sir Joseph's masterful disposition, comes of age, he treats his mother very much as his father did before him. He confidently informs Lady Mason "that by certain admixtures of ammonia and earths he could produce cereal results hitherto unknown to the farming world" (2). When Lady Mason tries to warn Lucius that experimental agriculture is expensive, he silences her as effectively as Sir Joseph had done: "I know what you are going to say, mother" (2). Among Lucius' projects is a plan to farm land that Lady Mason had rented to Samuel Dockwrath, who succeeded to the business of Sir Joseph's solicitor. Lady Mason cannot reveal her fear that if Lucius makes an enemy of Dockwrath, he may start looking among his predecessor's papers for evidence to harm her. She argues that Dockwrath needs the land to raise food for his sixteen children, but her humane arguments fail to influence her arrogant son.[3] Lucius reclaims the fields, and Dockwrath finds evidence that Sir Joseph's will is not genuine.

It is the central irony of Lady Mason's life that the baby for whose sake she resisted her husband's tyranny grows up into a man no less jealous in claiming his rights, no less resistant to feminine influence, than his father. The privileges she stole for her son only feed his arrogance. After Lady Mason learns that she will be accused of having perjured herself when she swore that her husband's will was genuine, she hopes to conceal the matter from Lucius so as to preserve some freedom of action for herself. Like his father, he is unresponsive to her feelings, and he is determined to act and speak for her. She decides to circumvent him, as she circumvented Sir Joseph.

Behind Lucius' back, Lady Mason appeals for aid to two powerful men: the barrister Mr. Furnival and her neighbor Sir Peregrine Orme. The former has the legal knowledge, the latter the social prestige, that Lady Mason needs to gain an acquittal. Lady Mason is willing to do anything to conciliate these men whose words have greater weight than hers. "It was necessary," the narrator claims, "that she should bind men to her cause, men powerful in the world and able to fight her battle with strong arms. She did so bind them with the only chains at her command" (35). Sex is the chain by which the still beautiful Lady Mason binds Mr. Furnival, a restless married man in his fifties. Visiting his chambers carefully dressed, she lets him "keep her hand [in his] for a minute or so, as though she did not notice it" (12). In gaining the support of chivalrous old Sir Peregrine, a combination of flattering helplessness and subtle sexual allure proves effective.

With Mr. Furnival and Sir Peregrine, as with her husband, Lady Mason must barter her beauty for the aid she needs, concealing her repugnance at the bargain. In her second trial, Lady Mason must defend herself with the voice of Mr. Furnival, just as, in forging the will, she spoke her own words in her husband's voice. By suggesting that Lady Mason's relationships with her son and her two male advisors resemble her relationship to her husband, Trollope can make a more general point about female helplessness than if he were to confine his story to an examination of the Mason marriage. Lady Mason is a potential angel driven to criminality because the men around her respond to sexual manipulation, but not to virtue. In the first half of the novel, she is trapped in a repetitive cycle of repression and deceit.

Lady Mason is freed from this trap by a woman very different from herself. Lady Mason has felt the effects of the commercial world's tendency to trade in women, but Edith Orme comes from the world of the gentry and has known only chivalrous protection. In the Orme family, we can see the ideal of womanhood in operation. When Mrs. Orme was widowed, she remained with her husband's father, Sir Peregrine, who "yielded to her in all things, and attended to her will as though she were a little queen, recognizing in her feminine weakness a sovereign power . . . having . . . for years indulged himself in a quixotic gallantry" (3) toward this cherished daughter. Lady Mason's husband offered her the exact sum he thought her to be worth; but Sir Peregrine conceived that "the softness of a woman's character should be preserved by a total absence of all pecuniary thoughts and cares" (3).

One of Lady Mason's most persistent problems is her inability to speak with effect, but Mrs. Orme, her slightest whim anticipated, finds happiness in silence. "Mrs. Orme was not a woman given to much speech . . . but she could make her few words go very far" (14). When Sir Peregrine asks Mrs. Orme to approve his plan to marry Lady Mason, Mrs. Orme is too kind to oppose him. "Many of the sweetest, kindest, best of women are weak in this way," the narrator notes approvingly. They cannot bear to "say hard, useful, wise words in opposition to the follies of those they love" (35). Mrs. Orme is an angel who influences not by rational argument, or even by gentle hints, but by her selfless refusal to speak at all. Chivalry has silenced her as effectively as tyranny silenced Lady Mason, but it does not matter because she always gets her way.

Or doesn't it? As Mrs. Orme's story progresses, Trollope shows us that even at its best, the Victorian family maims its women. Mrs. Orme has been protected not merely from evil but also from life in all its diversity, by her confinement in a sheltered home. To her father-in-law Mrs. Orme is "the purest of the pure . . . whose whiteness had never been sullied by contact with the world's dust" (56). Her life with Sir Peregrine is frighteningly empty: though she has spent twenty years in his home, she "had never while there made one really well-loved friend" (14). Mrs. Orme does indeed have the kind of purity the Victorians recommended for women: the purity of ignorance. But as she becomes a stronger, more thoughtful woman, through her accidental contact with Lady Mason's guilt, we realize that her capability for moral growth had been stifled by Sir Peregrine's protective care.

Overcome by a generous desire to save Sir Peregrine from the disgrace of marrying her, Lady Mason confesses her guilt. Sir Peregrine is so deeply committed to his conventional view of women as pure and passive creatures that it has never occurred to him that the gentle Lady Mason might be guilty. "You did it," he asks her incredulously, "and he, your husband, knew nothing of it?" (45). Sir Peregrine's simplistic view of moral issues makes him slow to understand that extenuating circumstances should soften his judgment of Lady Mason. Though the situation baffles him, Sir Peregrine simply assumes that, as the head of his household, *he* must decide what to do about Lady Mason. He is frantically determined to protect Mrs. Orme from contaminating intercourse with a criminal: "How was he to save his daughter from further contact with a woman such as this?" (45). It is both touching and comic that this doddering, impractical old man should determine to shelter a woman in her forties as if she were a child—and it is a relief that he fails. Sir Peregrine breaks his resolution to act as Mrs. Orme's guardian when he comes to see that "the weight of these tidings would be too much for him, if he did not share them with some one. So he made up his mind that he must tell them to her" (45).

The "unwonted vehemence" (45) of his daughter-in-law's response to the story surprises Sir Peregrine. When he tells Mrs. Orme that Lady Mason should "return to Orley Farm without being again seen by her, her woman's heart at once rebelled" (45), and she refuses to send Lady Mason away. Though she is not always logical, Mrs. Orme's grasp of the complex moral issues involved is far more sophisticated than Sir Peregrine's. And she shows herself capable of practical action, concealing the breach between Lady

Mason and Sir Peregrine so as not to jeopardize Lady Mason's chances of an acquittal. Having come, by a bizarre accident that Sir Peregrine would certainly have prevented if he could, to love this sinner, Mrs. Orme will not betray her love. Because Sir Peregrine believes that female purity should be equated with ignorance of evil, he finds Mrs. Orme's conduct disturbing. "It went sorely against the grain with him when it was proposed that there should still exist a close intimacy between the one cherished lady of his household and the woman who had been guilty of so base a crime. It seemed to him that he might touch pitch and not be defiled;— he or any man belonging to him. But he could not reconcile it to himself that the widow of his son should run such risk" (46).

But Mrs. Orme perseveres, and her arrangements succeed: the Ormes' support helps Lady Mason gain the acquittal to which she is morally, if not legally, entitled. Further, Mrs. Orme's love touches Lady Mason and helps her to repent her crime. Mrs. Orme, however, could not have accomplished these things had Sir Peregrine continued to protect her from the necessity for moral choice. If Mrs. Orme helps Lady Mason leave the world of commerce and enter that of morality, Lady Mason is no less effective in helping Mrs. Orme leave the moral limbo in which she has existed for so long.

Mrs. Orme shows a new self-confidence and capability for action when Sir Peregrine, moved by Lady Mason's decision to return the property, tells Mrs. Orme that he wants to renew their engagement. For the first time, Mrs. Orme finds the strength to speak wise, but painful words: she tells him that " 'it is all over now'. . . in the softest, sweetest, lowest voice" (76). Sheltered and innocent, Mrs. Orme lived in silence, but experience gives her something to say and the power to say it effectively—without damaging her feminine kindness. "Edith," Sir Peregrine tells Mrs. Orme, "since you came to my house there has been an angel in it" (76). But Mrs. Orme is now a different sort of angel from what she once was—an experienced angel who has felt "a touch of sympathy . . . [with] the old Bailey Jew lawyer" (64) hired to defend the criminal she loves.

Though Mrs. Orme "was good, and pure, and straightminded," the narrator asserts that "Lady Mason was greater than she in force of character,—a stronger woman in every way, endowed with more force of will, with more power of mind, with greater energy, and a swifter flow of words" (60). The weak woman, sheltered from experience by the patriarchal family at its best, only learned by accident that she was capable of moral growth, while the strong woman could not accept the limitations it placed upon her freedom of action. Their contrasted experiences indict Victorian society. Even when it is functioning as it should, it restricts women's development—and when the men to whom it grants power abuse their trust, it harms women more seriously still.[4]

In *Orley Farm* Trollope encounters a problem that has no precedent in his earlier novels, which treated women conservatively. *Orley Farm* makes a subversive point through a sensational example, and Trollope must take special care to present his criminal heroine in a manner that will prevent readers from condemning her out of hand. Therefore he does not reveal Lady Mason's guilt until the novel is more than half over, though by that time he has introduced plenty of evidence that she may be guilty. In the opening sections, the poignant nature of Lady Mason's early experiences, her exemplary conduct to her husband, her quiet life after his death, and her devotion to her son are all stressed. When Trollope gives his readers access to Lady Mason's thoughts, he shows only her pain and anxiety, cutting off these sequences artificially, at the moment when she might well begin to reflect on her guilt. Though readers know that Lady Mason uses questionable means to gain the support of powerful men, this originally suggests that she is terrified by the disgrace a new trial will bring, rather than that she is guilty. Indeed the reader is at first encouraged to draw the same false, but conventional, conclusion about Lady Mason's horror at the prospect of a new trial that several male characters draw: "We must remember that she is a woman, and therefore weaker than you or I" (26).

Thus Trollope establishes sympathy for Lady Mason before allowing readers to suspect that she may be guilty. Knowledge of her virtues grows along with suspicion, and like Mrs. Orme, readers come to love Lady Mason before receiving proof of her guilt. Condemnation does not overwhelm sympathy even when Lady Mason confesses her crime to Sir Peregrine. At this point, the narrator ventures "to hope, that Lady Mason's confession . . . will not have taken anybody by surprise" (45). And in fact he has told his tale so skillfully that readers can accept the revelation without those "revulsions of feeling" (45)—either of surprise or of condemnation—that the narrative is carefully structured to prevent.

Later the narrator emphasizes Lady Mason's remorse, while other characters extenuate her guilt by stressing the special circumstances of her case. "Wretched miserable woman, but yet so worthy of pity!" (45), the narrator exclaims after she confesses, and Mr. Furnival notes that Lady Mason's "character was one which might have graced a better destiny" (78). In the end, even Sir Peregrine forgives Lady Mason: "To me she is the same as though she had never done that deed. . . . Can I say because she did one startling thing that the total of her sin is greater than mine?" (79).

Thus, by the timing of his revelations, the narrator sustains respect for a female felon, but he never acknowledges how manipulative he has been. "I may, perhaps, be thought to owe an apology to my readers in that I have asked their sympathy for a woman who had so sinned as to have placed her beyond the general sympathy of the world at large," he notes accurately. He is not, however, being quite so honest when he claims, "As I have told her story that sympathy has grown upon myself till I have learned to forgive her, and to feel that I too could have regarded her as a friend" (79). The narrator disarms his readers by the pretense that the process of discovery through which he has carefully led them is one that he himself accidentally experienced.

The narrator's voice, no less than his timing, helps persuade readers of *Orley Farm* to see women in unusual ways. As Geoffrey Harvey remarks, Trollope's capacity to convince readers to question conventional beliefs "depends on his [initial] creation of shared conventional values. His narrator praises public schools, inveighs against public examinations, and extols domestic contentment,"[5] and so gets under the reader's guard before suggesting any unorthodox ideas. On issues concerning women, the narrator of *Orley Farm* certainly does operate in this way. He generalizes with blandly conventional confidence about woman's place and nature, paying *homage en passant* to a variety of pleasant truisms. "An instinct implanted from the birth" teaches naturally good girls "the expediency of a staid demeanor" around men (19), he claims. The narrator is appalled that girls who hunt should be almost "as independent when going across the country as the young men who accompanied them" and agrees with "many of their neighbors" that their families ought not to allow them such freedom (28).

But this conventional narrator also fills his narrative with a variety of slightly subversive observations about women, observations that become more frequent as the work progresses. These subversive remarks almost always refer to particular characters and situations, for the most sweeping generalizations remain conservative in tone. Thus an ill-used matron is casually denominated the "wife and slave" of her husband (1). Lucius Mason is faulted for his belief in male supremacy: "In truth he understood nothing of a woman's strength" (63). At some cost to consistency, the narrator covertly undermines the conventional view of women he frequently articulates. But he never alters his tone so dramatically as to startle or offend his readers. *Orley Farm* is the first of Trollope's novels to use this manipulative technique to introduce unorthodox ideas about women.

The way Trollope narrates Lady Mason's story is not the only strategy by which he subverts conservative notions about women. The stories of several aging couples also promote this aim. To many critics, *Orley Farm*'s subplots, like those of *The Bertrams*, seem irrelevant. P. D. Edwards agrees with Michael Sadleir that these "limp sub-plots" have no other function than to provide the " 'variety and sectional interest' demanded by part issue."[6] But the subplots dealing with middle-aged marriage develop the idea organizing the main plot: that men who do not mistreat women often shelter them so completely that they never become autonomous human beings. These subplots interact with the main plot to undermine the cherished theory of home as society's moral hope, the very theory which *The Three Clerks* and *Framley Parsonage* endorsed so enthusiastically. In all of these plots the family fails to humanize the commercial world—and in several of them commercialism invades the family itself, causing spouses to treat each other like business associates, or even competitors.

Lady Mason is by no means the only wife in *Orley Farm* whose husband sees his marriage as a mere transaction. The solicitor's wife, Miriam Dockwrath, "was overworked, and had too many cares, and her lord was a tyrant to her rather than a husband" (5). Dockwrath regards his wife in economic terms: as a factory for producing children and a domestic drudge to be exploited with no more compunction than factory owners felt toward their expendable hands. Instead of being softened by his wife's mild nature, Dockwrath finds it annoying and systematically cuts her off from those she loves. The narrator cynically claims that other husbands also react in this way: "There are men who take a delight in abusing those special friends whom their wives best love" (1).

If Miriam's story is told in a key of low pathos, the tale of Mrs. Moulder, the commercial traveler's wife, repeats the same ideas in a farcical mode. For Moulder, marriage is a bargain in which he guarantees that his wife will not want for "plenty of the best of eating; and for linen and silks and such like" (24), while she waits unoccupied in her empty house for the rare occasions when he needs her services. And if he receives imperfect service on these visits, Moulder can "make himself extremely unpleasant," as he reminds his wife of the terms of their agreement: " 'What the d——— are you for?' he would say. . . . 'It ain't much I ask of you in return for your keep'" (24).

Orley Farm is filled with marriages that do not fit the ideal pattern. The Furnival marriage is the most striking of these precisely because Mrs. Furnival is the sort of woman who would certainly have earned a husband's love in Trollope's earlier novels. "As a poor man Mr. Furnival had been an excellent husband," but then "success and money had come,—and Mrs. Furnival sometimes found herself not quite so happy as she had been when watching beside him in the days of their poverty" (10). Mr. Furnival loses interest in his aging, limited wife in spite of her selfless nature. In their younger days, she had taken her tea black so that "his large breakfast-cup might be whitened to his liking . . . and in stinting herself had found her own reward" (11). She wants nothing more than to go on making sacrifices for her husband, but he no longer needs them— and he neglects her cruelly. The Furnivals demonstrate that a wife's self-abnegation will not necessarily earn the desired response from her husband—particularly if years of drudgery have made her "stout and solid" (11) in appearance and dull in conversation.[7]

Undercutting the novel's usual pattern of exploitative husband, victimized wife, are Joseph Mason, the younger, and his parsimonious mate. Like Dockwrath, Moulder, and Furnival, Mrs. Mason runs her household on commercial principles—starving her husband and children, while buying herself every possible indulgence. But although Mrs. Mason is not a victim like *Orley Farm*'s other wives, neither does she manage to dominate her husband. Further, the novel's depiction of her marriage forwards its critique of the theory that home provides an uplifting refuge from the commercial world. In most of *Orley Farm*'s families, the hubands, not the wives, have been corrupted by commerce, but Lady Mason and Mrs. Mason prove that women are not as immune to commercializing pressures as the Victorians liked to believe. Mrs. Mason, indeed, has been completely corrupted by the prevailing greed— a frightening reversal of the ideal.

If the stories of these women resemble Lady Mason's in stressing the helplessness of the average wife and the commercialization of marriage, the story of Lady Staveley echoes the tale of Mrs. Orme in a lighter tone. The Staveley family approaches the Victorian ideal even more closely than the Ormes: a wise, loving father, a mother happily bound up in her household, three charming children. But there is more than a hint that Lady Staveley, toward whom the narrator's tone alternates between sentimental indulgence and mild contempt, has, like Mrs. Orme, been overprotected. Though Lady Staveley is "a good, motherly, warm-hearted woman" (19), she has neither absorbing work to do nor much knowledge of the world around her. Consequently, she has become obsessed with petty details of household management and with the virtues of her family, which she exaggerates absurdly. She thinks "a great deal about her flowers and fruit, believing that no one else had them so excellent . . . she thought also a great deal about her children, who were all swans,—though, as she often observed with a happy sigh, those of her neighbors were so uncommonly like geese" (19).

Pride in her family, hostility to outsiders, and the ignorance that sustains those emotions are all disturbing concomitants of Lady Staveley's feminine virtues. When her daughter Madeline falls in love with a poor though intelligent man, she cannot understand her daughter's choice and childishly tries to interfere with what is clearly a *fait accompli*. Sheltered and indulged, Lady Staveley has a weak grip on reality even where the emotions, supposedly a woman's area of expertise, are concerned. No bizarre accident, like the one that favored Mrs. Orme, helps her to grow up, and she remains a stunted human being.

The middle-aged wives in *Orley Farm*'s subplots help to generalize the critique of the angel-in-the-house ideal which its main plot suggests. The romantic subplots involving the novel's two ingenues, however, pull in an opposing direction. Naturally intelligent, "able to hold her own with the old as well as with the young" (10), Lady Mason's counterpart, Sophia Furnival, acts the role of an innocent and sweet young lady, "mild and gentle to girls less gifted . . . possessing an eye that could fall softly to the ground, as a woman's eye always should fall upon occasions" (10). Like Lady Mason, Sophia is an actress whose femininity is not quite real. But where Lady Mason's dishonesty was forced upon her by the pressure of circumstances, Sophia chooses falsehood of her own free will.

Mrs. Orme's young alter ego, Madeline Staveley, however, truly is the feminine creature that Sophia pretends to be. Her movements are "soft, graceful, and fawnlike as should be those of a young girl" (19); she loves her parents and is content at home. The narrator uses extremely prescriptive language in discussing Sophia and Madeline; moreover, his tone never suggests that Madeline is lacking in any way. Unlike her mother, she is intelligent as well as loving. Nor does the narrator imply that greater knowledge of Sophia would deepen our sympathy for her, as it did for Lady Mason. Excusing a young man for falling in love with Sophia, the narrator explains that his readers "have had a much better opportunity of looking into the character of Miss Furnival than [this suitor] had had" (66). To know her better is to like her less. These subplots end with old-fashioned poetic justice: Madeline marries, and Sophia loses both the lovers with whom she has been heartlessly toying.

But perhaps these romantic subplots are undermined by the context of pervasive female frustration in which Trollope places them; they are undoubtedly undermined by the fact that several of their characters diverge disturbingly from their prototypes in traditional romantic comedy. Sophia does resemble Lady Mason in being too strong to fit easily into the prescribed female role. Lady Mason, under pressure, tells one great falsehood, while Sophia's whole persona is a continuous deception. Obviously it is easier to forgive Lady Mason, but it is also true that Sophia's rational, cool character, which would be admirable in a man, is something a marriageable girl might want to conceal. Because *Orley Farm* shows dishonesty to be the natural weapon of powerless women, it is hard to censure Sophia's dishonesty quite as much as we presumably ought. Nor does her loss of the conceited Augustus Staveley and the arrogant Lucius Mason as prospective husbands seem a terrible punishment.

Madeline marries Felix Graham, a barrister with a taste for the rational reconstruction of society—always an ominous preference in Trollope's view. Felix is a "rationalist" when it comes to women, as well. He has undertaken the education of a poor girl, Mary Snow, whom he is molding into the perfect wife. Felix's enterprise suggests his lack of respect for a woman's independence, as well as his belief that reality can easily be squeezed into an ideal shape. Both Mary's nature and his own, however, prove less malleable than Felix thought. She falls in love with another man, and he gives up his molding project to marry Madeline. But gentle Madeline's happiness with this overconfident man—a somewhat inadequate comic hero—does not seem quite assured.[8] Her other suitor, young Peregrine Orme, is probably right that he himself would "have made her a better husband. . . . He was more akin to her . . . in tenderness of heart" (80). The dissatisfaction with romantic comedy so often displayed by Trollope's later work first makes itself felt in the flawed resolution of this slightly perfunctory subplot.

The romantic subplots in *Orley Farm* perform a complex function. Their traditional tone and almost traditional content help to soften the adverse effect that the disturbing main plot and the other sub-versive subplots might have had on conventional readers. But at the same time, the serenely optimistic and conventional romantic subplots are undermined, at least to some extent, by pessimistic material surrounding them.[9] In a society that has systematically maimed so many women, Madeline is not likely to escape unscathed.

"The Ideal Woman Is a Prig"—*The Small House at Allington*

Trollope's increasing concern with the complex problems of real women is shown by his choice of the sinful, yet fascinating Lady Mason as the protagonist of *Orley Farm*. But the book's ingenue, Madeline Staveley, is as nice, and as dull, as the idealized romantic heroines of the earlier novels. *The Small House at Allington,* however, really is a novel *about* its ingenue—a perversely intriguing character, neither vapid like Linda Woodward, nor wholly admirable like Mary Thorne. Lily Dale is the first of Trollope's romantic heroines who is indisputably the most interesting character of the novel in which she appears. And this is so because *The Small House at Allington* ceases to affirm Victorian ideals of romance and begins to attack them, developing its critique through the contrasted personalities of Lily and her sister Bell. Freed from a purely affirmative role, the romantic heroine moves in unprecedented directions.[10]

The Small House at Allington and its successor *Rachel Ray* offer a number of new departures. Instead of placing the ingenue at the center of a conventional, but perfunctory, comic subplot, these novels focus upon the experiences of their ingenues, showing how the social world they live in prevents their stories from ending as romantic comedy should, in the achievement of a truly satisfactory marriage. *Rachel Ray,* as we shall see shortly, preserves the form of romantic comedy while subverting its basic assumptions, but *The Small House at Allington* does not even do that. In *The Small House at Allington, Rachel Ray, Can You Forgive Her?,* and *Miss Mackenzie,* the experiences of the romantic heroine move from the periphery to the very center. But those experiences no longer fit the patterns of comedy so neatly as did the experiences of Trollope's earlier ingenues.

The Small House at Allington dramatizes the way unrealistic ideas about men, women, and courtship can destroy love. As many critics have remarked, the novel frustrates the reader's desire for its "natural" comic conclusion: the marriage of Lily and John Eames. This resolution, however, is impossible not because Lily is a faulty woman—preferring pain to pleasure—as has often been argued,[11] but rather because she tries to govern her conduct by a set of unrealistic conventions.[12] Lily attempts to follow the standard code of feminine behavior in courtship, and because she is a strong and intelligent girl, she manages to do so with remarkable consistency. Thus she reveals the nature of that code more clearly than a less dedicated adherent could. Lily's failure is more the fault of convention than of her own peculiarities: a social rather than a psychological tragedy.

Lily and her sister Bell, girls of dissimilar temperaments, hold different views about men and women. Critics have had difficulty in evaluating Lily's character because her manner is at variance with her convictions. Lily is a lively, outspoken girl, so it is easy to underestimate the influence of convention on her behavior and to hold her personally responsible for mistaken decisions that were actually dictated by commonly accepted rules of conduct. The problem with Bell is just the reverse, for she is far more independent than her manner implies. Superficially, Lily seems free-spirited, while Bell appears to be stereotypically quiet and proper. Lily calls Adolphus Crosbie a "swell," and Bell reproves her for talking slang. Lily is the one who teases the men, while Bell sits demurely by. When Crosbie asks Lily to play croquet at dusk, for example, she tells him the absence of light will not matter, since he plays "quite independently of the hoops" (I, 3). Bell's sense of humor is seen only by her mother and sister, and even with them, she prefers not to discuss her feelings. But Lily talks openly of her most intimate thoughts.

But if we look at their convictions about social issues in general, and about woman's nature and destiny in particular, it turns out that Lily's views are far more conventional than Bell's. Self-reliance and perseverance are the qualities Bell admires, without distinction either of class or of sex. She rejects several commonplace notions about middle-class marriage: that marriage is a woman's profession; that a woman ought to rise in the social hierarchy by making a good marriage, provided she truly loves the man she accepts; that a lady is a delicate creature whose husband should support her in idleness; and that love is the center of a woman's existence. In fact, Bell's silence turns out to be her way of protecting a view of the world that, she well knows, is not shared by her associates. Her convictions go underground where they can be safe from pressures she does not feel strong enough to resist. *The Small House at Allington* contains several scenes that show Bell assenting politely to propositions whose truth she inwardly disputes "with all the strength of her heart and mind" (I, 9). And this survival strategy does work. No one disapproves of Bell.

Bell does not find much to admire in the Victorian class system. She tells her sister that she despises aristocratic society, because it is closed to virtuous people who lack birth and fashion, but Lily disagrees. "After all," Lily argues, "think how much work [aristocrats] do. . . . They have all the governing in their hands, and get very little money for doing it." "Worse luck for the country," Bell answers. "The country seems to do pretty well," Lily contends, "but you're a radical, Bell. My belief is, you wouldn't be a lady if you could help it." "I'd sooner be an honest woman," is Bell's reply. Later we learn that "this was an old subject of dispute" (II, 14).

Just as Bell refuses to believe in the innate superiority of aristocrats, so too she is unwilling to accept standard definitions of masculinity and femininity. When the novel opens, Bell is nursing a secret anger against Dr. Crofts, who had once appeared to be in love with her, but did not make her an offer of marriage. Bell knows that Crofts, who is not earning a comfortable income, was prevented from proposing by his conventional views of female delicacy. Crofts will not marry unless he can provide his wife with the protected domestic environment in which she can function as an ornamental angel. "A man may undergo what he likes for himself," Crofts tells Bell, "but he has no right to make a woman undergo poverty" (I, 9). Bell accepts this explanation with her usual reserve, but internally she dissents: " 'As if a woman cannot bear more than a man!' she said to herself" (I, 9). Bell wishes she could earn her own money, but knowing that this is impracticable, would at least like to prove within the home that she can work as hard as any man. "Income should not be considered at all" (I, 6) in planning marriages, she asserts firmly.

Bell's anger at Crofts results from real disagreement, and not merely from frustrated affection. She is not interested in Crofts because he can offer her social advancement, but because he needs her. She rejects his middle-class ideal of marriage, in which a sheltered wife proves her worth by her moral sensitivity rather than by her practical activities. Democratic Bell prefers a working-class model of marriage in which a husband and wife become economic partners, sharing hardship on equal terms. And so, demonstrating the characteristic Dale tendency to take extreme positions, she decides that she and Crofts will never marry: "If there was anything in the world as to which Isabella Dale was quite certain, it was this—that she was not in love with Dr. Crofts" (I, 20).

Bell feels doubly sure that she does not love Crofts because, after their love affair has stalled, she finds herself attracted to Adolphus Crosbie. "I once fancied that I cared for Dr. Crofts, but it was only fancy," she tells Lily, and then her unwillingness to reveal her aberrant tendencies prevents her from going on to explain that "her knowledge on that point was assured to her, because since that day she had felt that she might have learned to love another man" (I, 27). Here Bell is judging her feelings in terms of the conventional idea that a woman who truly loves one man should not be susceptible to the attractions of another. This is precisely the idea that will destroy Lily's chances for happiness, but Bell comes to see it as a mistaken notion. When Crofts finally decides to propose, Bell feels nothing but joy and forgets all about the "infidelity" she once took as proof that she did not love him.

Bell ultimately rejects the conventional views about love upon which Lily's bark is wrecked. She does not believe that Crofts is faultless. She does not want to advance into a state of luxurious prosperity through his means. She knows that she can live happily without him, because she did it during the years when poverty prevented him from proposing. She knows also that he is not the only possible man for her. Love will be an important part of her life, but not its all-consuming center—work will be significant as well. Bell's subplot concludes with a happy marriage, as romantic comedy should, but it does so only because her conception of marriage differs dramatically from the one convention recommended for a girl of her class. Bell's lightly sketched story is the first of the "progressive comedies," the joyous conclusions of which are premised on unconventional notions about the sexes, that become so important in Trollope's later books.

Like Bell, Lily is a theoretician with extreme ideas about love—and the word "theory" comes up frequently when the narrator discusses her views. Unlike Bell, however, Lily states her theories vigorously because they are so conventional that she is sure they can only redound to her credit. Instead of proving that she is a rebel, her outgoing manner is actually the consequence of her conservative convictions. In *An Autobiography* Trollope remarked on Lily's popularity with readers, but added, "In the love with which she has been greeted I have hardly joined with much enthusiasm, feeling that she is somewhat of a female prig" (10). According to the *Oxford English Dictionary*, a prig "cultivates or affects a propriety of culture . . . or morals, which offends or bores others." A quotation from a work written in 1877 illustrates this usage: "The ideal woman is a prig."[13] Lily is indeed a priggish woman, determined to live up to a cultural ideal of feminine behavior whose value seems to her indisputable. But to Trollope, at this point in his career, Lily's ostentatious orthodoxy was disturbing.

And it is, I think, this odd combination of qualities in Lily which disturbs modern readers: she asserts her views openly because their very conventionality gives her the courage to do so. When Bell, voicing her usual commitment to the protective value of decorum, tells Lily that it is not nice to talk slang, Lily answers, a bit smugly, "I'd like to be nice—if I knew how" (I, 2). The narrator agrees with Lily's implication that she is already an expert on niceness: "If she knew how! There is no knowing how, for a girl, in that matter. If nature and her mother have not done it for her, there is no hope for her. . . . I may say that nature and her mother had been sufficiently efficacious for Lilian Dale in this respect" (I, 2). A little slang flows quite charmingly from the lips of a girl whose theories and conduct are so quintessentially nice—as Lily is well aware. Lily accepts all the conventional notions about class, love, and marriage that Bell rejects. A believer in the divine right of kings, she accepts the sexual hierarchy as well. Lily thinks "that some decent income should be considered as indispensible before love could be entertained" (I, 6), because she endorses the view that women are delicate creatures, whose manly husbands must protect them from the rougher side of life. When she accepts a man in less than opulent circumstances, her conception of how she might help him stretches no further than needlework. She believes that a woman should advance herself by marrying her superior in age and achievement. And so Crosbie's godlike air of success attracts Lily to him. While they are engaged, Lily regards Crosbie not merely as her husband, but as her "master" (II, 27). She thinks of their marriage as an unequal relationship in which he condescends and she receives benefits: "Remember all that he is to give up for my sake!—And what can I do for him in return? What have I got to give him?" (I, 6).

Lily believes both that men are intended to rule wives, whom they surpass in knowledge and power, and that men are women's moral and emotional inferiors—a closely related tenet of the usual Victorian view of the sexes. From Lily's perspective Crosbie is making a great sacrifice in marrying a country girl, a sacrifice that should not really be expected, given the selfishness which men's worldly experience fosters. When he fails to write her, she excuses him on the grounds that men "never recognized the hunger and thirst after letters which women feel when away from those whom they love" (I, 27). And later, when she reflects on the terrible speed with which Crosbie jilted her, she justifies him by saying, "Men are not the same as women" (II, 27). His cruelty seems to her so naturally male that she refuses to hold him accountable for it, telling her friends repeatedly, "I am not blaming him, remember" (II, 24). Lily believes that it is natural for a man to regret an imprudent engagement because she thinks that love, which is everything to a woman, is only a fraction of a man's life.

Lily is no less conventional in her views concerning the behavior in courtship that is appropriate for each sex. Lily's theory is that "a girl should never show any preference for a man till circumstances should have fully entitled him to such a manifestation, [and then she should] make no drawback on her love, but pour it forth for his benefit with all her strength" (I, 7). This was indeed the usual Victorian way of reconciling two conflicting aspects of woman's nature: innocence and susceptibility to emotion. In giving her emotional side full rein as soon as a proposal has conferred authorization to do so, Lily wells knows that there is "a risk. He who was now everything to her might die . . . he might neglect her, desert her, or misuse her. But she had resolved to trust in everything" (I, 13). Trollope stresses Lily's awareness of danger to show that she is consciously, with some difficulty, striving to follow her theories. She does not merely blunder into trouble.

Because the husband is his wife's master, an engaged girl, in Lily's view, must learn how to subjugate her own feelings to those of her fiance. During their engagement, Lily tries to convince herself that Crosbie's views admit no disagreement. When he tells her that he plans to leave Allington, Lily feels upset that he seems eager to go, but does "not allow herself to suppose that he could propose anything that was unkind" (I, 12). As time passes, however, she finds that it is more difficult than she had imagined to submit her judgment to his, for she soon begins to discover that in spite of the masculinity that attracted her, he is not perfect. She cannot help resenting his ungracious behavior, but then, according to her theory, she has to reproach herself for her resentment. "I forget how much he is giving up for me; and then, when anything annoys him, I make it worse instead of comforting him" (I, 7). The idea of woman as selfless comforter to man proves hard to put into practice.

Lily accepts Crosbie without really knowing him because she thinks that a man's most significant attributes are his surface attributes: fashion, maturity, and an air of mastery and success. "I was so proud of having him," she tells Bell later, "that I gave myself up to him all at once. . . . Who could expect that such an engagement should be lasting?" (II, 14). She did not look for sensitivity or moral excellence in him because she thought of these as feminine qualities.

When Crosbie starts to reveal the seamier side of his personality to Lily, she is extremely disturbed, but her theories about men help her to minimize the implications of his behavior./Bitterly disappointed to discover that Lily will have no fortune, Crosbie tells her that he has decided to postpone their marriage and continue with his bachelor life in London. As the narrator says, "he was ungenerous" (I, 15), and Lily feels this, "though she would not acknowledge it even to herself" (15). That he would rather defer marriage than give up his expensive habits, which include entanglements with loose women, does upset her, and she turns away when he tries to kiss her. But when he asks her, "Are you angry with me?" she again reminds herself that it is a woman's duty to forgive and a man's nature to be selfish, insensitive, and even immoral—so she controls her anger. " 'Oh, no! Adolphus; how can I be angry with you?' And then she turned to him and gave him her face to kiss almost before he had again asked for it. 'He shall not think that I am unkind to him . . .' she said to herself" (I, 15).

Lily's theories lead her to engage herself to a man whose character she does not understand; they tell her to submit to him even when he starts to reveal his moral mediocrity. Furthermore, her submissive, worshipping behavior produces an ambivalent response in Crosbie. At first her "way of flattering her lover without any intention of flattery on her part, had put Crosbie into a seventh heaven" (I, 6). But soon he begins to feel burdened by her unflagging attention to his every gesture. The narrator uses calculatedly ambiguous language to describe Lily's behavior during her engagement; so predictably girlish is Lily that her charm begins to cloy. While eating his dinner, Crosbie reflects that his coffee "would soon be handed to him by a sweet girl who would have tripped across the two gardens on purpose to perform for him this service" (I, 7). When Crosbie visits her home, Lily curtsies with ostentatious deference, looking "like some wondrous flower that had bloomed upon the carpet . . . smiling, oh, so sweetly" (I, 9). Having chosen, conventionally, an oh-so-sweet girl, who trips rather than walks, who abases herself in stylized attitudes, and who endlessly describes her devotion in a "silvery voice" (I, 7), Crosbie is frightened by the tenacity with which she clings to him.

And so he jilts her for Lady Alexandrina De Courcy, who has little to recommend her except that she offers an escape from Lily. For Crosbie, as for Lily, the union of masterful husband, worshipful wife, proves less attractive in actuality than it had appeared in theory. Fleeing from Lily's emotional demands, Crosbie overcompensates and marries a woman who has no feeling whatsoever for others. Lily is left to decide if she can accept a new suitor, John Eames. Her decision that she will never love again results from her conventional ideas about love, as they affected her relationship with Crosbie and her reaction to its termination.

Lily's subjugation to Crosbie explains her inability to recover when he jilts her. Her theories of female subordination told her that she must surrender herself to her lover from the moment of their engagement. In several brief, but surprisingly frank, passages, Trollope suggests that in addition to giving Crosbie her mind, Lily gave him more of her body than most young ladies would have dared to do. When he and Lily said their good-nights in a secluded nook, passionate embraces were the rule, and after he leaves her, Lily is tormented by sexual guilt. In her efforts to live up to her theories about generous love, she sinned against her equally orthodox theories of feminine purity, as she later comes to feel.

When she explains to her mother why she can never marry John Eames, this is on her mind. "I am married to that other man," she says with difficulty. "When he kissed me I kissed him again, and I longed for his kisses" (II, 27). Later she reflects, "When he held me . . . in his arms, I told myself that it was right, because he was my husband" (II, 27). Only by convincing herself that she is "widowed" (II, 27) can she retain her self-respect when she remembers her sexual involvement with Crosbie, but though a widow, she cannot remarry because her "husband" still lives. Since a feminine woman cannot transfer her love as a man may do, Lily preserves her self-respect by remaining loyal to Crosbie, though he has married another. "I cannot change myself because he is changed," she tells John Eames, again revealing her view that decency is a feminine attribute. "I should be disgraced in my own eyes if I admitted the love of another man, after—after—. . . . These things are different with a man" (II, 24). The internal contradictions of her theory place poor Lily in this untenable position.

If Lily were to look impartially at the way she allowed an inferior man to use and discard her, she would indeed feel foolish and soiled. But her theories provide her with a more palatable way of interpreting what has happened. She convinces herself that Crosbie's behavior, given the nature of men, was not only excusable, but justifiable. Men are ambitious; so in jilting her for an earl's daughter, Crosbie behaved naturally. "I have forgiven him altogether," Lily tells her mother, "and I think that he was right" (II, 27). He failed, in her view, only when he imagined that he could be happy with a simple country girl—a mistake, rather than a sin. If Crosbie was right in the line of conduct he pursued, then Lily herself committed no serious error of judgment in trusting him as she did. It was a misfortune and not a disgrace.

But though Lily's theories give her a way of interpreting Crosbie's character that minimizes her humiliation, they also make it difficult for her to love again. If she does not cling to her belief in the moral inferiority of men in general, she will have to acknowledge how stupid she was to love the unusually flawed Crosbie. But if she does cling to her conventional beliefs about love, she can only accept another man as she accepted Crosbie: with complete surrender of self. Crosbie was able to hurt Lily deeply because she gave herself to him unreservedly. Had she not allowed herself to become a "creature utterly in his power" (I, 15), her mistake would not have been so devastating. Having learned to what pain such self-abnegation can lead, she is unable to repeat the venture. And even if she could, the irresolute John Eames is not the man an intelligent young woman would be inclined to worship. Lily will never again be a flower in the carpet for any man, but the idea of becoming one on Johnny's behalf is particularly absurd. Many readers feel that Lily could have been happy with John, and perhaps they are right—but such happiness could be found only in a more equal marriage than the unbalanced union Lily's theories recommend.

Lily is a typical Dale in her tendency to take extreme positions— and she espouses a revealingly extreme version of the Victorian love code. An idealist, she thinks reality can be forced to follow theory. Bell also tends toward extremes, but she is doctrinaire in her commitment to a down-to-earth, practical view of life. The contrast between them is suggested by their conversation about a romantic novel both have read. "It was a matter of course," Bell says contemptuously, that the book's heroine was right to marry its hero. "It always is right in the novels. That's why I don't like them. They are too sweet." But Lily retorts that she likes novels precisely because "they are so sweet. . . . A novel should tell you not what you are to get, but what you'd like to get" (II, 12). Lily prefers the ideal to the real. When her dreams are shattered, she rejects "real" marriage altogether and clings to the "sweet" theories of femininity and masculinity that caused her sufferings.[14] By her stubborn endorsement of convention, Lily finds an acceptably feminine way to express the assertive nature that characterizes the Dales. But she forfeits the comic resolution.

The farcical subplot concerning John Eames's London misadventures both reflects and belittles the novel's main plot, extending its critique of conventional notions about men and women. Both plots suggest that if a penniless woman is to succeed in life, she can do so only by marrying a successful man who is likely to regard a union with her as an entrapment. This is the nightmare side of Lily's lovely dream of middle-class marriage. Amelia Roper's unmaidenly attempt to force John Eames into wedlock is not so different from Lily's conventionally proper relationship to Crosbie as it originally seems.[15] Amelia, the first person to realize that John is a competent young man, responds to this no less sincerely than Lily did to Crosbie's air of success. When Amelia tells John, "I didn't think ever to have cared for a man as I have cared for you" (II, 29), she means it. Amelia really does love John, and she loves him, in part, because he offers her a chance of escaping slavery as an assistant in her mother's sordid boardinghouse.

Lily does not pursue Crosbie immodestly, but the same motives influence her. She feels "triumphant satisfaction" that Crosbie is "her bird, the spoil of her own gun, the product of such capacity as she had in her, on which she was to live" (I, 13). This startling metaphor suggests that a woman who cannot earn a comfortable income will be forced to cannibalize a man, whether or not she is naturally so inclined. When women must hunt men in order to live well before the world, or to live at all, financial and emotional considerations mingle strangely, engendering a destructive state of distrust. Perhaps it is for this reason that *The Small House at Allington* does not include a single happily married couple among its characters. The farcical subplot drives home the point that Lily's is a common misfortune, caused more by social forces than by her own character.

The narrator of *Orley Farm* has to perform the difficult task of evoking sympathy for his dishonest heroine. His tone is reassuringly conventional, but he subverts the ideas he ostentatiously espouses and gradually moves the reader toward a more compassionate understanding of Lady Mason's character. Because the narrative voice is so skillfully handled in *Orley Farm,* Trollope succeeds there in an endeavor he had attempted unsuccessfully in *The Noble Jilt* and *The Bertrams*: to center his work upon a rebellious heroine without sacrificing either reader sympathy or thematic consistency. But the narrator of *The Small House at Allington* performs a very different rhetorical function: he must suggest the ideas that will show readers how destructive Lily's conventional view of love is to her happiness, without sounding so revolutionary that he forfeits their trust. Where *Orley Farm*'s narrator had to move his readers toward a heroine whom they might otherwise condemn too harshly, *The Small House*'s narrator must distance readers from a heroine whose conventional views they might otherwise accept too easily.

The narrator of *The Small House at Allington* has been called "sharper and more cynical" than the narrators of the earlier novels, and this is an accurate assessment.[16] But it is also important to note that the narrator's cynicism is quiet and unobtrusive. We have already discussed the faintly parodic language with which the narrator describes Lily's girlish charm, but this is only one of his methods for subtly distancing readers from her. This narrator never supports Lily's conventional views on love by the sort of sentimental generalizations that the earlier narrators favored. When the narrator describes Lily's theories, he rarely comments upon them and certainly never endorses them. But he persistently calls attention to the disenchanting details of women's lives under the rule of Victorian custom: "The little sacrifices of society are all made by women" (I, 13). "Women are more accustomed than men to long, dull, unemployed hours" (II, 2). As these details accumulate, they undercut Lily's idealistic views.

This cynical narrator also sneers quietly at male pomposity and female emotionalism: "Men are cowards before women until they become tyrants; and are easy dupes, till of a sudden they recognize the fact that it is pleasanter to be the victimizer than the victim,— and as easy" (I, 14). When Crosbie leaves her, Lily watches him as long as her eyes can be "blessed with some view of his departing back" (I, 16). Sometimes the narrator (in a positively Flaubertian manner) refrains from comment and allows the juxtaposition of details to make a disturbing point for him. On one such occasion, the narrator gives us Crosbie's thoughts on the engagement—"Of course I must suffer,—suffer damnably"—and then wonders "what was the state of Lily's mind at the same moment?" Lily, it turns out, is reproaching herself because, no matter how hard she tries, she is unable to show Crosbie "how thoroughly and how perfectly she loved him" (I, 7). Sometimes the narrator's comments upon minor characters tacitly imply a judgment of Lily which he does not choose to state openly. Thus he expresses his disapproval of Mrs. Dale's decision to live a life of perpetual widowhood for the advantage of her daughters, a conventionally self-sacrificing decision that resembles several Lily will later make: "I think that Mrs. Dale was wrong" (I, 3). From this we can infer that he might have reservations about Lily's views as well.

Though he never sounds like an advocate for women's rights, the narrator of *The Small House* does try to prevent his readers from identifying too closely with the heroine he sentimentally introduced to them as "dear Lily Dale" (2). The falsely reassuring type of narrator Trollope used in *The Warden* and *Barchester Towers* unsettles the ordinary Victorian reader's view of women in *Orley Farm*—the earliest of Trollope's novels to deploy in its handling of this emotionally charged topic the manipulative techniques of narration he had developed to deal with other issues. But in *The Small House at Allington* he develops new narrative techniques for subverting the orthodox notions embraced by his idealistic heroine, while retaining the trust of his conventional readers.

Comic Convention in *Rachel Ray*

Virtually every critic who has written about *Rachel Ray* (1863) classifies the novel as a heartwarming romance, closely modeled on the kind of stage comedy in which "two young people meet, fall in love in a moment, are separated by artificial obstacles, and are finally united."[17] Rachel Ray and Luke Rowan, the romantic leads, receive general admiration from critics as "two healthy-minded young people"[18] by means of whose ideal love "society itself is cured of its slight neurosis, an uneasiness about sex, and is thus revitalized."[19] But the same critics who see *Rachel Ray* as a perfect romantic comedy are puzzled by the perfunctory quality of its comic plot. "The obstacles [to Luke and Rachel's union] are so slight that even with some dilatoriness on the author's part they are barely enough to keep the book going till the end," one critic writes.[20] Another agrees that the opposition to the marriage "never becomes fully credible,"[21] while a third argues that Rachel and Luke are such ideal lovers that they soon dwindle into mere "ciphers of faithfulness, and real conflict disappears."[22]

Rachel Ray's comic plot certainly is thin—indeed it seems so insufficient to support a four-hundred-page novel that one might wonder whether the work really is a straightforward romantic comedy after all. And closer examination does reveal tensions between form and content suggesting that this novel, disguised in a suspiciously inadequate manner as comedy itself, subtly subverts the idea that comic form can depict a society that does not grant autonomy and responsibility to women. In *The Small House at Allington* Trollope showed how the heroine's conventional notions about love prevented her story from ending, as romantic comedy should, in her marriage to the hero. In *Rachel Ray* he suggests that the power relations of Victorian marriage make the comic ending a matter for less than total rejoicing. These two novels show Trollope's growing irritation at the powerless position of women and the unrealistic rules by which they were expected to live. Because of this irritation, he begins to undercut the comic form that he had used straight-forwardly in novels like *Doctor Thorne* and *Framley Parsonage*. But he handles the feminist subtexts of *The Small House* and *Rachel Ray* with great caution and tact. In *Rachel Ray*, indeed, he is so tactful that its subversive elements have done no more than to arouse vague suspicions that its comic plot is not quite satisfactory.

Rachel Ray's comic romance begins when a newcomer to Bas-elhurst, Luke Rowan, falls in love with Rachel Ray, whose once genteel family lives in reduced circumstances. Rachel's family fears that Luke's intentions may not be honorable. Misunderstandings ensue and the marriage is celebrated only on the book's conclud-ing page. But the novel's substance is not to be found in these slight misunderstandings. Looking beyond the romantic comedy, we discover that most of the novel portrays a series of power struggles, many of them connected only tangentially to the love story itself.[23]

Rachel is involved in one such conflict, Luke in several others. As they battle their adversaries it becomes clear that these two lovers are not quite what we expect the heroes and heroines of romantic comedy to be, for both prove exceptionally strong-willed and harsh in their treatment of others. Because the novel also suggests, through its minor characters, that the institution of marriage offers a wife little power, its conclusion, superficially so joyous, actually has ominous implications for Rachel. Having proved herself able to act independently, Rachel enters a relationship that does not promise her much scope for independent action. And because women in this novel are fond of power—not indirect power to influence men, but direct power to shape the world according to their own de-sires—the reader's misgivings about Rachel's marriage must be extended to marriage in general. In the world of *Rachel Ray*, the love match that concludes comedy is usually, for women at least, little more than an attractively disguised trap.

Victorian readers certainly could have read *Rachel Ray* as a simple tale affirming conventional ideas about love and marriage, though they would have had to ignore the ironies surrounding the book's use of comic form. The narrative voice of *Rachel Ray* keeps this interpretive option open for the conservative reader. The narrator, who never explicitly questions the notion that he is telling a traditional love story, occasionally generalizes about femininity and manliness in sentimentally orthodox terms. But, as we shall see shortly, this narrator also notes many disturbing details that undermine commonplace Victorian notions about the sexes. The narrator himself does not appear to comprehend the full significance of these details, which thus remain scattered through the story in a manner that leaves readers free to ignore them. Though his tone is less cynical, the narrator of *Rachel Ray* resembles the narrator of *The Small House at Allington* in assuming a stance that may distance alert readers slightly from the views of a conventional heroine.

The inhabitants of Baselhurst are engaged in a variety of serious disputes, and although money is often involved, the central object of nearly every conflict the novel examines is power rather than wealth. The most important conflict takes place between Rachel and her Evangelical widowed sister Mrs. Prime for control of Rachel's future. Mrs. Prime, who would like Rachel to spend her days sewing for the poor, regards Luke Rowan as a dangerous acquaintance. Rachel is attracted to Luke and repelled by her sister's charitable schemes, but she is telling her mother the truth when she claims that the real issue is not pleasure, but power: "I won't be ruled by her" (5). Rachel's "expression of unrelenting purpose" (5) when she says this surprises her mother, and the conflict escalates rapidly.

A second power struggle develops between Luke Rowan and Mr. Tappitt, a share of whose brewery Luke has inherited. On his arrival at the brewery, Luke discovers that "a sour and muddy stream . . . flowed from [its] vats; a beverage disagreeable to the palate" (3), and he is fired with an ambition to produce good beer. Tappitt, however, has managed to earn his living as a brewer of bad beer and can hardly believe that Luke's proposed improvements will not bring disaster. Luke decides to force Tappitt to retire. His intention is "to be master" (10), but Tappitt also feels that "for continual mastery [in the brewery] it was worth his while to make a fight" (10). So a contest for "mastery"—a key word in the novel—develops, although Luke has offered to buy Tappitt out on generous terms. Again, power proves more desirable than tangible benefits.

"A love of power" (1) is the peculiar vice of Mrs. Prime, who as a widow controls her own fortune. Mrs. Prime loves this money only as it helps her to gratify her ruling passion. "Mrs. Prime liked to be more powerful at . . . charitable meetings than her sister labourers in the same vineyard, and . . . achieved this power by the means of her money" (1), the narrator remarks. Mrs. Prime receives a proposal from her clergyman, Mr. Prong, a prototypical Evangelical hypocrite. Often in nineteenth-century English fiction, such characters reveal that greed is their strongest motivation, but in this one respect Mr. Prong does not run true to type. The lonely Mrs. Prime accepts his proposal on condition that she retain control over her fortune. But later she learns that she cannot attain this end without the cooperation of her intended husband. Mr. Prong is poor and if his main concern were simply to better his financial position, he would marry Mrs. Prime even though "she had burdened her promise with certain pecuniary conditions" (24). Yet he resolves "never to yield on the money question," for he cannot give up "that absolute headship and perfect mastery, which . . . should belong to the husband as husband" (24). Mrs. Prime knows that mastery is Mr. Prong's ultimate aim. "It is not that he wants my money for the money's sake," she tells her mother, "but that he chooses to dictate to me how I shall use it" (23). And since Mrs. Prime will not accept dictation, Mr. Prong does indeed lose both wife and money over the issue of marital authority.

Mr. Prong is also involved in a power struggle with a neighboring clergyman, Dr. Harford. An Act of Parliament has divided Dr. Harford's parish in two, the new parish becoming the benefice of Mr. Prong. Dr. Harford reacts to this assault with unclerical violence, not because "this was a question touching his pocket. . . . His pocket would be in some degree benefitted. . . . It was no question of money. . . . His parish had been invaded and his clerical authority mutilated" (18). Solely because he has lost clerical power, "hatred of Mr. Prong" becomes "the strongest passion of Dr. Harford's heart" (18).

There is a parliamentary election in *Rachel Ray,* as in several other Trollope novels. Here, however, the election is just one of many

Baselhurst power struggles. Nominally the conservative candidate is Butler Cornbury, the local squire—but in fact, Butler has decided to stand only at the instigation of his wife, who does nearly all his campaigning for him. Alone among the members of her family, Mrs. Cornbury values power more than money: "The [opposition] were striving to frighten the Cornbury people out of the field by the fear of the probable expenditure; and had it not been for the good courage of Mrs. Butler Cornbury would probably have succeeded in doing so" (17). Because of Mrs. Cornbury's courage, Butler wins the election, and it is certainly arguable that the wife, not the husband, was the real candidate.

These power struggles, several of which involve women, suggest that the desire to rule is a potent one, motivating males and females in equal proportions. Many women here use what direct power they have intelligently and responsibly—unlike the ambitious viragoes of novels like *Barchester Towers* and *Doctor Thorne*. Yet the novel's treatment of women's social position, especially within marriage, suggests no less emphatically that women are able to wield power only in unusual circumstances. In this world a woman's actions, and often her very words as well, are dictated to her by men.

Through its analysis of the relationship between Mr. Tappitt and his wife, the novel examines the power structure of an average Victorian marriage. Tappitt holds the purse strings, and Mrs. Tappitt must resort to those traditional methods of the weak, wheedling and misrepresentation, when she has any expensive end in view. Having decided to give a ball, Mrs. Tappitt and her daughters are "too judicious . . . to commit themselves by the presumption of any such term" (5)—for "ball" implies expense and is sure to provoke a refusal from the paterfamilias. Instead they dub the festivity an "evening tea party" (5). "Dogs fight with their teeth, and horses with their heels; swans with their wings, and cats with their claws;—so also do women use such weapons as nature has provided for them" (14), says the narrator—not unsympathetically—about this sort of feminine deviousness. Even a "good wife" like Mrs. Tappitt, who accepts the idea of female subordination, often finds the powerlessness of her position "vexatious to her spirit" (6).

The problems of subservience, however, take a more serious form for Mrs. Tappitt when her husband's quarrel with Luke Rowan about the brewery escalates. Tappitt refuses Luke's generous offer to buy him out, because he cannot bring himself to resign his control over the brewery. Quite unused by the habits of either his marriage or his business life to yielding or sharing power, Tappitt considers fighting Luke with the help of unscrupulous attorneys who, as he himself is quite aware in his more lucid moments, will take his money though they know he has no chance of victory. Mrs. Tappitt sees that if she does not stop her husband the family will be ruined. Unlike the other struggles in *Rachel Ray,* this conflict is not for permanent domination, which Mrs. Tappitt never dreams of trying to claim. It is a struggle to achieve one well-defined object.

Though Mrs. Tappitt, in this marital tussle, clearly has reason on her side, the power relations within her family are such that she is almost unable to prevent her husband from ruining them all. When his wife remonstrates with him, Tappitt tells her that verbal aggression is both unfitting and unfeminine: "Margaret, I must tell you once for all that that is not the way in which I like you to speak to me" (27). Mrs. Tappitt does not dispute the general proposition that a wife's duty is to suffer and be still: "I know I'm bound to submit, and I hope I have submitted. Very hard it has been sometimes when I've seen things going as they have gone; but I've remembered my duty as a wife, and I've held my tongue" (27). But she wants to make an exception to this rule of silence for situations in which the family—a wife's peculiar care—is threatened. In defense of her children's livelihood, Mrs. Tappitt thinks that even a feminine female has the right to speak. Tappitt responds by screaming "Woman!" (27) at his wife, as a gentle reminder of her place, for he has no better argument to employ.

Mrs. Tappitt wins her battle not only because she is in the right but also because of the accidental fact that Tappitt comes home drunk from a political banquet. When his powers of self-assertion have been diminished by an acute hangover, Mrs. Tappitt manages to convince him to take the only course that, as he himself knows, will avert disaster. The luck Mrs. Tappitt needs in order to prevail here, and the deplorably opportunistic tactics she is forced to employ, make a disturbing point about the power relations of marriage. Mrs. Tappitt has adjusted to subordination in marriage, though she has not found it an easy task. She occupies a middle position between two other characters, one of whom, Rachel's widowed mother Mrs. Ray, is ideally suited to the restrictions of marriage, while the other, Mrs. Butler Cornbury, evades those restrictions altogether. The novel's analysis of these two women completes the background against which Rachel's developing relation to Luke, and the comic conclusion itself, must be viewed.

Mrs. Ray is a real angel in the house, "a sweet-tempered, good-humoured, loving, timid woman" (1), not merely willing to accept direction from others but positively unable to live without it. While the other women in the novel seek power, Mrs. Ray fears it. Such a woman, the narrator remarks, must live her life in subordination to someone and if she has no husband she will "swear conjugal obedience sometimes to her cook, sometimes to her grandchild, sometimes to her lawyer. . . . To some standing corner, post, or stump, she will find her way and attach herself, and there will she be married" (1). Mrs. Ray desperately needs an authority to obey because she is pathologically lacking in critical intelligence: "It never occurred to her to question any word that was said to her" (1). With a good husband, such a woman can be happy. But when Trollope suggests that acceptance of her husband's authority is an unmitigated blessing only for a woman who is totally unable to use her head, he does not place marriage in a very favorable light. When the narrator, in one of his sentimental moments, remarks that Mrs. Ray is "a woman all over" (1), he seems to be missing the point. Mrs. Ray is indeed a parody of Victorian femininity, but in her refusal to think for herself, she differs from the other women in this novel.

Mrs. Butler Cornbury escapes the conflict between a desire for power and a powerless social position that troubles most of *Rachel Ray's* female characters, because exceptional circumstances have given her exceptional power over both her own spouse and society in general. Money, talent, and an appreciative husband give Mrs.

Cornbury a degree of influence within her own family that no other woman in the novel approaches. Though Butler is "the eldest son of the most puissant squire within five miles of Baselhurst" (5), he badly needed the fortune brought to him by his wife, whose father inherited large sums from "the most surprising number of unmarried uncles and aunts that ever a man had" (26). In addition, Mrs. Cornbury's combination of "good temper, good digestion, good intellects, and good looks" (26) has won the admiration of her husband, who knows that her charm gives "soul and spirit to daily life at Cornbury Grange" (26). And finally, Mrs. Cornbury is fortunate to have married a modest man, happy in his social position and without the desire to dominate that characterizes many men in *Rachel Ray*. Butler is not embarrassed to admit that his wife is the "general" (26) of the family forces.

In the world at large, Mrs. Cornbury's combination of high status and personal charm enables her to assert herself far more freely than the other female characters even attempt to do, yet no one accuses her of behaving in an unfeminine manner. Rachel's response to Mrs. Cornbury is typical of the way others react to her. Though she believes in feminine subordination and though she sees that Mrs. Cornbury always "chooses to have her own way," Rachel will not censure her charming, prominent friend, inconsistently excusing Mrs. Cornbury's willfulness on the ground that "she is so good-humoured" (8). But no other assertive woman in the novel escapes severe criticism. In fact, Mrs. Cornbury's position in society is so unusual that people have trouble remembering to which sex she belongs. When Mrs. Cornbury electioneers for her husband at the brewery, Tappitt remarks that "women don't know anything about [politics]," meaning to insult only his wife and quite "forgetting that Mrs. Cornbury was a woman" (17).

Mrs. Cornbury is a vivid character, but her husband remains shadowy and makes only a few brief appearances. Perhaps Trollope feared to focus too much attention on the Cornbury marriage. Had he let his readers learn more about Butler's relationship with his wife, Trollope would have made it harder for them to overlook how subversive his treatment of relations between the sexes in *Rachel Ray* actually is. For though Butler violates Victorian norms by allowing his wife to wear the pants, he is perfectly happy and never loses his dignity. Precisely because this unconventional marriage works so well, Trollope chooses not to make it a prominent feature of his novel. In the facile way that—almost offstage—she obtains power, Mrs. Cornbury seems to inhabit a different world from the constricting one in which the more ordinary female characters must struggle.[24]

But Rachel herself, penniless and in love with a domineering man, is certainly an inhabitant of that world. In both her strength of character and her desire to obey accepted standards of feminine behavior, Rachel resembles Mrs. Tappitt. Throughout the novel Rachel is willing to assert herself only in feminine ways. Knowing that a woman has the right to marry if a proper candidate presents himself, Rachel is quick to use this right in her battle with her sister over Luke's attentions. Armed with the authority of her clergyman, Mr. Comfort, who has approved Luke as a suitor, Rachel resists her sister, "almost savagely . . . resolved to fight" (3) and succeeds in becoming engaged to Luke. But she feels free to battle with Mrs. Prime only in the interests of a traditional feminine prerogative. In this respect, Rachel resembles both Lady Mason and Lily Dale, who also find within the set of customs that has rendered them powerless a justification for some kind of twisted self-assertion.

One of the things that attracts Rachel to Luke is his "masculine" force of character, while he likes the "feminine" timidity she shows in his presence. "What a woman she is!" he thinks, "so womanly in everything" (4). But under pressure Rachel's womanly sweetness disappears. Withdrawing his earlier sanction, Mr. Comfort tells Mrs. Ray she must order Rachel to end her engagement to Luke. Comfort bases his decision on gossip about Luke's finances, gossip which, as even the unworldly Rachel realizes, is highly implausible. But a lifetime of laying down the spiritual law has given him great confidence in his own judgment.

When Rachel hears that she must reject Luke and that even the form of her letter has been dictated by Mr. Comfort, the strength of character she developed during her conflict with Mrs. Prime makes it hard for her to submit. "She hatch[es] within her mind plans of disobedience,—dreadful plans" (20). She knows, however, that she cannot execute these plans, for such rebelliousness would certainly cost her Luke's respect. "She was bound by her woman's lot to maintain her womanly purity. Let her suffer as she might there was nothing for her but obedience" (20). But Rachel sees that though it would be disastrous to rebel openly, the feminine strategy of passive resistance is practicable. "As she thought of this injury," the narrator comments, "that fierce look of which I have spoken came across her brow! She would obey her pastors and masters. . . . But she could never again be soft and pliable within their hands" (20). Rachel writes to Luke as she has been commanded to do, though she tries to suggest, between the lines, that she is writing under duress. Luke does not even reply and Rachel carries out her plan to punish her mother and Mr. Comfort by the unvarying misery of her demeanor.

Naturally this punishment falls far more heavily on Mrs. Ray, who like Rachel herself was only obeying her pastors and masters in the course of action she adopted, than it does on Mr. Comfort. Luke reacts to Rachel's letter by punishing her in the same unfair way, though he is quite aware that girls are not free and that Rachel "couldn't write just what letter [she] liked, as he could" (23). The only difference between them is that Rachel punishes her mother quietly, almost secretly, for she knows that open aggression is unfeminine, whereas Luke punishes Rachel quite openly, with his usual masculine vigor. Thus, as their romantic difficulties progress, Rachel and Luke both prove themselves inflexible, masterful, and harsh to those they love, in defense of what they conventionally see as their rights. Though he knows that her letter was dictated by others, Luke allows Rachel to suffer for months after he is in a position to clear his character and return to her, and Rachel is equally slow to forgive her mother.

The comic hero and heroine of *Rachel Ray* are assertive youngsters indeed. Luke can hardly open his mouth without some variant of the line "I mean to have my own way" (16) emerging, and Rachel proves similarly fierce and hard when she can demonstrate these qualities without violating the code of feminine behavior. Comparison with Lord Lufton and Lucy Robarts of *Framley Parsonage* suggests the degree to which Luke and Rachel deviate from the stereotypes of likable young lovers, but Trollope had already paved the way for this kind of unorthodox ingenue with his characterization of Lily Dale. By the end of the book, the reader realizes that a marriage between two such unyielding temperaments may not prove harmonious. But Rachel herself never perceives this because of her commitment both to traditional ideas concerning feminine and masculine behavior and to comic form as the best shape a woman's life can assume. For Rachel, as for comedy, marriage is the only happy ending.

From the start, Rachel advocates feminine submission and masculine dominance, and so does Luke. When Mrs. Ray remarks on Luke's willfulness, Rachel answers, "He's what people call imperious; but that isn't bad in a man, is it?" (16). Luke, in turn, loves Rachel for what he sees as her womanly softness. Even her obedience in the matter of the letter, though it offends him, causes him to love "her with a surer love . . . than he had ever felt before" (26), for it proves her deference to authority. But neither Luke nor Rachel sees that although, in accordance with her principles, she means "to be ruled by" (14) and "to serve" (30) him as his wife, her struggles to win that position have taught her some effective strategies for getting her own way. Such a woman may find it painful to submit, when her strong will comes inevitably into conflict with her husband's.

In the end, Rachel gets the man she wanted all along, but she gets him on terms that may not prove satisfactory for long. She achieves the pleasures of love, wealth, and status at the price of renouncing power. Mrs. Prime, on the other hand, in breaking her engagement with Mr. Prong, renounces the comforts marriage can bring to retain the power that control of her own money gives her. And that is indeed the choice the society depicted in *Rachel Ray* offers to all but the luckiest women: power accompanied by loneliness and disapproval, or pleasure and social acceptance in a state of passivity. The comic form of the novel suggests that Rachel is correct in choosing the pleasures of marriage, and Mrs. Prime mistaken in accepting isolation as the price for a very limited degree of power. But because the novel's characters, women as well as men, generally prefer power to pleasure, Rachel's choice is called into question. In fact, neither option is really acceptable.

The obstacles separating the lovers of romantic comedy usually fall into two classes. Either the society they live in is corrupt and must solve the problems preventing their union—as is pretty much the case in *Doctor Thorne*—or else the lovers themselves need to grow before they can unite—as in the Katie-Charley subplot of *The Three Clerks*. In *Rachel Ray*, a combination of defective social institutions and their own defective characters keep the lovers apart. Only chance reunites them: when he is able to prove that his financial standing is sound, Luke can return to Rachel in triumph, and, so soothed, is finally willing to take her back. His character does not change at all. And though the society depicted in the novel eases its repressive sexual attitudes, it does not liberalize the choices it offers to women—a far more serious problem. The novel's comic plot seems thin precisely because the social and personal healing we expect has not taken place.

Suspicion is cast on *Rachel Ray*'s comic conclusion by the absence of the changes that ought to prepare for it. And so it should not surprise the reader that when Rachel and Luke wed, the atmosphere is grim: they "were married on New Year's Day . . . and afterwards made a short marriage trip to Penzance and the Land's End. It was cold weather for pleasure-travelling" (30). It is indeed cold weather for honeymoons in this novel, but with her marriage journey—as with her views of marriage in general and of her husband's character in particular—Rachel affirms the conventional and ideal at the expense of ignoring reality. "Rachel when she returned could not bear to be told that it had been cold. There was no winter, she said, at Penzance" (30). Like the comic form of the novel itself, these superficially touching and romantic words conceal devastating ironies. The novel has ended in marriage, but it has also shown that without changes in the alternatives available to women, its ostensibly positive conclusion does not promise its heroine the happiness she expects. Without reform, Trollope suggests, Victorian society can produce only pale, unconvincing imitations of romantic comedy.

Repression and Freedom in *Can You Forgive Her?*

By contrast with *Rachel Ray,* where the subtext asserting women's need for power was carefully hidden beneath the bland surface of a romantic comedy, *Can You Forgive Her?* explicitly articulates two interpretive options, one hostile to its many rebellious women, the other sympathetic with their plight. The narrator of *Can You Forgive Her?* just isn't sure how to explain the story he is telling. He oscillates uncomfortably between interpretations of character and motive that endorse the conventional male viewpoint and interpretations that exonerate the novel's angry, unconventional women. The narrator fails to resolve most of the interpretive issues raised by *Can You Forgive Her?*, but he states the antifeminist case more vigorously in the early portions of the novel than he does towards its conclusion. As the novel progresses, the commentary on its female characters shifts subtly, away from censure, toward exculpation.

At the outset, for example, the narrator is fairly sure that Alice Vavasor is in the grip of feminist delusions aroused by "a flock of learned ladies" (11) when she breaks her engagement to the gentlemanly John Grey. The narrator mentions Grey's repressive treatment of Alice, but does not see it as a significant motive for her behavior. By the end, however, the narrator has become certain that Alice could not accept Grey's unspoken assumption that he would be the dominant partner in their marriage, although he still alludes occasionally to her pride as one reason why she broke the engagement.[25] The narrator remarks toward the novel's close that on the subject of how they should live as a married couple, Grey "had never argued . . . with [Alice]. . . . He had not condescended so far as that. . . . But she could not become unambitious, tranquil, [and] fond of retirement . . . without being allowed even the poor grace of owning herself to be convinced. If a man takes a dog with him from the country up to town, the dog must live a town life without knowing the reason why. . . . But a woman should not be treated like a dog" (63). Only after drawing the reader into the tale by his reassuring portrait of Grey does the narrator begin to show this "perfect" gentleman in a less flattering light. But he never attacks

Grey so vigorously as to force the unwilling reader to acknowledge that Alice was justified in jilting him.

By keeping two interpretive options open, but gradually shifting the balance between them, Trollope minimizes the risk of offense while moving conventional readers toward greater sympathy with such initially unappealing women as Alice the jilt, Glencora Palliser the would-be adulteress, Kate Vavasor the confirmed spinster, and Mrs. Greenow the sex-starved widow. The "dual" narrative style also acts as a continual reminder that men and women see the world from different angles. This reminder is important, for the diametrically opposed alternatives Victorian England offers to men and women turn out to be a central theme in the novel.

That the narrator of *Can You Forgive Her?* cannot resolve many of the issues he raises suggests another subversive possibility: his tale is more complex than he realizes and the concepts he is using to analyze it are not quite appropriate. One reason the narrator has such trouble deciding how to apportion blame among his characters is that he attempts—persistently, though not consistently—to judge their behavior according to Victorian notions of manliness and femininity. But the novel's action undermines these conventional ideas. The accusation that a woman is unfeminine, for example, loses its bite in a novel that shows conventional standards of femininity to be unrealistically narrow. When the narrator makes a conventional judgment, he often seems uneasily aware that it is inadequate to the complexities with which he is dealing and reverses himself almost instantly.[26] This happens with special frequency in the latter portions of the novel, after the narrator begins to sense that his conventional analyses have not proved very useful. As the novel closes, the narrator says that Alice's reluctance to renew her engagement to Grey resulted from her "wish . . . to undergo the punishment she had deserved" for jilting him. But the narrative has shown that Alice had good reason to reject Grey, and so the narrator speedily changes his mind, attributing her conduct to "that feeling of rebellion which [Grey's] masterful spirit had ever produced in her" (74).

Like *Rachel Ray*, *Can You Forgive Her?* describes women who need more freedom and power than their lives allow them. Indeed, the novel is an anatomy of women's options in a world controlled by men—a descriptive classification of unattractive possibilities, highlighting the economic, social, and emotional restrictions to which Victorian society subjects women.[27] The three main plots concern a marriageable girl, a wife, and a widow. But the novel also contains a major character who is a confirmed spinster—in addition to a cast-off mistress and a prostitute, who make striking cameo appearances. Thus it covers the entire range of women's experience. None of its women, rich or poor, is satisfied with the opportunities her life has provided. The discarded mistress and the prostitute are pathetic creatures on the verge of starvation, while the wealthier women experience subtler forms of sexual and economic oppression.

But this is only half the story, for *Can You Forgive Her?* demonstrates that the destructive repression Victorian society visits on women is the mirror image of the destructive liberty it allows to men. Though critics have largely overlooked this fact, *Can You Forgive Her?* gives nearly as much consideration to the problems that the code of masculinity causes for its male characters as it does to the problems the ideal of femininity creates for its women. The women of *Can You Forgive Her?* suffer from repression, but its men suffer almost as dramatically from liberty. Too much freedom to express their natural inclinations can prevent men from learning to make the compromises that are necessary in human relationships. In *Can You Forgive Her?*, Trollope subverts both the prescriptive code of femininity and the permissive code of manliness. The novel implies that because the two codes ultimately derive from a single theory of male and female nature, they cannot be understood in isolation from one another. Both sexes are shown to be victims of a system that, according to the narrator of *The Way We Live Now*, "taught . . . that every vice might be forgiven in a man . . . though every virtue was expected from a woman" (2).

Each of the four main female characters of *Can You Forgive Her?* finds that the code of feminine behavior allows her insufficient scope to express her feelings or to pursue her aims. The Victorians' ideal woman found happiness in serving others and had no ambitions outside the domestic sphere. It is easy to see that few real women could develop contentedly within the bounds of an ideal that directs all women to live in the same way and to want the same things. Alice, Glencora, Kate, and Mrs. Greenow are all accused—by the narrator, by other characters, or by their own consciences—of feeling "unfeminine" emotions, or acting in "unfeminine" ways. The novel's title might refer to any one of them; all need forgiveness for violating the rules of womanly conduct.

Alice jilts John Grey because she cannot bear the subordinate position that he expects her to occupy as his wife. But like many of Trollope's rebellious women, she lacks the confidence to reject the conventions she has violated and reproaches herself for having "behaved badly . . . in a manner which the world will call unfeminine" (32) by refusing to marry the man she loves. In a passage that has been quoted as evidence of Trollope's hostility to feminism, the narrator mocks the political ambitions that Alice left Grey to pursue.[28] She would, he says, have liked to be "the wife of the leader of a Radical opposition . . . and to have kept up for him his seditious correspondence while he lay in the Tower" (11)—an absurd, romantic dream.

But in reading this passage we should note that although Alice is politically radical, she remains conservative in her views on the woman question—"not so far advanced as to think that women should be lawyers and doctors" (11). For this very reason she cannot formulate her political aspirations in a way that makes sense. Indeed, she cannot articulate them at all and so remains "silent, having things to say but not knowing in what words to put them" (3) when she tries to tell Grey what she wants from life. Alice's belief in the ideal of femininity makes her emotional rebellion against its implications appear absurd. Her conservative convictions prevent her from proposing new options for women, and so she can only fantasize pathetically about carrying secret messages in her stays. She sounds foolish not because she is too feminist but because she is not feminist enough.

The honest and passionate Glencora rebels in a very different manner, but her rebellion is equally unsuccessful. In her daily life, Glencora has to deal with far more terrible pressures than those that affect the relatively independent Alice. Glencora's family forced her into a marriage of convenience that proved more repressive than she had expected. Plantagenet Palliser finds his wife's use of such slangy expressions as "the long and the short of it" (49) intolerably unladylike and wants her to be a model of propriety at the age of twenty. Glencora uses her wit to attack the conventions that limit women's freedom, and she dreams of eloping with a lover. But Glencora never acts on her most rebellious impulses. She knows that such action would be suicidal, and so she can do no more than vent her bitterness in a stream of angry witticisms. The narrator asserts that Glencora is "not softly delicate in all her ways . . . not . . . at all points a lady," but excuses her by pointing out that "had Fate so willed it she would have been a thorough gentleman" (49). Had she not been born into the wrong sex, Glencora's life might have been happy enough, but she is a woman, and her rebellion, like Alice's, is doomed from the start.

Kate Vavasor does not rebel against woman's lot so directly as Alice and Glencora, but Trollope makes it clear that she is at least as ill-suited to it as they. Kate is an active woman, uninterested in marriage, whose upright, courageous character provokes her grandfather to say, "I wish you had been a boy" (53). Given the passivity demanded of women, however, Kate's only opportunity for action comes through her participation in the activities of her brother George. Her identification with the opposite sex has generated some serious conflicts about her own sexuality. "Oh, heavens! how I envy him!" (31), she says when she imagines George caressing Alice. Without George's activities to plan and his emotions to share, Kate, as she herself realizes, would "have nothing to do in the world;— literally nothing—nothing—nothing—nothing!" (6). In the end, George fails Kate, and she is indeed left purposeless. Alice and Glencora rebel against repression; Kate tries to evade it and is equally unsuccessful.

Only Mrs. Greenow can manipulate the conventions governing women's behavior so that they do not frustrate her desire to control her own life or her longing for sexual fulfillment. The comic way she accelerates her mourning, in order to remarry without having to wait the customary two years after her husband's death, demonstrates her magical power to evade the restrictions that gall other women. But if she did not feel them to be restrictions, she would not need to evade them as she does. Perhaps the most striking proof of Mrs. Greenow's extraordinary power is the narrator's failure to censure either her "taste for masterdom" (7) or her openly expressed interest in sex.

Though the novel's principal women are very different from one another, none of them can conform to Victorian society's ideal of feminine conduct. That they cannot conform even when, as in Alice's case, they are fully convinced they should, undermines the authority of the ideal itself. However, none of the novel's four principal men—though all are flawed—is ever described as "unmanly." The Victorians had an ideal of gentlemanly behavior, which was related to, though not dependent on, social class. There was a lot of talk about "nature's gentleman," but everybody knew that it was easier to achieve the combination of honesty, courtesy, and kindness that defined the gentleman if one had the proper education and a degree of financial independence.[29] It was not easy to live up to the ideal of gentlemanly conduct, but being a gentleman is not the same thing as being masculine: the latter task was less demanding. One could not identify an "ideal man" who was an exact counterpart to the "ideal woman" so often described. For the notion that men want different things and serve society in different ways was an intrinsic part of the conception of masculinity. Only one kind of woman could be feminine, but many types of men—from the dedicated cleric to the fearless soldier—could be manly.

Unlike the ideal woman, the masculine man is not defined by his negations but by a series of positive attributes. He is ambitious, competitive, industrious, rational, and purposive. He is the master of his own emotions. He controls every situation and rarely appears at a disadvantage. It is natural for the manly man to want many things: success, variety, pleasure, achievement, dominance. He may also want to stand well with his own conscience. If his desires lead him outside the bounds of morality, his wrongdoing is not inexcusable, like the wrongdoing of a woman—for he is naturally a creature of desire.

Because the code governing masculine behavior is permissive, it provides no help if the man's natural bent needs restraint. And this becomes a problem for the four male protagonists of *Can You Forgive Her?*, who embody four symmetrically balanced aspects of the complex Victorian notion of masculinity. Alice's two suitors, Grey and Vavasor, incarnate the opposed masculine qualities of control and violence; Glencora's husband and her ex-lover, Burgo Fitzgerald, embody the equally opposed masculine passions for work and pleasure. Through this complex scheme, Trollope demonstrates that the code of masculinity can accommodate opposites.[30]

John Grey is neither the perfect gentleman nor the insensitive tyrant that the narrator's inconsistent remarks by turns describe. Rather he is a man who, like the other three male protagonists, has found an element of the Victorian notion of manliness suitable to his temperament and has built a persona upon it. Grey embodies that portion of the code that directs a masculine man to be rational, decisive, in control of any situation, never mastered by emotion.

A look at Grey's boyhood may help to explain why he was attracted by this particular definition of masculinity. The only child of a widowed clergyman, Grey was "brought up under his father's eye, having been sent to no public school" (10). Thus Grey escaped the rough conditions for which public schools were notorious; he went to Cambridge, the university located close to his home, refusing to venture farther afield to attend Oxford. Then, in the narrator's words, he "sat himself down, near to his college friends . . . in the house which his father had built" (10), on an income of fifteen hundred a year.

The hint of contempt in the phrase "sat himself down" implies that there is something odd about the course of action Grey has chosen. Why should a man in his early twenties, with an adequate but by no means magnificent income, choose to live in an ugly country, devoting himself desultorily to books and varying his existence only by an occasional visit to London to complete "some slight literary transaction" (10)? And Grey lives this way even though he finds it very boring! After his engagement to Alice, indeed, Grey wonders "much that he should have been content to pass so long a portion of his life in the dull seclusion which he had endured" (10).

Grey's choice of "early retirement" may be related to the habits fostered by his childhood among elderly clergymen. He fears the conflict to which most boys become inured and would rather endure considerable tedium than risk failure by entering a profession. But, obviously, he does not want to live in a manner that others find contemptible, so he does have a problem. The code of masculine decorum provides Grey with a solution to his difficulty. Since dignity, rationality, and control, no less than activity, ambition, and a fighting spirit, are elements of manliness, Grey can present a masculine persona to the world by becoming an exemplar of the former set of qualities, even though he ignores the latter set completely. And this is exactly what he does, in the unconscious way people usually accommodate to social pressure.

Grey's fear of imprudence, conflict, and loss of dignity is almost pathological. Though he lives well within his income, he worries about the money he is spending on his garden, fearing "in his prudence" that "the glass-houses were so good and so extensive" as to constitute a sort of folie de grandeur (10). Though he emerges the victor when George Vavasor attacks him, "the [mere] reflection that he had been concerned in a row was in itself enough to make John Grey wretched" (52). Grey studiously maintains his calm demeanor, asserting by his every gesture that he is completely in control.

Grey's relationships with others are conditioned by his need to defend the fragile image he has created. An intimate friend is with him when he receives the letter in which Alice announces that she has engaged herself to George. As Grey reads Alice's letter, he suffers "as, probably, he had never suffered before. But there was nothing in his countenance to show that he was in pain" (36). He is unable to confide in his friend, saying significantly that "there are things which a man cannot tell" (36). According to Grey's ideas of manliness, a man should not reveal defeat even to his closest friend. And so complete is Grey's self-control that, when Alice breaks their engagement, he fools her into thinking he does not much care.

Alice's desire that he enter public life almost certainly terrified Grey, to whom thoughts of contesting an election or being pelted with eggs would have been absolute anathema. But the convention of masculine supremacy allows him to avoid an argument he might not win, and Grey takes advantage of it, refusing to discuss a change in his lifestyle. The motive behind Grey's repressive behavior toward Alice becomes evident at the end of the novel when Plantagenet Palliser encourages him to enter politics. When Grey tells Palliser that he wants only to live an honest life, Palliser answers that a man can "live honestly and be a Member of Parliament as well." Because he has refused so persistently to discuss the subject, Grey is shaken by this obvious point. Reflecting on Grey's response, the narrator comments that "it is astonishing how strong a man may be to those around him,—how impregnable may be his exterior, while within he feels himself to be as weak as water, and as unstable as chaff" (74). Grey comes to see that his refusal to enter politics was motivated by fear and decides to try it. But (true to form) he cannot bring himself to make openly the "terrible acknowledgments of his own faults" (74) that are Alice's due.

Unlike Grey, George Vavasor is a man of naturally aggressive temperament. When "hardly more than a boy" (4), he attacked a burglar who was about to sneak into his sister's room. George wrested the man's chisel from his hand, and killed him with it, receiving a wound that scarred his face. In an age which took crime seriously and admired the manliness of a fighting spirit, George's exploit seemed completely laudable. Alice certainly reacts in this way: "The scar had never been ugly to her. She knew the story, and when he was her lover she had taken pride in the mark of the wound" (5).

From this beginning, George goes on to become a master of every form of violent conflict, acquiring a certain celebrity in the process. "Men who had known him well said that he could fence and shoot with a pistol as few men care to do in these peaceable days. Since volunteering had come up, he had become a captain of Volunteers, and had won prizes with his rifle" (4). When George knocks down his employer "with a blow between the eyes," he claims that he has good reasons for doing so. "The deed was looked upon with approving eyes by many men of good standing" (4), who help him to find another job.

Thus far, at least, George's behavior conforms to the ideal of fighting, right-minded masculinity celebrated in such Victorian novels as *Tom Brown's Schooldays*. And George receives nearly as much admiration for embodying this aspect of "manliness" as John Grey does for his rational self-control. But George's fighting spirit begins to get out of hand. A man who has won success by asserting his own will runs the risk of developing a habit of violent self-assertion and of becoming less scrupulous about the ends he pursues. George quarrels with his grandfather, who has refused to help him borrow on the prospect of his inheritance, and spends his savings trying to force an entrance into Parliament. He lives in a room that has "a special place adapted for his pistols, others for his foils, and again another for his whips" (12). Rivalry, dominance, and courage have become obsessions. When he considers re-engaging himself to Alice, he feels more "keenly alive to the pleasure of taking from John Grey the prize which John Grey had so nearly taken from him" (30), than he is to the prospect of recovering his love. While recklessly pursuing parliamentary ambitions, he consoles himself by reflecting, "Nobody shall say I hadn't the courage to play the game out" (13).

As he becomes more addicted to getting his own way, George rationalizes his behavior by questioning the moral code that originally restrained his violence. He develops "certain Bohemian propensities,—a love of absolute independence in his thoughts as well as actions." He comes to worship murderers as "great men" who have "looked the whole thing in the face" and who have rightly concluded that "all scruples and squeamishness are bosh,—child's tales" (51). He fantasizes murder with increasing frequency. And so George drifts away from an ideal of personal strength used in the service of laudable ends, toward the worship of pure force that is so disturbing an element in such Victorian thinkers as the later Carlyle. Gradually George's violence grows less purposive, until finally he attacks his sister and John Grey in pointless rages that injure his real interests. Where Grey's version of manliness erred on the side of caution, limiting his development, George's version carries him outside the bounds of convention and so destroys him.

Plantagenet Palliser incarnates yet another aspect of Victorian masculinity: devotion to socially valuable work. Though he is "surrounded by all the temptations of luxury and pleasure," he chooses to work at politics "with the grinding energy of a young penniless barrister . . . . He was listened to [in Parliament] as a laborious man . . . who, dull though he be, was worthy of confidence. . . . He rather prided himself on being dull" (24). Like Grey and Vavasor, Palliser makes himself into an embodiment of the kind of masculinity that suits his temperament. Naturally dull and conscientious, he earns respect by becoming a dull and conscientious public figure.

But Palliser finds that the course he has chosen creates its own problems—and in this way, too, he resembles Grey and Vavasor. The devotion to work that was part of the code of manly behavior stunted personal development. Convinced that a dry style is necessary to success in his work, Palliser demonstrates this tendency in a particularly clear form. He marries for public reasons: to gain an income appropriate to his station and to produce an heir to the Omnium dukedom. His marriage with Glencora "in a point of view regarding business, had been a complete success" (24), but in personal terms it was an equally complete failure, for if Palliser "was dull as a statesman he was more dull in private life" (24). Palliser's neglect of his personal life is so complete that he rarely has sexual relations with his wife. "He seldom gives over work till after one, and sometimes goes on till three. It's the only thing he likes, I believe" (23), Glencora says ruefully as she prepares to go to bed alone on the first of many similar occasions. Palliser sees no connection between his nocturnal behavior and Glencora's tardiness in conceiving a child: perhaps the most dramatic proof of how little this authoritative politician knows about everyday human reality.

Glencora's adulterous longings, which result so directly from sexual and emotional neglect, cannot be cured by her own efforts. Only a thorough reformation of Palliser's behavior can save his marriage, and luckily his desire to stand well with his conscience makes him willing to reform when he understands how deficient a husband he has been. He gives up an opportunity to become Chancellor of the Exchequer in order to take his wife abroad. Suddenly he begins going "to bed early, having no figures which now claimed his attention" (62)—and Glencora becomes pregnant immediately.[31] After realizing that his brand of masculinity has nearly destroyed his marriage, Palliser moderates his devotion to work. But he remains a limited human being.

Even the self-destructive Burgo Fitzgerald is, in his way, a manly man, for he devotes his life to pleasure, one of the things men "naturally" desire. Like the other men in *Can You Forgive Her?*, Burgo has developed the kind of masculinity that was encouraged by his disposition and circumstances. "Born in the purple of the English aristocracy," the sweet-tempered, careless Burgo "when he came of age . . . was master of a sufficient fortune to make it quite out of the question that he should be asked to earn his bread" (18), but was not rich enough to aspire to a political career. Pleasure is the career naturally marked out for such young aristocrats. The narrator implies that Burgo is just living as many people expect a *man* in his position to live, when he says that Burgo had "no idea that it behoved him as a man to do anything but eat and drink" (18). His family is still supporting him as he approaches thirty, drinking curacao at breakfast and seducing the maids.

Readers of *Can You Forgive Her?* may find the narrator's reiterated sympathy with "poor Burgo" (29, 76) surprising, for surely Burgo, born in the purple, naturally sweet-tempered, and startlingly beautiful, is one of the fortunate ones of the earth. But these ostensible advantages actually helped to destroy Burgo, who might have done better had more been expected of him, had "his eyes been less brightly blue, and his face less godlike in form" (29), his birth less exalted, and so forth. At the end of the novel, the narrator wonders whether Glencora's "purple-born" (80) baby boy will have a better chance of happiness than an ordinary child. Though the question remains unanswered, Burgo's experiences are not encouraging in their implications for Glencora's son.

Nor are they encouraging in their implications for men in general. Burgo is an unusually privileged man, but the liberty to develop along undesirable lines is one that every male shares —to some extent. Limited only by society's lax code of manly behavior, the novel's four principal men are all, compared to its restricted women, "purple born." These men suffer from insufficient guidance, and, as we have seen, this causes serious difficulties for each of them.

The men of *Can You Forgive Her?* must struggle with the consequences of excessive freedom, but precisely because they are the victims of freedom and not of repression, it is reasonable to hold them responsible for their own fates.

The women, however, suffer from pressures that greatly limit their freedom of choice. Alice cannot find the exciting life she seeks within the bounds of the conventions she venerates. Shrinking back against the cold stone wall of a graveyard, she agrees to marry Grey, telling him bitterly, "You win everything,—always" (74). She had no chance of escape, because the alternative she sought just was not there. Glencora gains some self-respect by bearing a male heir—who will help perpetuate the social order that has victimized her.[32] Kate, unable to live through her brother, has nothing to live for except the task of repaying the money he stole from Alice.[33] And even Mrs. Greenow gains no more in life's lottery than the privilege of reclaiming a harmless scapegrace. But these women settle for so little because their world offers them nothing better. We should not call their aspirations mistaken or stupid, as several critics have done, because they fail to achieve those aspirations.[34] Nor should the pleasant tone of the novel's conclusion blind us to its gloomy content.

By the time *Can You Forgive Her?* ends, then, the reader may suspect that more is at stake than the question of which characters stand in need of forgiveness and why. Victorian views of femininity *and* masculinity—not individual women and men—have been on trial. Somewhat covertly, but nonetheless forcefully, those views have been condemned.

The Parable of *Miss Mackenzie*

In *Miss Mackenzie* Trollope asks a new question: what would a woman, who had led a restricted life into middle-age, do with money and freedom if they were suddenly presented to her? Formally *Miss Mackenzie* is a romantic comedy, ending with its heroine's marriage. The narrator's cheerful tone, like the novel's comic form, implies that a satisfying romantic tale is being told. But the novel diverges from the classic comic pattern in several ways.[35] The romantic climax occurs at the wrong time, the hero is half-hearted about his love, and the heroine's experiences, up to the moment of the technically happy resolution, are exaggeratedly grim. All this creates tensions between form and content similar to those in *Rachel Ray* and in the main plot of *Can You Forgive Her?*, but the issues involved are different.

Unlike Alice Vavasor, Margaret Mackenzie does not want scope for action outside the domestic sphere. Her aims are feminine: marriage and the opportunities for fulfillment that it provides. And unlike Rachel Ray, she seems to be a woman who would find wifely subordination easy to tolerate. Her determined pursuit of sex, love, and pleasure, however, is not quite acceptable behavior for an aging spinster in Victorian society. Margaret finds it difficult to achieve her modest aims in a world that tells the superfluous woman to accept her own superfluity and live for others. The romantic resolution of *Can You Forgive Her?* was unsatisfying because Alice had aspirations that marriage could not fulfill—but the resolution of *Miss Mackenzie* is unsatisfying because the marriage the heroine makes is not the romantic union she sought.

When the thirty-six-year-old Margaret Mackenzie inherits a fortune from her invalid brother, she is very nearly a tabula rasa as far as outward experiences are concerned. Her childhood "in her father's house had been dull and monotonous" (I, 1), and at nineteen "she was transferred" (I, 1), like a parcel, to her brother's home, where her isolation was even more complete. For "fifteen years, her life had been very weary. A moated grange in the country is bad enough for the life of any Mariana, but a moated grange in town is much worse" (I, 1). After her brother's death, Margaret must learn to make even the most elementary distinctions before she can begin to act for herself: "She told herself over and over again that wealth entailed duties as well as privileges; but she had no clear idea what were the duties so entailed, or what were the privileges. How could she have obtained any clear idea on the subject in that prison which she had inhabited for so many years?" (I, 2).

But Margaret, like other prisoners, has developed a rich imaginary life to compensate for the poverty of her real one. During her many years of "sad, sombre, and . . . almost . . . silent" (I, 2) confinement,

Margaret records the feelings she cannot vocalize in "quires of manuscript"—journals, poems, and, more surprisingly, "outspoken" love letters, "which had never been sent, or been intended to be sent, to any destination" (I, 1). In a hostile environment, her individuality and passion manage to survive, but only by going underground. Margaret's experiences suggest that the natural response to repression is secrecy. She finds safety by playing the negative role in which society has cast her, "a silent, stupid old maid" (I, 1). Her sexual desires, her capacity to think clearly, and her power to use language have all been inhibited—though not destroyed—by the circumstances of her life.

Money, in the world of *Miss Mackenzie,* is power, and only when she inherits a fortune can Margaret begin to develop. She hopes to meet "clever people, nice people, bright people" (I, 1) and if possible to marry. The feminine woman does not, of course, long immodestly for marriage—she waits for love to take her unawares. And so Margaret comes close to violating the code of femininity when she frankly tells her surviving brother Tom that "it was on the cards that she herself might marry" (I, 1). Her brother is "much surprised that she should dare to declare her thoughts" (I, 1), for until this point she has passively played the part of selfless angel in which her relatives have cast her.

Although Margaret is unconventional enough to admit she wants marriage, she is not willing to make the far more damning admission that sex plays a large part in her longing. But Trollope's interest in the effects of repression on women's sexuality had been building for years, as his tactful explorations of the issue in *Orley Farm* and *The Small House at Allington* indicate. And so, in a scene that was remarkably outspoken for the prudish 1860s, Margaret does acknowledge to herself that she is searching for passion. "Was she beyond all aptitude for billing and cooing, if billing and cooing might chance to come her way? . . . She got up and looked at herself in the mirror. . . . Her hand touched the outline of her cheek, and she knew that something of the fresh bloom of youth was still there. . . . She pulled her scarf tighter across her bosom, feeling her own form, and then she leaned forward and kissed herself in the glass" (I, 9).[36]

The thought of trying to satisfy her desire for pleasant society, much less for billing and cooing, seems audacious to Margaret, who knows that society frowns on worldly, demanding spinsters. Powerful emotions drive Margaret to "rebel," but she cannot reject the standards of femininity by which her conduct would be condemned, or overcome the fear that she will disgrace herself by pursuing her own ends. In this respect, she resembles such heroines as Caroline Waddington, Lady Mason, and Alice Vavasor, all of whom assert themselves, but lack confidence in their right to do so. The interesting thing about Margaret's rebellion is that it frightens her even though it is so very mild. "Would it not have been easier for her," she wonders, "easier and more comfortable,—to have abandoned all ideas of the world, and have put herself at once under the tutelage and protection of some clergyman who would have told her how to give away her money, and prepare herself in the right way for a comfortable death-bed?" (I, 2)—to have returned, that is, to the living death of self-suppression under male authority, which society approves for women in her position. Though Margaret finally does decide to "give the world a trial" (I, 2), the desire to avoid censure by returning to "her former obscurity and dependence" (I, 12) never disappears. Tentatively, then, Margaret begins to search for a lovable husband. Soon her substantial fortune, well-preserved appearance, and sweet disposition, in descending order of importance, have attracted three suitors. But Margaret's situation is not enviable, for none of the suitors offers what she is looking for. Trollope stresses this point by burdening them with three nicely contrasted—and extremely serious—flaws.

First in the field is Margaret's cousin, John Ball, the widowed father of nine. In his youth Ball was clever and passionate. But a large family in conjunction with small means crushed his spirit. He tried to increase his capital through speculation and gradually became obsessed with wealth, while losing interest in everything else: "He was always thinking of his money" (I, 6). When John Ball proposes to Margaret, her self-abnegating side is tempted by his need for her money and services. "When he told her of the heavy duties which might fall to her lot as his wife, he almost made her think that it might be well for her to marry him" (I, 7). But she cannot quite bring herself to renounce the joyful fulfillment of a romantic marriage for the grimmer satisfaction of "sacrificial duties" (I, 9) well done. "Of romance in [John Ball] there was nothing left. . . . It was not only that his head was bald, but that his eye was dull, and his step slow. The juices of life had been pressed out of him" (I, 9). Margaret has spent her youth nursing worn-out men, and she is not ready to sign on for another term under only slightly improved circumstances. Ball has none of the sex appeal for which she is searching.

After rejecting Ball, Margaret acquires two other suitors: Samuel Rubb, her brother's partner, and the curate Mr. Maguire. Like Ball, both of these men are mainly interested in Margaret's money. Margaret finds Rubb attractive, but he is simply not a gentleman in education, dress, or manners. Though she wishes to reject the conventions that have so trammeled her, to assert her right to marry a man for love "even though he might not be a gentleman," Margaret finds herself unable to "go down among the Rubbs . . . and give up the society of [her own class]" (I, 10). Social standing without physical attraction is not enough to make Ball an acceptable husband, but attraction without social suitability is equally unacceptable.

Superficially Maguire combines the best qualities of Rubb and Ball. A gentleman by profession, he possesses some personal attractions: "dark hair . . . good figure . . . expressive mouth" (I, 11). But Mr. Maguire also "squinted horribly" (I, 9), and this physical flaw is the outward sign of a serious moral flaw. For Maguire is a canting evangelical hypocrite. Although Maguire is the worst of her three suitors, the inexperienced Margaret almost accepts him because, unlike Ball and Rubb, he seems to possess something close to the combination of gentility and magnetism for which she is searching—in spite of his horrifying squint. Margaret's plight suggests that a woman will not necessarily be offered a satisfying marriage even if she is attractive and has money of her own.

But just as Margaret decides to accept Maguire, she learns that a legal error has been made and that her entire fortune is almost certainly the property of John Ball. Margaret's response to this loss of freedom is—paradoxically, but quite believably—one of relief.

Though her money had given her the illusion of choice, it was only an illusion, for none of the marriages within her reach promised her happiness. Even an unusually powerful woman in Victorian society cannot have her own way, as Margaret discovers. She has come to "hate her money [which] had brought her nothing but tribulation and disappointment" (II, 1). The search for fulfillment was fraught with such difficulty that Margaret is positively pleased to give it up, and to place herself "under the guidance of her cousin [John Ball] . . . pledged to do nothing of which he would disapprove" (II, 9).

At this point, however, another reversal occurs. When John Ball sees how passively Margaret reacts to misfortune, his lukewarm feeling for her becomes passionate, and he renews his proposal. Margaret's helplessness awakens real love in John Ball. He gets a pleasant sensation of masculine power from the "soft, womanly trusting weakness" with which she appeals to him (II, 5) and from the way she "clung to him and trusted him . . . though he was going to take from her everything that had been hers" (II, 5). Margaret rich and independent could not rejuvenate Ball, but Margaret weak and passive transforms him into a young lover: "He took her, and kissed her lips, and told her that he would take care of her, and watch for her, and keep her, if possible, from trouble" (II, 5). Ball's hair does not quite grow back, but in other respects he improves dramatically.

Margaret's expectations are now considerably lower than they once were, and she accepts the altered John Ball with real pleasure. When Ball acquires Margaret's money, he also gains masculine appeal in her eyes, and she suddenly finds him a thrilling lover. "The poetry had come to be a fact, and the romance had turned itself into reality," rhapsodizes the narrator when Ball proposes (II, 5). If *Miss Mackenzie* ended here, we might agree with James Kincaid that it is a straightforward romantic comedy about the rejuvenating power of love—though we would have to note that the novel's characters define love in terms of male dominance and female submission.[37]

But *Miss Mackenzie* is only two-thirds over when Margaret accepts John Ball's renewed proposal. It is too early for the comic conclusion we think we have witnessed, and sure enough, further troubles develop almost immediately. Although the narrator shows little awareness that anything disturbing has occurred, Ball's reaction to these troubles should undermine the reader's approval of the match. Margaret intercepts Ball—on his way to bed—to refute a false accusation made against her by Maguire. But this small act of self-assertion gets Margaret into trouble. Her boldness in calling him into her bedroom and her passionate manner frighten Ball, who is attracted mainly by her submissive side. He starts to see Margaret (both literally and figuratively) as a loose woman: "The loose sleeve of her dressing-gown had fallen back, and he could see that her arm was round and white, and very fair. Was she conversant with such tricks as these?" (II, 7). As is the case with other assertive women in Trollope's novels, Margaret's fears that she might inadvertently go too far prove to have been well founded.

Though Margaret was relieved to surrender control of her destiny to John Ball, she cannot renounce her newly acquired strength of character. Two years of wealth and freedom gave her a voice, if they did nothing else for her. No longer the silent, timid creature of the novel's early sections, she defends herself firmly against the charge that she is unfit to marry Ball, and when he responds evasively, "a gleam of anger flashed from her eyes" (II, 7). Ball is upset by Margaret's pride. He wants her, but he wants her helpless and submissive: "He did not like to think that all authority over her was passing out of his hands. . . . He was prepared to receive her tears and excuses, and we may say that, in all probability, he would have pardoned her had she wept before him and excused herself" (II, 7). But Margaret has done no wrong and will not weep.

For several months, Ball is much troubled. He loves Margaret, but he hates her independence. Weakly, he postpones his decision, telling himself he will reconsider the matter after the lawyers have reached a final settlement about Margaret's fortune. When he meets Margaret, his behavior maddens her, for he ignores her suffering and speaks "as though there was nothing to be regretted by anybody, except the fact that he could not get possession of the property as quick as he wished" (II, 10). Thus the rejuvenated John Ball disappears, and his old careworn self, obsessed with money and inattentive to the emotions, emerges once more. Even when the question of the fortune has been settled, he cannot decide what to do about Margaret, and renews his proposal only when a friend pressures him to do so. Margaret, about to become a hospital nurse, is happy to marry him. But their match at the end of the novel is not the romantic triumph she had anticipated earlier. She now understands the weakness of his character, while he fears the strength she has developed. Even during the proposal scene, Ball keeps wandering off into irrelevant lamentations about the money he has lost. " 'It has been unjust, has it not?' said he, piteously, thinking of his injuries . . . [though] he knew that this was not the kind of conversation which he desired to commence" (II, 14). But he has a hard time leaving the subject of money for that of love.

The marriage that once looked joyous now seems acceptable only because Margaret's other possibilities are bleak. "Her destiny was in [Ball's] hands to such a degree that she felt his power over her to amount almost to a cruelty" (II, 11), and she must be delighted when he uses that power mercifully. She is now happy to get him, even though he has relapsed into the apathy that originally made him distasteful to her. Thus *Miss Mackenzie,* like *Can You Forgive Her?* and *Rachel Ray,* ends with a union that is less pleasing than the usual celebratory marriages of comedy. When the narrator says that Margaret accepted her marriage "thankfully, quietly, and with an enduring satisfaction, as it became such a woman to do" (II, 15), the reader understands why such a woman must be thankful for such a marriage and finds the remark somewhat ambiguous.

P. D. Edwards thinks that *Miss Mackenzie* is a far-fetched novel that deals "a number of blows to the reader's credulity." These blows include the improbabilities surrounding Margaret's loss of fortune and the incredible ignorance of genteel manners that Samuel Rubb displays.[38] It is possible, however, that Trollope used a far-fetched plot and a cast of ludicrously unattractive minor characters in *Miss Mackenzie* precisely because the work is a parable about the lives of women in Victorian England, rather than a completely realistic novel. If *Miss Mackenzie* is a parable, then the farcically exaggerated deficiencies of Rubb and the other suitors, as well as the unaccountable legal developments that emphasize Margaret's helplessness, can be defended. For on this hypothesis, we would expect Margaret's experiences to be both revealingly typical and revealingly extreme.

And so they are. Margaret's girlhood is an exaggerated and prolonged, but completely recognizable, version of the upbringing most middle-class girls received. The ideal of femininity demanded reserve and self-suppression from middle-class girls, while it doomed them to very restricted lives. The intellectual and sexual development of these girls tended to be repressed almost as thoroughly as Margaret's was—and like her they may well have hidden unconventional desires beneath their placid exteriors. If they let their assertive impulses be seen, as Margaret did, they risked the sort of disapproval she encountered. Margaret's unsatisfactory suitors, her helpless position when she accepts Ball, and her dependence on him after the engagement are also exaggerated versions of commonplace problems. Through this heightened reinterpretation of the "ordinary" woman's experience, Trollope makes some disturbing points about the position of women.

Miss Mackenzie's symbolically suggestive plot implies that Margaret is a representative Victorian woman, and its narrative style reinforces this point. James Kincaid rightly observes that the novel's narrator "spends most of his time nudging us into identification with Miss Mackenzie by mock apologies."[39] Margaret is a very mild rebel indeed, but many Victorians would have thought her interest in sex and pleasure unsuitable to a maiden lady of such advanced age. When the narrator jokingly excuses Margaret for desiring to bill and coo, for wanting to have some fun, or for getting angry when people mistreat her—as he continually does—he encourages us to ask why so many apologies are necessary for such ordinary desires. In a tactful, understated way, this plethora of excuses implies that ordinary readers are likely to judge women's conduct by absurdly narrow standards.

When the narrator generalizes about women, he sometimes reassures the reader by endorsing the conventional standards by which Margaret's assertive tendencies would be judged unfeminine or abnormal. But far more frequently he takes the position that Margaret's ostensibly deviant impulses are by no means unusual. "Like all other single ladies, she was very nervous about her money" (I, 3), he notes on one such occasion. "She was doing what we all do" (I, 6) in searching for friends she could be proud of, he claims on another. The reader is also given extensive access to Margaret's thoughts, which show her to be a decent woman struggling with a series of unpleasant dilemmas—though the cheerful narrator never acknowledges how distasteful her options really are. These elements of *Miss Mackenzie*'s narrative style urge readers to question the standards by which Margaret would be found deficient. They quietly suggest that she is a sort of Everywoman.

Trollope also emphasizes the typicality of Margaret's experiences by ironically relating them to two literary prototypes. In her girl-hood, Margaret is "Mariana in a moated grange," waiting for a suitor who never comes, and in her maturity she becomes the patient Griselda, cruelly abused by the man she loves. These two parallels stress the passive suffering of women both as maids and as wives, though the narrator's lighthearted tone in developing them softens their impact. Margaret, like Griselda, must wait patiently for a man to regret his mistreatment of her, but she does not wait with Griselda's complete passivity. When John Ball's mother attacks her, Margaret defends herself angrily, a "modern Griselda . . . galvanized into vitality" (II, 10). Further, the introduction of a character named Mrs. Chaucer Munro, at the very moment when everyone is referring to Margaret as "Griselda," prods readers to recall "The Clerk's Tale," where Griselda's story is told. There Chaucer shows that Griselda may well encourage Walter's mania by her quiescence in enduring his cruelty. "Oh noble wives, in highest prudence bred,/ Allow no such humility to nail your tongues," Chaucer advises lightly in his envoy to the tale.[40] In the end, then, the parallel implies that it is not desirable for a modern woman to imitate Griselda's patience. But because the modern woman is nearly as powerless as Griselda was centuries earlier, circumstances often force her to make the attempt.[41]

Miss Mackenzie suggests that even the least rebellious women may nurse secret desires for sex, pleasure, and self-expression. But their world offers them only the choice between Mariana in youth and Griselda in middle age. Should they move beyond these roles, they risk both censure and self-reproach. Safety is to be found only in the acceptance of severe restriction, the kind of restriction Margaret accepts when she marries the decent but limited John Ball. Though the comic form and the narrator's pleasant tone help to screen this disturbing interpretive possibility from the conventional reader, Margaret's story is a parable about women's unsatisfactory options and the small blessings for which they must be grateful.

Depths and Surfaces in *The Claverings*

In *The Claverings,* a novel about self-deception and hypocrisy, Trollope uses a deceptive, "hypocritical" form to develop his theme. Though conventional on the surface, the novel ultimately rejects the very conventions by which it appears to be organized. As we have seen, tensions between form and content characterize the novels immediately preceding *The Claverings.* But the subversive elements of these novels are better hidden than the subversive elements here. In *Rachel Ray,* for example, the subtext concerning women's desire for power is so well disguised that it has gone almost unnoticed by critics. But nearly every critic who discusses *The Claverings* notices that its narrator's conventional interpretation of his story is unconvincing, that its resolution is displeasing, or that its ironic content undermines the blandly comic form.[42] Andrew Wright uses a revealing simile to describe the tensions between form and content in this disturbing novel: "*The Claverings* has a special kind of unpleasantness, like a bad smell in what appears to be a good room, which seems less and less good as the smell becomes more pervasive."[43] One cannot avoid feeling that something is rotten in *The Claverings* because it goes a long way toward closing off the interpretive escape routes for conventional readers, which the earlier novels carefully kept open.

The main plot of *The Claverings* initially appears to be both a traditional romantic comedy in form and a conventional moral tale in content. Julia Brabazon, who jilts her fiancé Harry Clavering in favor of the rich roué Lord Ongar, is punished by a horrible marriage, a ruined reputation, and the loss of the man she loves. For a while she functions as a blocking character, preventing Harry's marriage to the long-suffering Florence Burton. In the end, however, Florence's goodness triumphs, and she is united to Harry amid general rejoicing. But tone, timing, and above all characterization in *The Claverings* encourage the reader to look critically at its surface elements. Just as the novel's characters substitute idealized images for the unsatisfactory realities of their lives, so too does its moralistic brand of comic form simplify the complex issues it raises. Thus, the novel offers a commentary on the kind of comedy it pretends to be.

The characters in *The Claverings* are not, for the most part, very likable, but they conceal their defects and feel little guilt about their dishonesty. They pretend to be ideal people united in ideal family relationships and reproach themselves when the truth slips out. In fact, they incarnate Victorian hypocrisy about money, sex, and the joys of domesticity.[44] Thus, although Mr. Clavering, Harry's clergyman father, hates his nephew, Sir Hugh, he dines with him occasionally so "that there might be no recognized quarrel" (2) between them to cause scandal in the parish. When Sir Hugh and his brother are lost at sea, Harry— who can't stand either of them, and who will now inherit Hugh's estate—reports the tragedy "with the usual amount of epithets . . . terrible, awful, shocking,—the saddest thing that had ever happened!" (44). Although this sort of hypocrisy does not usually loom large in Trollope's novels, one could cover pages with examples of the way characters in *The Claverings* distort reality for public consumption.

The Claverings examines four marriages: two of them ostensibly successful, but actually less ideal than they appear,[45] the other two grotesque and frightening failures. At first, the narrator gives us a positive impression of the marriage between Mr. Clavering and his admirable wife. Smoking cigars "was the only vice with which Mr. Clavering could be charged," the narrator claims indulgently. "He was a kind, soft-hearted, gracious man, tender to his wife, whom he ever regarded as the angel of his house" (2). But no sooner does the narrator draw this picture of conventional bliss than he begins to show that the marriage is only superficially blissful. In spite of his angelic wife's example, Mr. Clavering "had sunk into idleness," telling himself daily, "I see a better path . . . but I follow ever the worse" (2). His wife reacts as people usually do in this novel: she strives to preserve the appearance of harmony, though the reality is gone. "She had given [her husband] up, [but] not with disdainful rejection, nor with contempt in her eye, or censure in her voice, not with diminution of love or of outward respect" (2). As the novel progresses, Mrs. Clavering struggles to treat her husband with the proper deference—to sustain their image as a happy family ruled by a wise patriarch—while she quietly represses the laziness and snobbery that mar his character. They still love one another, but all is not as ideal as it appears. The narrator presents this marriage to the reader so as to emphasize the discrepancy between its surface and the underlying reality.

Nor is the marriage of the engineer Theodore Burton and his wife Cecilia as harmonious as narrator, husband, and wife unite to suggest. Cecilia constantly claims that her husband is perfect: "Theodore tells me everything," she says rhapsodically and not very plausibly to a new friend. "I don't think there's a drain planned under a railway-bank, but that he shows it me in some way; and I feel so grateful for it" (8). But every time we see the Burtons in action, they are squabbling. "I don't think women recognize any difference in flavours," Theodore remarks condescendingly. "I should not mind this, if it were not that they are generally proud of the deficiency." Cecilia, stung, accuses men of expressing an equally childish pride in their musical ignorance. Little complaints, which are more revealing than she realizes, punctuate Cecilia's praise of her husband. "I'm so glad that you have been here a little before him," she tells a visitor, "when he's here I shan't get in a word" (8). Soon Cecilia embarks on a platonic flirtation with Harry, who "made love to [her] over her children's beds" (15), and secretly undertakes a project of which Theodore would surely disapprove. And so the reader learns that this marriage is fraught with unacknowledged strains, which result from Cecilia's difficulties in adjusting to wifely subordination. "I don't think . . . I care so much about my own way as some women do," she tells Theodore with unconscious irony. "I am sure I always think your opinion is better than my own;—that is, in most things" (40). Cecilia hates independent women like Julia precisely because her own efforts to submit to her husband have cost her so dearly.

The failed marriage of Sir Hugh and Hermione is quite unlike these marriages, which, though not ideal, are normal mixtures of good and bad feelings. Sir Hugh, a man "fond of pleasure and fond of money" (1), is "very secret in his own affairs, never telling his wife anything about them" (11). He leaves her alone on his gloomy estate, while he enjoys himself in London, and takes "a delight in being thus overharsh in his harshness to her. He proved to himself thus not only that he was master, but that he would be master without any let or drawback, without compunctions, and even without excuses for his ill-conduct" (35). Trollope's minute-by-minute account of Sir Hugh's brief visit home before leaving on a long fishing trip suggests that he has stopped having sexual relations with his wife, whose "washed-out, dowdy prettinesses" (35) now repel him—neither the first time that Trollope has hinted at sexual problems he cannot discuss openly, nor the first time that he has portrayed a married woman who is not getting as much sexual attention as she would like. The narrator endorses her sister Julia's view that Hermione has been no more than a "body-slave to Hugh Clavering" (15); at Hugh's death he claims she should be called "the enfranchised slave" (44) rather than the poor widow.

The marriage of Julia and Lord Ongar, who "had had delirium tremens, and was a worn-out miserable object" (2), is even more nightmarish than her sister's grim union. His friends having convinced Lord Ongar that "his only chance of saving himself lay in marriage," he purchases Julia "at the price of a brilliant settlement" (3). A few months later the newly widowed Julia returns and discusses her marriage with Harry Clavering. When her husband found, Julia tells Harry euphemistically, "that he had been wrong in marrying me, that he did not want the thing which he had thought would suit him . . . he strove to get another man to take me off his hands" (7). A friend of the Ongars lets Harry know that, unlike many old roués who marry young brides, Lord Ongar "was not man enough to be jealous" (14) of his wife. The narrator says that the revelations he heard about the Ongars "almost made Harry Clavering's hair stand on end, and . . . must not be repeated here" (14). Apparently Lord Ongar was both impotent with his wife and involved in vices too grotesque to mention in a respectable work of fiction. For respectable fiction, like the characters in *The Claverings*, must put a decorous gloss on the unpalatable realities its readers want to ignore.

The main plot of *The Claverings* is played out against the background of these four marriages. The marriages of Mr. Clavering and the Burtons demonstrate the Victorian tendency to idealize the angel wife and the appreciative husband. The marriages of Sir Hugh and the Ongars dramatize the terrible results that ensue when society encourages male selfishness and then grants men almost absolute power to neglect or abuse their helpless wives. The novel's treatment of these two unsuccessful marriages also reveals how propriety prevents the discussion of sexual problems. The marriages in *The Claverings* predispose readers to look suspiciously at Victorian notions about domestic bliss, as well as at the human tendency to reshape experience in the light of an ideal. The picture of marriage this novel draws urges its readers to sympathize with the economic, social, and sexual plight of women, which it depicts in more frightening terms than do Trollope's earlier works. These attitudes help to guide readers towards an interpretation of the novel's main plot that diverges from the one its surface elements suggest.

When *The Claverings* opens, Julia has just jilted Harry because she is convinced that, given her extravagant habits and his unstable character, a marriage between them would not work. Though Julia would like to enter a profession, she knows she has to "be married well, or to go out like a snuff of a candle" (1). She resolves to "do her duty by her future lord. The duty would be doubtless disagreeable, but she would do it with all the more diligence on that account" (3). Her cynical brother-in-law Sir Hugh, however, thinks her marriage will be more difficult than she anticipates: "Julia will find she has caught a Tartar" (3). Though Julia convinces herself that "she had not many regrets" (3) about losing Harry, she thinks of him continuously as she plans her wedding. Immediately after the ceremony she reflects that "she had chosen her profession, as Harry Clavering had chosen his; and having so far succeeded, she would do her best to make her success perfect" (3).

Thus far it seems as if Trollope is preparing a conventional moral fable for his readers. The ambitious Julia, having rejected love in favor of money, has failed to repress her feelings for her old lover and is about to find her new husband more difficult than she expects. Readers naturally anticipate that Julia's marriage will founder and that she will discover too late that her love for Harry is more enduring than she imagined—anticipate, in fact, exactly what *did* happen to Caroline Waddington after she married Henry Harcourt in *The Bertrams*. And for a while the story seems to be developing, in so extreme a manner that we may suspect a touch of parody, along these lines. We have already seen how quickly Julia's marriage ends in disaster. When she returns to England, her natural male protector, Sir Hugh, believing the false rumors about her sexual misconduct that her husband circulated, decides not to receive her. Taking this as proof of her guilt, society follows suit and Julia finds herself alone. Though she tries to believe that her large income will suffice for happiness, she can enjoy nothing in her friendless condition. The narrator invents a melodramatic refrain to emphasize Julia's desolation: "The price was in her hands," he says again and again, but "the apples had . . . turned to ashes between her teeth" (12). And, as expected, she realizes that only through Harry's love will "the flavour . . . come back to the apples" (16). But Harry is engaged to Florence Burton, and so Julia feels "herself tempted to do as Judas did,—to go out and hang herself" (12).

Retribution for violating the code of feminine delicacy could hardly be more extreme, but Julia in fact does not receive Judas' punishment for her betrayal of love. She reaches her nadir halfway through the novel—not, as one might have expected, at its close. And then Trollope begins to rehabilitate her, restoring to her both the reader's respect and a measure of contentment.[46] In the first place, Harry's vacillating behavior gradually convinces everyone that "Providence was making a great mistake when she expected him to earn his bread" (48), and thus validates Julia's judgment that he was unfit to support a penniless wife. Her crime, then, was not rejecting Harry but marrying Lord Ongar, a crime that the reader, considering the pressure to marry prudently to which upper-class women were subjected, may well excuse.

Second, Julia's willingness to acknowledge her own misconduct, in combination with her honesty and generosity under trying circumstances, raises her in the reader's estimation. Her moral judgments are acute and fair. She admits that she sold herself, "as a beast is sold," and she sees that in ignoring her humanity men have treated her as she treated herself (25). She decides to make restitution for her sin by returning her ill-gotten gains to Lord Ongar's family, but they refuse to take back her income—thus proving that they do not condemn her as harshly as she condemns herself. Through Julia's scrupulousness, however, "an intimacy, and at last a close friendship, was formed between her and the relatives of her deceased lord" (48).

By the end of the novel, Julia is well on her way to social rehabilitation. And since she has been ostracized for sexual sins she did not commit—her mercenary marriage itself having done her no harm socially—the reader must agree that Julia's rehabilitation is deserved. Her strength of character makes it easy to believe her final promise to Harry: "You shall never hear of my being downhearted" (48). The lasting unhappiness we expect for Julia does not materialize, and the ashen apples disappear from the text. Though the narrator never acknowledges that Julia has grown in stature, neither does he try to conceal it. Critics agree that Julia emerges as the novel's most interesting character and as an admirable woman, even though she once sold herself for gain.[47] Victorian readers might have had more trouble reading this novel as an indictment of an impure woman than they would have had in reading *The Bertrams* as an indictment of Caroline, or *Can You Forgive Her?* as an indictment of Alice.

If, in his characterization of Julia, Trollope convinces his readers to respect a woman who has sinned against feminine purity, in his characterization of Florence Burton he gently undermines the notion that the domestic angel is the most admirable kind of woman.[48] The generally conventional, or at least reserved, narrator of *The Claverings* does not openly attack Florence any more than he openly praises Julia, but the amount of attention he pays to each tells a different story. Where the narrator has to struggle for paragraphs to capture Julia's complexity, he reduces Florence to little more than a cliche: a "nice girl" who makes "quiet domesticities" (4) attractive. In describing Florence, the narrator alternates between sentimental bromides and suspiciously flat language that suggests how uninteresting her goodness really is: one chapter dealing with her love troubles is titled "Florence Burton Packs up a Packet."

Florence, though perfectly feminine in the modest demands she makes of life, is just not as wise as the more experienced Julia. After a whirlwind courtship, which is so dull that the narrator does not bother to describe it, Harry and Florence become engaged. This premature climax parallels the premature punishment Julia suffers. It is one of those hurried resolutions that should alert Trollope's attentive reader to an approaching attack on the assumptions of romantic comedy. After the engagement, Florence, like Julia, concludes that Harry should not marry on a small income, for he "would not be happy as a poor man" (9). But where Julia knew that her unstable lover could not bear the strain of a long engagement, Florence foolishly decides that "Harry must wait" (9).

Because she is committed to the proposition that a woman should worship her lover, it is not surprising that Florence persistently ignores Harry's weak side. But her ignorance of his real nature appears foolish rather than noble. At one point she even recommends "a little flirtation" (9) as an antidote to the boredom of a long engagement, failing to realize that Harry—who is "ever making love to women" (15)—already has a positively dangerous talent for flirtation. Harry, irritated by being told to wait, falls in love with Julia and nearly betrays Florence. All of this suggests that Julia understands Harry far better than Florence, who is certain that "honesty and truth were written on every line of his face" (16), at the very moment when he is secretly planning to jilt her. Florence's view of Harry demonstrates the tendency to make reality conform to theory, which so many characters in this novel display.

When Cecilia delicately prepares to tell Florence of Harry's infidelity, Florence, unsure of what is to be revealed, demands the whole truth: "Look here, Cecilia; if it be anything touching himself or his own character, I will put up with it. . . . Though he had been a murderer, if that were possible, I would not leave him. I will never leave him unless he leaves me" (32). Cecilia asserts that Harry has not left Florence but is considering it—and the wounded Florence speedily descends from the high horse of eternal feminine constancy. "I do not want to see him, and I am glad that he has gone away" (32), she tells Cecilia huffily, causing Cecilia to respond with some justice, "You said you would not leave him, unless he left you" (32). Julia's powerful character gradually wins the reader's respect, but Florence's predictable perfection grows less appealing as Trollope suggests how much distortion her idealism involves.

Further, *The Claverings'* only subplot, which concerns the courtship of Harry's sister Fanny by the curate, Mr. Saul, undercuts Florence's standards of judgment in selecting a lover. Saul is, morally, everything that Harry is not: dedicated to his work, constant in his love, able to endure privation in the pursuit of laudable ends. But unlike Harry, Saul is neither charming, nor good-looking, nor well born, and therefore he is the sort of man "from whom young women seem to be as far removed in the way of love as though they belonged to some other species" (6). Everyone in the novel finds it odd that Fanny does finally fall in love with this "very good young man," because, as Harry (who certainly ought to know) remarks, "Girls don't fall in love with men because they're good" (34). And the reader also finds it odd, for in novels a man with "a thin hatchet face, and unwholesome stubbly chin" (34) seldom wins a beautiful girl like Fanny.

Florence, impressed by Harry's style, makes a more familiar choice and one that the reader is initially more inclined to applaud. But Saul grows to "larger dimensions as regarded spirit, manhood, and heart" (34) in the reader's estimation, and Fanny's peculiar choice is validated. Harry correspondingly shrinks, and so readers may become critical of the conventional criteria by which Florence selected him—as well as of the many romantic novels that tacitly approve those criteria. One peculiar consequence of a double standard that demands purity from women, but not from men, is that the angelic woman feels little interest in finding a male angel. In a scene that is heavy with irony at her expense, Florence thinks about

Saul's virtue, and then, turning her thoughts "to her own matters," congratulates herself on gaining "such a lover as Harry Clavering" (16), a lover so much more desirable than the unglamorous Saul.

Superficially Harry and Florence's tale is both comic and moralistic. The ambitious Julia is the obstacle separating the lovers, and when Harry decides to give her up, he makes the "right" choice by marrying the virtuous Florence. But beneath the novel's simple surface, complex tensions develop. The comic conclusion is undercut because Julia is not nearly as deficient as the plot structure implies, while Florence is not nearly as admirable. And it is undercut because Harry himself is even less of a prize than most of Trollope's weak young heroes: "the man . . . was not worth the passion" (37).

The novel's failure to settle the question of which woman Harry "really" loves also undermines its resolution. Most critics conclude that Harry should have married Julia because his feeling for her is more uniquely personal than his feeling for Florence, whom he chose because she was, by conventional standards, "fitter to be his wife" (4).[49] Julia remarks shrewdly that "men are not always fond of perfection. The angels may be too angelic for this world" (37)— and Harry proves her point when he considers telling Florence that his heart "had returned to one who was in all respects less perfect than she" (25).

But nonetheless it is inaccurate to say that Harry loves Julia rather than Florence. In fact, he loves them both—and it is significant that he does. When Harry returns to Florence, the narrator rightly argues that it is impossible to tell whether the declaration of renewed love he made her was "wholly true or only partially so" (41). Comic form and Victorian convention both say that there is only one true love, one right choice, one happy ending. And the right choice for a man is always the angelic woman—even if the right choice for a woman is not usually the angelic man. But the realities of love that emerge from Harry's story are too complex, and even perverse, to fit this simple, moralistic scheme.

The Claverings does not resolve the striking difficulties it raises. Its "angelic" women—Mrs. Clavering, Cecilia, and Florence—ultimately get what they want, but they are not elevated morally over the "erring" Julia, as Adela was elevated over Caroline in *The Ber-*

trams, a novel that handled similar contrasts in a much less subversive manner. In *The Claverings*—to a far greater extent than in any of Trollope's earlier novels—the unresolved tensions between conventional surfaces and the murky depths underlying them are themselves the theme.

After Hugh and Archie Clavering die, the narrator wonders what sort of funeral sermon ought to be preached for two such worthless men. "I should not myself have liked the duty of preaching an eulogistic sermon on the lives and death of Hugh Clavering and his brother Archie," he protests. "What had either of them ever done to merit a good word from any man?" (44). The narrator would have liked to tell the truth about their selfishness, but in the hypocritical world of *The Claverings* so honest a sermon is unthinkable. Is this hyprocrisy good or bad, the narrator wonders? Looked at from one point of view, he thinks, the eulogistic sermon that convention demands might have a positive effect. "It is well that some respect should be maintained from the low in station towards those who are high, even when no respect has been deserved" (44)—and such a sermon would encourage his dependents to think respectfully of Sir Hugh. But the narrator finally concludes that dishonest eulogy must be judged harmful if we "take into our calculation, in giving our award on this subject, the permanent utility of all truth, and the permanent injury of all falsehood" (44). And that, obviously, is what we ought to do.

This subtle point is, I think, crucial in understanding *The Claverings*, a novel filled with people who tell pious lies to preserve appearances. These lies are motivated by a desire to sustain belief in widely shared values, and they seem so justifiable that people are proud of telling them. If we recall Trollope's view that the Victorian novelist is supposed to be a "preacher of sermons," we can see how all this fits together. Like a false eulogy, the romantic comedy that endorses conventional notions about men, women, and love is a well-intentioned attempt to make recalcitrant reality conform to theory. But the novelist must consider something more than his role as the upholder of Victorian pieties when he writes his fiction. He must consider the permanent blessing conferred by artistic truth and the permanent injury done by artistic falsehood. In refusing, more firmly than ever before, to "preach" the conventional eulogy of pure women like Florence or to give the conventional warning against independent women like Julia, in mocking the moralistic comedy his public expected, Trollope affirms these "eternal" considerations. And at the same time he rejects the well-intentioned deceptions practiced by his characters, by society, and by a great deal of Victorian fiction.

Progressive Comedy in *The Belton Estate*

In *The Belton Estate*, Trollope attacks the double standard that punished women harshly for sexual misconduct it tolerated in men. Later on, this subject became something of an idée fixe for him, helping to organize such works as *The Vicar of Bullhampton, Is He Popenjoy?* and *Dr. Wortle's School*. But although *The Belton Estate* is the first of Trollope's novels to treat this potentially offensive theme at length, its approach is by no means tentative. *The Belton Estate* does not defer to its readers by keeping open the possibility of a conventional interpretation—as Trollope's novels of the early 1860s did. Even more definitively than *The Claverings, The Belton Estate* resists a conservative reading. The narrative voice, the interaction between subplots, and the development of the characters encourage the reader to sympathize with a fallen woman—and to enjoy a comedy premised upon progressive views of women.

The narrator of *The Belton Estate* differs from the narrators of the ambiguous novels Trollope wrote in the early 1860s. Those narrators were typically inconsistent or unconvincing in their conventional analyses of the female characters, moving the reader toward greater sympathy with dissatisfied women, while leaving open the possibility of a less unorthodox reading. But more than any of his predecessors, including the narrator of *The Claverings*, this narrator vigorously defends rebellious women. When he mentions unimportant customs of "feminine" behavior—like the "waspish" waist, which he claims ladies have rejected because they choose "in their more advanced state of knowledge" to look healthy rather than delicate (4)—he takes the side of reform. And when he discusses more controversial issues, he does the same. "In ordinary marriages," he notes approvingly, without regard for the male-supremacist reader, "the stronger and the greater takes the lead, whether clothed in petticoats, or in coat, waistcoat, and trousers" (11). *The Belton Estate* is the first of Trollope's novels to employ a narrator who is consistently—though not immoderately—feminist.

The Belton Estate audaciously parallels the situation of its virtuous heroine, Clara Amedroz, with that of the fallen Mary Askerton. Their problems are similar, and Clara comes close to making a marriage as intolerable as the one from which Mrs. Askerton fled under the protection of a lover. Clara needs great good luck in order to avoid this fate because the conventions guiding Victorian women make it difficult for the passionate woman to select a husband who will make her happy. In telling Mrs. Askerton's story, Trollope attacks the double standard of sexual morality directly; in telling Clara's, he attacks the views of male and female nature on which that standard is ultimately based.

Clara's experiences demonstrate that the customs governing inheritance encourage ruthless discrimination in favor of males. When the novel opens, Clara has "never done harm to anyone" (1), but her interests have nonetheless been sacrificed to those of her dissolute brother Charles. Mr. Amedroz saw his son's vicious behavior as masculine and glamorous. He felt a certain "delight in the stories which reached him of his son's vagaries" (1) and repeatedly paid his debts. Mr. Amedroz finally sacrifices even "the life assurances which were to have made provision for his daughter" (1) in a doomed attempt to save the property for his heir. But Charles, far past saving, commits suicide.

Mr. Amedroz salves his conscience for placing his worthless son's interests before those of his worthy daughter by reflecting that Clara may inherit something from her wealthy aunt, Mrs. Winterfield. But Mrs. Winterfield, "one of those women who have always believed that their own sex is in every respect inferior to the other" (7), subordinates Clara's interests to those of her worldly, hypocritical nephew, Captain Aylmer, as surely as her father subordinated them to those of her brother. Mrs. Winterfield is by no means the only woman in Trollope's novels who internalizes conventional notions about male supremacy and female subordination. Most of them do so to some extent. And this is not surprising if we consider how pervasive those notions were and how dangerous it would have been for a woman to reject them altogether. But Mrs. Winterfield is the most unjust of the male-supremacist women Trollope had yet portrayed.

Mr. Amedroz acknowledges his daughter's moral superiority to his son, though nothing follows from this insight. But Mrs. Winterfield, blinded by her prejudice in favor of men, never even realizes that her niece is a better human being than her nephew. Clara was raised by Mrs. Winterfield, a rigidly conservative supporter of low church views. But Clara does not "belong to that school of divinity in which her aunt shone" and feels that had she "left the old woman in doubt on this subject, she would have been a hypocrite" (1). Clara wants to be honest with her aunt because the view of women as pure and pious creatures suggests that they "are absolutely false if they be not sincere" in religious matters (1)—though some hypocrisy is tacitly permitted to men, who are not naturally so pious. Trying to live by this rule of the moral code females must obey, Clara violates another provision: that unmarried girls should submit to the guidance of their families. She cannot both retain her self-respect by eschewing hypocrisy and obey her aunt. Clara learns that because of its complexity and internal inconsistencies, the code of feminine conduct is almost impossible to follow—as Lily Dale had discovered in *The Small House at Allington*.

Captain Aylmer's relations with Mrs. Winterfield, however, are governed by an easier set of imperatives. "Being a man and a Member of Parliament" (1), as the narrator tartly notes, he can easily escape the penitential Sundays at his aunt's house. As Clara tells Aylmer, men like him "sail always under false pretenses," pleading business whenever they want to avoid something. The elastic moral code society applies to them permits them to "think [they] do [their] duty" in spite of this dishonesty (7). Although Aylmer is no more enthusiastically low church than Clara herself, he easily conceals his coolness from his aunt. Mrs. Winterfield's belief that her nephew shares her religious opinions and her conventional conviction that landed property "must all go together" (1) to a male heir convince her that she ought leave Aylmer everything and Clara nothing.

It is Clara's peculiar, but symbolically significant, fate to be thrice disinherited in favor of men—for her father's estate is entailed on Will Belton. Clara can avoid destitution only if Aylmer or Will gives her part of the property he inherited at her expense. The most convenient way for either heir to share his spoils with Clara is to marry her, and both do propose. Though Clara is in a much better position than many young ladies to identify the right man, she nearly marries the wrong one. By tracing the process of learning Clara undergoes, Trollope shows how social convention pressures a woman to err in this irremediable decision. And if a woman does marry an inappropriate man, her marriage may well disintegrate as Mrs. Askerton's ill-assorted marriage did.

When *The Belton Estate* opens, Clara is by no means a passive young girl. At twenty-five, she has weathered the tragedy of her brother's suicide, cared for her ailing father, and voiced her disagreement with her aunt. Clara has reflected with some resentment upon the position of young women: "Women—women, that is, of my age—are such slaves! We are forced to give an obedience for which we can see no cause. . . . The true reason is that we are dependent" (7). But it is not merely her experiences and character that appear to give Clara an excellent chance of choosing a satisfactory husband. For Clara is also favored in that one of her suitors is an exceptional man, while the other is ordinary at best, a circumstance that should simplify the process of choice. Will Belton is almost an ideal suitor, handsome, rich, and passionately in love with Clara. And he possesses an even more important qualification in the excellence of his character: "He was a man fit to guide a wife, very good-humoured,—and good-tempered also, anxious to give pleasure to others . . . as good a husband as a girl could have" (4). In fact, Will falls short of perfection in only one way: he is not quite a gentleman in manner or education, though he certainly is one in feeling.

Aylmer has the education Will lacks, and he too can afford to support a wife. But in other respects he is greatly Will's inferior. He avails himself of every opportunity for hypocrisy that his world offers to men. Nor is he at all generous. When his aunt, on her deathbed, repents disinheriting Clara, Aylmer suggests that the bare pittance of fifteen hundred pounds would be an appropriate legacy. Aylmer is not handsome and responds coldly to women. "He was not," as the narrator remarks, "a man to break his heart for a girl" (10), and his interest in Clara varies in inverse proportion to her availability.[50] He seems to have such exaggerated ideas about feminine delicacy that warmth in a woman disgusts him. In this respect, Aylmer resembles John Ball of *Miss Mackenzie*, but his fear of female sexuality is far more extreme. From the start Clara knows that Will is both a better man and a more passionate lover than Aylmer.

Not only is Will superior to Aylmer, but Clara really does find Will irresistible. Though Clara rejects Will's first proposal because she thinks she loves Aylmer, Will's sexual power over her becomes evident early in the story. When Will visits her, she gets up early to give him coffee in her dressing gown, though she knows that this will only encourage his attentions: "She hardly understood, herself, why she was doing this. She knew that it should be her object to avoid any further special conversation" (6). The narrator suggests what her motive might be, when he describes how a man would respond: "Who has not seen some such girl when she has come down early, without the full completeness of her morning toilet, and yet nicer, fresher, prettier to the eye of him who is so favoured, than she has ever been in more formal attire? And what man who has been so favoured has not loved her who has so favoured him?" (6). As the novel progresses, it becomes clear that Clara is encouraging Will's passion.

But in spite of Will's moral superiority to Aylmer, which she acknowledges, and in spite of her attraction to Will, of which she is dimly conscious, Clara believes she loves Aylmer and accepts his proposal. How can an intelligent woman like Clara make so foolish a mistake? The answer is to be found in the conventions about courtship that have guided her choice. For though Clara fumes against the restrictions to which women are subject, the Victorian moral code has a deep hold upon her. In considering various lines of conduct, she frequently asks herself what "her own feminine purity demanded" (18) before deciding what to do. Unhappy in her independence, she longs to renounce it when she can safely do so.

Clara dislikes Aylmer's shallowness and hypocrisy, but because she sees these qualities as normal male characteristics, she is willing to tolerate them. When Clara compares her suitors, she thinks that "were they two to meet in her presence—the captain and the farmer,—. . . she might have to blush for her cousin" (7). And, indeed, she loves Captain Aylmer because he is a man for whom she need not blush, a socially correct man, if not a morally distinguished one: "She liked his position in the world; she liked the feeling that he was a man of influence; perhaps she liked to think that to some extent he was a man of fashion" (11). But why should Clara blush for Will, who is so decent and so handsome?

When a Victorian lady married her social inferior, her friends were certain to disapprove. For what could motivate her wish to associate familiarly with a man whose mind was less refined than her own, except an indelicate longing for marriage at any cost, or a positively aberrant degree of sexual attraction? Clara seems to feel subconsciously that if she can love the chilly but respectable Aylmer, her choice will demonstrate her feminine delicacy; to choose Will would imply that she is so responsive to his unconcealed passion for her that his social inferiority ceases to matter. She is unwilling to admit this and persistently denies her attraction to Will.

The Belton Estate's liberal narrator suggests that Clara's behavior is not aberrant when he asserts that young girls are sexually so repressed and frightened that they usually choose respectability over passion: "I am more often astonished by the prudence of girls than by their recklessness. A woman of thirty will often love well and not wisely; but the girls of twenty seem to me to like propriety of demeanor, decency of outward life, and a competence. . . . Clara was more than twenty; but she was not yet so far advanced in age as to have lost her taste for decency of demeanour" (11). This passage hints that it takes most women a long time to discover their sexuality and that they may marry the wrong man in the meantime. It is implied that Clara accepts the idea that men are much more highly sexed than women—for when Aylmer reveals his sexual coldness, kissing her dutifully with a "chilling kiss" (11), she seems genuinely surprised. That a sexual woman might come to grief by marrying a frigid husband has not occurred to her.[51] But it did occur to

Trollope, who had already treated the problem in the Glencora subplot of *Can You Forgive Her?*. When girls choose husbands without realizing that sex is important in marriage, they risk marital disaster.

Clara fails to understand how important conventional views about male worldliness and feminine delicacy have been in making her choose "the thinner and the meaner of the two men" who want to marry her (22). But no sooner is she engaged to Aylmer, than she begins to feel both his moral mediocrity and the strength of her attraction toward Will. At this point, however, another rule of feminine conduct comes into play, forbidding her to extricate herself from the engagement. Clara, delighted to have chosen so respectable a husband, hopes she can now give up the uncomfortable independence circumstances have thrust upon her. "Hitherto she had been independent. . . . Now she would put aside all that, and let him know that she recognized in him her lord and master as well as husband. To her father had been left no strength on which she could lean. . . . Now she would be dependent upon him who was to be her husband" (11). But Clara soon learns that it is not so easy for an intelligent woman to surrender her autonomy.

Aylmer's commitment to the ideal of asexual femininity makes him regret his offer to Clara as soon as he hears the "hearty tone" (10) of her acceptance. There is something comical in this picture of a man, who has conventionally assumed that his fiancée must be sexless, and a woman, who has conventionally assumed that hers must be passionate, discovering their joint mistake. The standard view of sexuality is inadequate, these scenes clearly imply. Sensing Aylmer's horror at her enthusiasm, Clara begins to mistrust him. He justifies her mistrust by allowing his mother to tyrannize over her. Lady Aylmer threatens to break the engagement unless Clara will stop seeing Mrs. Askerton.

And so Clara realizes that she cannot enjoy the easy pleasures of submission without a ruinous sacrifice of self-respect. She would like to obey the rules of feminine conduct, if her own conscience would permit her to do so—but it will not. As the narrator notes with his usual unconventionality, Clara advocates a theory "in accordance with which the wife is to bend herself in loving submission

before her husband—[a theory that] is very beautiful; and would
be good altogether if it could only be arranged that the husband
should be the stronger and the greater of the two. . . . But there
sometimes comes a terrible shipwreck, when the woman before
marriage has filled herself full with ideas of submission, and then
finds that her golden-headed god has got an iron body and feet of
clay" (11). Luckily for Clara, Aylmer's clay feet are so immense that
she notices them before making the terrible mistake of marrying
him.

As Clara comes to see just how deficient Aylmer is, Will looks
even more attractive to her, but she fails to draw from this the
logical conclusion that she loves Will, and has mistaken her feelings
about Aylmer. Thinking of Aylmer's ungenerous order that she
drop Mrs. Askerton, Clara realizes that, given his conventionality,
she is "hardly surprised at his doing it. Yet Captain Aylmer was
the man she loved!" (16). Whenever Clara tries to investigate her
feelings about Aylmer, she fails, because "she wished to think that
she loved him, as she could not endure the thought of having
accepted a man whom she did not love" (25), and so does not
investigate impartially. Clara does not question the standards of
delicacy by which Victorian women were expected to live. On the
contrary, she is so upset that she may have violated those standards
that she deceives herself about what has happened.

But Aylmer's coldness—in combination with her delight in Will's
devotion and her inability to stop provoking his outbursts of passion
with what appears to be "malice prepense" (22)—do finally force
Clara to reassess the situation. After much suffering, Clara concludes
that it is better to admit that she has sinned against feminine purity
than to marry Aylmer. She rejects him firmly, "but there remained
with her a feminine shame, which made it seem to her to be impossible that she should . . . as a consequence of that rejection,
accept Will Belton's hand" (28). This shame does not, however,
delay Clara and Will's marriage for long. Clara's common sense,
the passion she has tried to deny, and her gratitude to Will all plead
powerfully on the other side.

In fact, the happy ending of Clara and Will's story is never really
in doubt. For P. D. Edwards Clara's tardiness in accepting Will is

a flaw in the novel: "Every detail" of the story, he holds, "corroborates the rightness of Clara's choice, leaving us convinced, finally, that it was no choice at all, that only a moral imbecile could have failed to appreciate Will's superiority."[52] But Clara is no imbecile, and though she almost acts like one, she does so for understandable reasons—not because Trollope nodded. It takes Clara a long time to accept Will because she must learn to question the conventions that guide her toward Aylmer. Trollope draws an amusingly extreme contrast between Will and Aylmer—using all his talent to portray Will as "a paragon" (4), by far the nicest of his generally unimpressive young suitors—in order to clarify this very point. And it is for this reason, too, that Trollope stresses Clara's maturity and intelligence. If an impressive woman making a ludicrously easy choice so nearly comes to grief, the standards by which she is judging must be faulty indeed.

A woman bound by the laws of society to give her fidelity to a man she does not love, and a loyal, passionate lover waiting for her to turn to him—this describes both Clara's situation during most of *The Belton Estate* and Mrs. Askerton's situation during her unhappy marriage. Trollope pursues a complex rhetorical strategy to evoke sympathy for this fallen woman, who left her husband and lived with Colonel Askerton until her husband's death enabled them to marry.[53] When Trollope introduces Mrs. Askerton in the novel's opening chapters, he encourages readers' suspicions of a woman about whose past damaging rumors are circulating. Mrs. Askerton is intimate with Clara, but though Clara indignantly attributes the gossip about her to "lying, evil speaking, and slandering," she is aware that "there was something in [Mrs. Askerton's] modes of speech, and something also in her modes of thinking, which did not quite satisfy [her] aspirations . . . as to a friend" (2). Mrs. Askerton's superheated interest in sex and romance often annoys Clara, who knows that "nothing will stop [her friend] when [she] once get[s] into a vein of that kind" (2). The reader is encouraged to infer both that the rumors about Mrs. Askerton's past are true and that Mrs. Askerton committed adultery because she lacked the innate delicacy that distinguishes the feminine woman.

At first, then, Mrs. Askerton seems to confirm the view, which most Victorian readers doubtless brought to the novel, that only a bad woman can be guilty of sexual misconduct. But after luring the reader into the novel by implying that its fallen woman will be treated in a familiar manner, Trollope begins to soften the picture he has drawn of Mrs. Askerton. When Will Belton recognizes in her a woman he once knew under another name, the reader learns that the rumors about her past are indeed true. But Will says nothing to put Clara on her guard against her friend. And since Will is such a good man, his decision to respect this friendship may lead readers to question the position taken by the local rector and curate that a woman guilty of sexual irregularities should automatically be shunned.

Will identifies Mrs. Askerton as the former Miss Vigo in an odd way. "It so chanced," he tells Clara, "that I once saw that Miss Vigo in some trouble. I happened to meet her in company with a man who was—who was tipsy, in fact, and I had to relieve her. . . . And there was a look about Mrs. Askerton just now [i.e., a moment earlier when Will casually mentioned the resemblance] so like the look of that Miss Vigo then, that I cannot get rid of the idea" (5). Will recognizes Mrs. Askerton less because her face resembles Miss Vigo's than because her look of helpless suffering on both occasions was the same—and this encourages the reader to see her as a victim.

Later an old friend asserts that Mrs. Askerton's husband, Jack Berdmore, "was a man with whom a woman could hardly continue to live" (14). The narrator confirms this when he summarizes—in an offhand way that suggests that it is a common tale—Mrs. Askerton's life story: a story "of her first foolish engagement, her belief, her half-belief, in the man's reformation, of the miseries which resulted from his vices, of her escape and shame" (18). Mrs. Askerton apparently accepted the view that male nature excuses male misconduct. Though she only half-believed in Berdmore's reformation, the idea that a good woman can reform an erring man, and the disgrace attending a woman's admission that she has changed her love, kept her from breaking her engagement. Conventional notions about the sexes nearly caused Clara to marry the wrong man; Mrs. Askerton actually does it, for similar reasons. And a really bad marriage could easily end in adultery, even in Victorian times. Thus the ideas underlying the double standard increase the likelihood that a woman will commit a sexual sin.

Once Mrs. Askerton had left her husband, the double standard that harshly punishes women's sexual irregularities forced her to practice deceptions that might well have blunted her moral sensibilities. "My life has been a lie," she tells Clara sadly, "and yet how could I help it? I must live somewhere,—and how could I live anywhere without deceit?" (18). As the narrator sympathetically explains, "misfortunes had come upon [Mrs. Askerton] in life of a sort which are too apt to quench high nobility of mind in a woman. There are calamities which, by their natural tendencies . . . add strength to the growth of feminine virtues;—but then, again, there are other calamities which few women can bear without some . . . injury to . . . delicacy and tenderness. . . . In this, I think, the world is harder to women than to men; that a woman often loses much by the chance of adverse circumstances which a man only loses by his own misconduct" (21). The indelicacy that the reader originally identified as the cause of Mrs. Askerton's sexual misconduct is actually the result of that misconduct. After she sins, the ostracism she encounters forces her to carry on her battle "by dishonest intriguing" (21). No wonder that a woman who has never been allowed to forget her own sexual sin should be obsessed with sex.

As Mrs. Askerton's story develops, the reader begins to understand how difficult her life has been, and Trollope nurtures the sympathy this insight engenders. First, he shows that Mrs. Askerton, though her troubles may have impaired her delicacy, is still capable of generosity: she tries to convince Clara that because their friendship is injurious to Clara's prospects, Clara must renounce her. And her preoccupation with romance appears in a favorable light when she schemes to promote the match between Clara and Will.

Second, Trollope guides the reader's response to Mrs. Askerton by cleanly dividing the novel's likable characters from its despicable ones in terms of their reaction to her sin. Clara, Will, Will's saintly sister Mary, and the decent attorney Mr. Green agree that, considering her misfortunes and her later respectability, "all that woman's sins should be forgiven her" (32). The stupidly pious Mrs. Winterfield and the coldly proper Aylmers, on the other hand, are "comfortably horror-stricken . . . delightfully shocked" (17) by Mrs. Askerton's iniquity and wish to see her hounded out of society. So do the clergy, who get an unusually bad press in this novel.

Third, as the novel progresses, Trollope brings Colonel Askerton—originally a shadowy and disturbing character—more fully onstage and reveals how deeply he loves this woman who was once his mistress. His idle life, divided between shooting and reading French novels, seems at first to imply that he is a selfish, trivial man—probably, like his wife, obsessed with sex, if the French novels are any indication. An "ill-natured smile" (5) that crosses his face when Mrs. Askerton speculates about a marriage between Will and Clara suggests a disquieting cynicism about love.

But soon this unflattering picture softens, very much as the picture of Mrs. Askerton does. It becomes clear that Colonel Askerton must live in retirement for his wife's sake and that he quietly bears the tedium to which this subjects him. If he is a bit sour on the subject of marriage, he certainly has reason to be so. Gossiping tongues, he tells his wife lovingly, cannot reach him, "excepting so far as they may reach [him] through [her]" (21), and he protects her as best he can. His pleasure when Clara agrees to become his wife's visitor shows how much he has suffered in watching her suffering. Mrs. Askerton bursts into tears when she tells Clara of his goodness to her. By the end of the novel, Colonel Askerton's love for his wife has been idealized almost as dramatically as Will's love for Clara—though the Askertons have gotten a bit soiled in the course of their ordeal at the hands of society. With both couples, Trollope implies that the right man need not be the first man, and that when such a man is waiting on the sidelines, it may be difficult for a woman to remain faithful to her first foolish commitment.

Finally, Trollope increases the reader's sympathy for Mrs. Askerton by slyly attacking the unreflective religion that would condemn her, without considering the circumstances of her case. The local clergyman, Mr. Wright, is eager to defame Mrs. Askerton, falsely claiming that she and her husband are living under assumed names. In the heat of his passion for feminine purity, he is quite willing to spread unfounded rumors. The narrator criticizes the adherence to inhumane moral standards that characterizes Mrs. Winterfield's brand of religion. Why, he asks, if adherence to the old doctrines is all that salvation requires, "is it that the activity of man's mind is the only sure forerunner of man's progress?" (7). The narrator's mind is indeed active in questioning conventional religious beliefs. He mocks a clergyman who asks Clara to pray with him after her aunt's death, for failing in his "easy piety" to realize that "of all works in which man can engage himself, that of prayer is the most difficult" (9). And the narrator thinks that the unmerited suffering of cripples like Mary Belton should lead us "to inquire curiously within ourselves whether future compensation is to be given" (13). By mocking conventional piety and praising the inquiring mind—as well as by questioning conventional ideas about men and women—the narrator of *The Belton Estate* encourages readers to rethink the moral issues raised by Mrs. Askerton's story.

By the end of the novel, readers who would originally have shared the Aylmers' horror at Mrs. Askerton's conduct must either feel for her or resist the tendency of the entire book. But in affirming Mrs. Askerton's basic decency, readers of *The Belton Estate* must also reject the double standard by which she has been condemned— and this is easier to do since they have seen how close the views of male and female nature on which it is based came to wrecking Will and Clara's chances of happiness.

The successful lovers in this novel are willing to respect a woman's autonomy, to allow her to make a mistake and to feel sexual passion—to treat her, in short, as a human being, rather than as a sexless, selfless angel. Will and Colonel Askerton are wonderful men, but perhaps a bit too good to be true in their unwavering devotion to the women they love. To stress the idealized, fantastic nature of its comedy, Trollope concludes *The Belton Estate* with the most delightful, but also the most incredible, of comic festivals: the Beltons kill the fatted calf, and the Askertons come to dine with Captain Aylmer, the local squire, and the malicious Mr. Wright. Mrs. Askerton's social rehabilitation is merely asserted, for it cannot realistically be explained. No fallen woman could have regained her position in society so easily as Mrs. Askerton does. But the reader's pleasure in this impossible amnesty reinforces the novel's plea for reform.

A truly satisfying comic resolution for women, *The Belton Estate* implies, is possible only with extraordinary men like Will and Colonel Askerton. And it necessitates a vigorous and thorough rejection of many conventional notions about masculinity and femininity. Unlike the romantic conclusions of several earlier novels, which Trollope slyly undercuts, the conclusion of *The Belton Estate* is truly joyous and satisfying. But Victorian views about men, women, and love almost prevent its achievement. Where the happy ending of *Barchester Towers* is premised on a return to conservative notions about women, the progressive comedy of *The Belton Estate* depends on the rejection of those notions.

4 Comedy, Tragedy, and the Position of Women in the Later Novels

In the preceding pages, I have shown how Trollope's changing view of women is reflected in the changing form of his novels, especially in his handling of the comic plots he invariably includes. During the years separating *Framley Parsonage* from *The Belton Estate*, Trollope continued to supply the romantic comedy his public expected, even as he rejected the conservative view of woman's mission that romantic comedy was so well suited to express, and he devised a variety of ways to articulate unorthodox ideas about women without disrupting the conventions of the genre. The surface of Trollope's comic plots thus remains almost unruffled, even in the most subversive of these early works.

Trollope knew that his readers understood the conventions of romantic comedy, which they had encountered in an endless succession of plays and novels. When readers identified any given plot as a romantic comedy, that identification inclined them toward certain prefabricated critical judgments: the ingenue must be lovable, or at least redeemable; by the time he gets her, the hero must have demonstrated that he deserves her; their marriage must promise personal happiness and may offer social healing as well. If the story that Trollope told did not quite support these judgments, there was a good chance that its discordant elements would go unnoticed. Trollope could expect the public to read his subtly unorthodox romantic comedies as traditional comedies endorsing the proposition that marriage is the only "happy ending" for a woman. Thus he could pursue his artistic ends without sacrificing the popularity that the straightforward romantic comedy in such early novels as *Doctor Thorne* and *Framley Parsonage* had helped him win. And there was always the chance that if he presented his subversive notions about women cleverly enough, he would convert some of his readers without their realizing what was happening.

If I am right that the novels Trollope wrote from 1861 to 1865 use comic form to mask his sympathy for rebellious women, then the persistent tendency of his critics to see those novels as ultimately affirmative and conventional because they are technically comic suggests that he knew what he was doing. Trollope's critics sometimes complain that there is a disjunction between the comic form of a novel and its ironic content, but they privilege form over content and conclude that the reader "is supposed" to be satisfied with the tale that has been told because that tale is technically a romantic comedy. Thus George Levine argues that Trollope intends us to find the conclusion of Alice Vavasor's romantic comedy "beautiful and satifying," though her story demonstrates that she must make "impossible" accommodations to achieve that conclusion.[1] Levine sees this as a failure of Trollope's art. But surely Trollope had proved long before he wrote *Can You Forgive Her?* that he could create delightful, coherent, and conservative romantic comedy when he wanted to.

On other occasions, critics simply overlook the tensions surrounding the comic resolutions of Trollope's earlier novels. Because *Rachel Ray*'s deviations from classically comic form are so slight, few critics of the novel have noticed how Trollope compromises its conclusion. Even where a more obviously disturbing book like *Miss Mackenzie* is concerned, there is a tendency to assume that comedy must indeed end comically—and to ignore the fact that it does not. Thus P. D. Edwards argues that Margaret Mackenzie makes a "complete escape" from the social "abyss" of spinsterhood into which she has nearly toppled when she marries John Ball, an escape that "has something of a fairy-tale quality."[2] It is hard to see how marriage to a worn-out man with nine children and an evil mother-in-residence could be called a fairy-tale escape, even if the man is not a bad sort of fellow. Edwards' reading of *Miss Mackenzie* shows how easily form can overwhelm content where romantic comedy is at issue.

R. C. Terry, James Kincaid, and the authors of *Corrupt Relations,* among others, acknowledge that even in the earlier novels Trollope sometimes undercuts his romantic comedies by juxtaposing them against plots that suggest less orthodox views of women. "As one reads of the marriages in his work," Terry remarks, "one can only ask where the angel of light [whom Trollope exalts in his romantic comedies] has gone."[3] Kincaid makes a similar point when he argues that Madeline Staveley's comic romance is of such minor importance to *Orley Farm* that its very insignificance forces the reader "to recognize the central patterns of denial" traced in the stories of the novel's older women.[4] While these critics are correct that Trollope often subverts romantic comedy by placing it in a disturbing context, they fail to notice how many comic plots in the early novels are destroyed from within by the unorthodox way Trollope develops them. In dealing with the comic plots themselves, even those who acknowledge that Trollope's sympathies were often on the side of discontented women allow form to take precedence over content. Kincaid, for example, thinks that Trollope's novels typically use a blissful romantic comedy as the main plot. Though he acknowledges that the romance in any given novel may be undercut by the ironic plots surrounding it, Kincaid argues firmly that "opening the form through a manipulation of the main plot [itself] is rare in Trollope."[5]

But as the preceding chapters have demonstrated, Trollope's earlier novels developed many techniques whereby they undermine romantic comedy from within: the inadequate hero; the rigid heroine; the "angelic" heroine whose static perfection is unfavorably compared with the humanity of an erring foil; the use of parodically sentimental language to describe the ingenue; the premature comic resolution that proves to be no resolution at all; the "happy" ending that does not quite fit; the narrator who suggests unorthodox responses to an orthodox story. Because these techniques never disrupt the form of Trollope's early comedies, their importance has largely gone unnoticed. The critical consensus on the early novels either takes their comic plots straight, or holds that those plots are undermined only by the context in which Trollope places them. The critical response to *Can You Forgive Her?* and *The Claverings* offers only a partial exception to this generalization.

In the novels he wrote between 1865 and his death in 1882, however, Trollope began to take violent liberties with the form of romantic comedy in order to state the case for the independent woman more strongly. The romantic comedies of his later novels are often radically at variance with tradition in their plotting, in the character types they employ, in the patent unsuitability of their technically happy resolutions, or in the ideas about women upon which they are premised. In addition, Trollope's later novels investigate tragedy more thoroughly than his early works. He had experimented with this mode in *The Bertrams* and *Orley Farm*, but his later books reveal a growing fascination with its suitability as a tool for exploring the plight of women.

Because the late novels disrupt the form of romantic comedy so much more vigorously than the early ones—and because the late novels so often suggest that women's lives are tragic lives—Trollope's Victorian readers noticed that those novels treat women in unconventional ways, though they had largely overlooked the subversive elements in his earlier work. Despite the fact that attitudes toward women were growing more liberal as Trollope wrote them, his later novels were too liberal to please his public. Part of the falling off in Trollope's popularity during the 1870s undoubtedly resulted from the unorthodox view of women that the novels of this period suggested—their general pessimism was not the whole problem. One Victorian reader, Mrs. Oliphant, admired the early ingenues, but hated the "endless fluctuations"[6] in which Trollope's later heroines engage as they seek satisfactory lives in a world that denies them satisfactory choices. Nor has recent criticism been slow to notice that Trollope undermines his later romantic comedies from within.

In the following pages, I shall use evidence drawn from the period between the publication of *The Belton Estate* and Trollope's death to argue that the feminist sympathies of the later novels are often expressed through the same techniques of generic manipulation upon which the early novels relied. My readings of these novels have in some cases been anticipated, but my central argument has not: the early novels established the foundations of formal experiment upon which the far more experimental late novels build in developing their unorthodox views of women.

Romantic Comedy

Though Kincaid asserts that Trollope typically uses a romantic comedy as his main plot, he also acknowledges that Trollope sometimes belittles romantic comedy by relegating it to the sidelines, refusing to let it compete in intensity with a less generically predictable central plot. As I noted above, Kincaid argues that Trollope belittles Madeline Staveley's romantic comedy in just this way. But Kincaid thinks that Trollope develops Madeline's comedy *itself* in a completely traditional manner and in enough detail to carry conviction. The subversion comes from outside the subplot, not from within it, in Kincaid's view. In my discussion of *Orley Farm*, however, I suggest that perhaps Madeline's subplot is gently undermined from within by its perfunctory quality: Felix Graham is not sufficiently developed for us to feel sure that Madeline will be happy as his wife. He has some ominous qualities, and we do not see enough of him to conclude that they will disappear. In our eagerness for the comic conclusion, this plot hints, we are likely to surrender our critical faculties and seize whatever we are offered, inadequate though it may be.

When Trollope wrote *Dr. Wortle's School*, he pushed its comic romance much farther offstage. His refusal to develop this comedy to the point where the reader might find it convincing or satisfying clearly signals his impatience with the unrealistic assumptions upon which romantic comedy is often based. But in writing the absurdly perfunctory comic romance of *Dr. Wortle's School*, Trollope merely exaggerates a technique for mocking romantic comedy that *Orley Farm* had subtly pioneered.

Until the midpoint of *Dr. Wortle's School*, the only interaction between its two sketchily characterized teenage lovers, Mary Wortle and Lord Carstairs, is a brief lackluster chat about the fascinating, mature protagonists of the main plot: an agnostic American woman and the guilt-ridden Englishman with whom she is living in a bigamous union. Then Carstairs suddenly makes Mary an offer, which nothing but the conventions of romantic comedy could have prepared us to anticipate. Fearing that the engagement would be imprudent, Mary sends her lover away, but in Carstairs' absence, the two fathers arrange a marriage. Mary becomes engaged without having spoken one word of love, and the narrator winds up this subplot by remarking crabbily that "what might be, or would be, or was, the end of such folly, it is not my purpose here to tell" (Part V, 12). Far more openly than Trollope's earlier novels—but in a similar manner—*Dr. Wortle's School* ridicules readers' desire for the consoling certainties of romantic comedy by giving them its shadow, but not its substance.

The suspiciously undeveloped comic plot, however, is only one of several techniques for subverting romantic comedy that Trollope takes from his early novels and employs—with more openly destructive intent—in the later ones. Like *Rachel Ray, The Duke's Children* (1880) undermines comedy through its portrayal of an ingenue whose strength of purpose bodes ill for her happiness as the wife of the powerful man she marries. Rachel's quiet firmness pales, however, beside the fierce determination to have her own way that Mary Palliser displays. Rachel accepts her mother's right to forbid her marriage with Luke Rowan, and becomes angry only when her mother capriciously withdraws the sanction she had given the engagement. But even then Rachel does not try to change her mother's mind. Because Rachel's strategies for expressing resentment are so quietly feminine, few readers have seen anything ominous in the strength of purpose she develops.

Mary Palliser's threatening strength of will is, however, much harder to overlook. Though Mary promises her father "to try to do all that [he tells her]," when he forbids her marriage with the unsuitable Frank Tregear, she negates her concession completely by adding that she expects him to give his permission (11). She will not promise to refrain from communicating with Tregear. When Mary announces that "this is a matter in which [she] mean[s] to have [her] own way" (24), we realize that she is "a very self-willed young lady indeed" (24).

Mary resembles the earlier ingenues in asserting herself only to claim privileges that she believes are legitimately hers: "Being the child of rich parents she had the right to money. Being a woman she had a right to a husband. Having been born free she had a right to choose one for herself" (24). But she has a wider conception of her privileges than her predecessors, and the code of feminine behavior does not have the powerful hold upon her feelings that it had on theirs. When told of the delicacy that should characterize the feminine woman, Mary says contemptuously, "Of course I have to be—delicate. I don't quite know what the word means" (2). Though she recognizes her father's power, Mary goes far beyond earlier heroines in rejecting any obligation to submit to a parent's judgment or will: she would run away with Frank if the financial consequences of such a course were less disastrous.

None of the men in Mary's family sympathizes with her willfulness and unconventionality. Her undisciplined brother, Lord Silverbridge—who was thrown out of Oxford for painting the Dean's house scarlet—thinks she should submit: "As for supposing that girls are to have what they wish, that is nonsense" (30). Mary's almost equally undisciplined brother Gerald tells her she is unmaidenly in revealing her feelings for Tregear. Her father thinks that he has the right to compel Mary to yield even if he should "doom her to death, or perchance to madness" (50) by doing so. Although they finally consent to her marriage, Mary's father and brothers remain somewhat horrified by the determination she has displayed. They never offer her the sympathy she repeatedly tries to extract. The only male who takes Mary's side is Tregear himself, and he obviously has ulterior motives for doing so.

In other matters, however, Tregear is a very conservative man—and a conceited one as well. His callous behavior toward his first love, Mabel Grex, proves that he cares more about his own advancement than about the feelings of others. In an early draft of *The Duke's Children*, Tregear was portrayed as an unscrupulous adventurer, and he is not much more likable in the published version.[7] By the end of the novel, Mary has articulated a conception of her own rights that goes too far for any of the men in her family and has persistently pursued an aim that those men find positively disgraceful. How then will it be between her and the conservative, strong-willed Tregear—who is neither sweet nor tender, and who has supported her rebellion for purely selfish reasons?

After their reunion, Mary tells Frank that the suffering of the previous year "was worse for [her] than for [him]." When Frank demurs, Mary flatly contradicts him: "But it was, Frank; and therefore I ought to have it made up to me now" (79). Alas, that is not likely. Though their story ends as romantic comedy ought, the trouble that looms on the horizon for Mary and Frank will probably be more serious than the trouble that threatened Rachel Ray and Luke Rowan. Critics generally think Rachel a very sweet girl, but they find it more difficult to overlook the assertiveness that makes Mary such a disturbing ingenue.[8] Tregear has certainly met his match.

In the early novels, Trollope sometimes undermines his romantic comedies by concluding them in disturbing ways, and he uses this technique again, more dramatically, in his later work. When John Ball makes his romantic proposal to Margaret Mackenzie, and she accepts him with rapture, the reader is optimistic about their chances for happiness. But the conclusion is compromised by the disheartening information—about Ball himself and about the position of women—that Trollope reveals between the engagement and the marriage. So ironic a story cannot logically end with a comic celebration. Similar arguments might be made about the resolution of the Alice Vavasor plot in *Can You Forgive Her?* and that of *The Claverings*.

But in *The Eustace Diamonds* (1873), Trollope concludes his comic subplot with a conventional resolution that is far more patently illogical than any of the compromised comic conclusions in his earlier novels. The novelist must still pay lip service to the values for which the ingenue, Lucy Morris, stands—and to the necessities of romantic comedy—by rewarding her with marriage. But in the ironic world of *The Eustace Diamonds* it seems unnatural indeed that such a woman should receive her reward, for women here are objects to be appraised and traded; no one pays them reverence. Lucy's painful experiences, in conjunction with the implausible triumph that concludes them, hint that the angel in the house is an outmoded ideal—influential in fiction, powerless in reality. The transparently tacked-on quality of the novel's ending suggests that romantic comedy can now be salvaged only by strenuous intervention on the novelist's part.

The Eustace Diamonds leaves its readers in no doubt that Lucy's heart and intellect are faultless. But she lacks money, birth, and beauty. Though a more independent version of the type, Lucy resembles the angelic ingenues of Trollope's early novels. Her experiences, however, are gloomier than theirs, for her acquaintances universally believe that the external advantages she lacks are far more important than the internal ones she possesses. The constant cry that Lucy "has no beauty" (60) becomes a choral motif emphasizing the primacy of externals in this amoral world. As the novel's feminist narrator shrewdly suggests, people here believe the man to be "much more important than the woman," despite the fact that they have "a very bad opinion of men in general" (46). Nor are these two views so inconsistent with one another as they appear. Male misconduct is expected because important men are too busy "to act at all times with truth and sincerity" (46). On the same grounds, such misconduct is excused. Both morality and the woman who is (theoretically) supposed to embody it are at a discount in this milieu.

When Frank Greystock, a debt-ridden barrister with a large income, proposes to Lucy, she is ecstatic. But this premature climax is followed by a period of prolonged suffering that proves to Lucy how little anyone cares for the virtue that is her only asset.[9] The responses of Lucy's friends to the engagement range from astonishment to horror—although no one doubts that, personally, Lucy is "a treasure" (3), certain to prove an angelic mate. "Even dear old Lady Fawn," the novel's spokeswoman for the outmoded moral values, "had many times prophecied that [a marriage between Frank and Lucy] was quite impossible" (76). Frank's own family is still more cynical. His mother does all she can to convince Frank that he should jilt Lucy, arguing strangely that "Lucy had behaved badly in allowing herself to be loved by a man who ought to have loved money" (30).

Though Frank falls in love with Lucy's moral character, he shares the misogyny of the society this novel depicts, as well as its worship of success at any price. He believes that "affectation [is] necessary to a woman's character" (13), thinks that women are two-faced creatures who "hate each other so virulently" (18), and coolly denies the existence of the redundant woman problem. Like everyone else, he is obsessed with the money, rank, and beauty Lucy does not have. These attitudes cause him to repent his engagement and to neglect Lucy cruelly while he considers marrying the dishonest— but rich and lovely—Lizzie Eustace.

Lucy waits miserably for six months without a word of encouragement from anyone. And this is not surprising, for in fact Lucy herself is the only person in the novel who believes that her virtues are as valuable as Frank's social advantages, the only one who does not excuse his mistreatment of her. "She would ever think him to be a traitor [if he jilted her]," she decides. "Would not she have starved herself for him, could she so have served him? And yet he could bear for her sake no touch of delay in his prosperity" (76). That Lucy's suffering occurs almost entirely offstage suggests how very marginal a good woman is in the dark world of this novel. Though Margaret Mackenzie's marriage was also delayed by the instability of her lover and the low price society set on female virtue, her situation was brighter than Lucy's—for some of her friends did acknowledge that her excellence merited Ball's fidelity.

The narrator occasionally asserts that Frank may eventually come through, but most of the evidence implies that he will ratify his tacit repudiation of Lucy and that his treachery will be excused by an amoral, sexist society. Yet every reader knows that Frank will not actually jilt Lucy in the end. Because this subplot is the only one in *The Eustace Diamonds* that has any chance of turning out as romantic comedy ought, it must shape itself into comic form at whatever cost to probability.[10] And so Frank suddenly returns to Lucy, enveloped in a cloud of insubstantial excuses from the narrator. Frank, the attentive reader may well be surprised to hear, had always "been much nobler than his friends. . . . Hitherto [Lizzie's] money . . . had tempted him; but he had combated the temptation" (76). The narrator, in fact, follows a strategy similar to the one Lucy pursues from the moment Frank returns, when she altogether forgets "that she had for some time looked upon him as a traitor" (77). Everyone in the novel, Bill Overton rightly observes, acquiesces in the "very standards that have permitted [Frank's] misbehavior" when they offer him this "prodigal's welcome" after his gross misconduct.[11]

Even more perfunctory is the narrator's manner of excusing Frank's family, to pave the way for their joyous acceptance of Lucy: "She was received [at his home] with all the affection which Mrs. Greystock could show to an adopted daughter. Her quarrel had never been with Lucy personally,—but with the untoward fact that her son would not marry money" (77). This is unquestionably true, but since the motive underlying Mrs. Greystock's cruelty to Lucy was her denigration of personal qualities in favor of externals, it is also irrelevant.

Lucy deserves happiness in terms of the professed moral values of Victorian society and the conventions of Victorian fiction. But we cannot believe that she has really obtained it, given the nature of her lover and the real values of their milieu. For conventional romantic comedy exalting the angelic woman cannot plausibly take form in a world that has reduced all women to items of exchange. In such a world, angels are likely to finish last. Like the flawed resolutions of earlier novels, the inappropriate resolution of Lucy's story calls attention to the defects in Victorian mores that made a more satisfying one impossible.[12] But heartwarming, coherent comedy is more obviously impossible in *The Eustace Diamonds* than it was in *Miss Mackenzie*. So implausible is Lucy's technically comic tale, in fact, that its inclusion in *The Eustace Diamonds* forces a more thorough rejection of romantic comedy than its omission would do. Many critics read *Miss Mackenzie* as a dark, but pleasing, comedy. It is harder to miss the ironies that undercut Lucy's tale.

In *The Prime Minister* (1876), Trollope subverts romantic comedy by means of yet another technique borrowed from his earlier novels. Like *The Claverings*, *The Prime Minister* compares an ostensibly angelic ingenue with a woman who does not conform to the ideal of selfless femininity. The ingenue is rewarded by a happy marriage;

her foil ends up defeated, in ironic limbo. But as the story progresses, the ingenue comes to seem less perfect, while the foil grows in stature. Unlike the resolution of *The Eustace Diamonds,* the endings of *The Claverings* and *The Prime Minister* are believable enough, but their meaning has been called into question by the subversive portrayal of the central female characters. Although *The Claverings* and *The Prime Minister* use the same method to undermine romantic comedy and the feminine ideal, the later novel uses it with greater audacity: Emily Wharton, its putatively angelic ingenue, is a much more perverse creature than Florence Burton. And Glencora Palliser, Emily's foil, is a more determined rebel than Julia Ongar, who committed only one sin before returning to the paths of virtue. Critical response to the two novels suggests how much more openly *The Prime Minister* denigrates its ingenue. Only a few recent critics have noticed that Florence is a bit shallow, but a larger number dislike Emily intensely.[13]

Neither of *The Prime Minister*'s two plots initially looks like a romantic comedy: one tells the story of Glencora's struggle with her husband over the role she should play in his political career, the other describes Emily's nightmare marriage to the adventurer Ferdinand Lopez. The plot concerning Emily's fate, however, does double duty. Her old lover, Arthur Fletcher, is waiting loyally for her terrible marriage to end, and the reader knows that she will eventually accept him. Trollope provides the union of true lovers that readers wanted, but before they reach it, they must read the harrowing story of a disintegrating marriage that was itself a love match. For the first time, Trollope's subversion of romantic comedy definitely went too far: press and public repudiated the novel.

Through its two main plots, *The Prime Minister* contrasts two opposed types of womanhood. Emily is distinguished, the narrator remarks with apparent approval, by "a clearness of intellect joined with that feminine sweetness which has its most frequent foundation in self-denial" (5). Throughout the novel, Emily engages in a painfully earnest—yet increasingly unsuccessful—endeavor to obey the code of feminine behavior to the letter. But Glencora is "fresh, untrammelled, without many prejudices which afflict other ladies, and free from the bonds by which they are cramped and confined"

(8). Though the narrator never argues explicitly that Emily is trying to live by an impossible set of standards and never claims that Glencora is the more attractive of the two, these ideas emerge clearly from the text.

Emily knows that her only chance to escape from the "arrogance . . . stiffness and . . . ignorance" (24) that make the peaceful world of the Tory squirearchy so claustrophobic is by marrying a different sort of man from her childhood friend Arthur Fletcher. In addition, the male-supremacist Emily finds Arthur lacking in "that dignity of a superior being which a husband should possess" (39). Hoping to make good use of the one free decision society allows a feminine woman, she chooses the cosmopolitan Ferdinand Lopez, whose confident demeanor convinces her that he is "big enough to be her master" (39). She hopes that marriage to him will both enlarge her social horizons and make the subordination she desires a satisfying reality. Her choice demonstrates the blend of unconscious revolt and sincere conventionality that characterizes Emily throughout the novel.

Emily also knows that although a girl cannot be forced to accept any man, she has no right to marry against the wishes of her parents. So when her father violently vetoes Lopez, Emily is quick to promise the obedience of a dutiful daughter: "If you say it shall not be so, it shall not. I will do as you bid me" (5). But Emily's mode of obedience reveals a subconscious strategy for getting her own way, without violating the feminine code: "She would obey, but would take care to show [her father] that she was made miserable by obeying" (9). Never reflecting how antagonistic her behavior is to the spirit of self-denial by which a woman should be motivated, Emily soon gains her father's consent.

Lopez is as determined to dominate his wife as Emily is to subordinate herself, yet the marriage does not turn out as either expects. Lopez promises himself that his wife will "learn to look at the world with his eyes" (25), and Emily fully intends to do so. But as Emily plumbs the depths of her husband's dishonesty, she cannot keep her vow. She reminds herself legalistically that her marriage "had been for better or worse" and that as a dutiful wife she must love her husband even if he were "to prove himself the worst of men" (31). But no resolutions can prevent her from frowning expressively as Lopez reveals his greed, nor can she stop herself from "unconsciously and involuntarily" (31) comparing him with Arthur. Emily soon finds herself treating her husband as she treated her father: with a technically feminine submission quite inadequate to hide the anger she cannot repress.

Unlike Emily's father, Lopez is not softened by an obedience that masks neither her suffering nor her disapproval. Lopez believes in male supremacy as firmly as Emily does, but as an outsider to English society, who has learned its manners by rote, he does not quite understand the limits of a power that other men use more tactfully, if no less tyrannically. In this area, as in others, "respectable" Englishmen know better than to reveal their allegiance to the values Lopez openly espouses.[14] When Lopez argues that he has a right to control his wife absolutely, no matter how badly he behaves, his claims are hardly more extreme than those her gentlemanly father made in forbidding her marriage without even offering an explanation. Emily's ill-concealed reservations goad Lopez on to ever more violent attempts to reduce her to submission. For the first time Trollope takes a strong-minded, but conventional, ingenue past her marriage to a domineering man—and proves that her commitment to male dominance cannot avert disaster.

Like Lily Dale—an earlier heroine who also failed to live up to her conservative convictions about the sexes when circumstances called her bluff—Emily continues to endorse the code. And after Lopez' death, she continues to take unconscious advantage of the possibilities for quietly feminine aggression it offers. "It was forbidden to her, she believed, by all the canons of womanhood even to think of love again. There ought to be nothing left for her but crape and weepers" (67). If a residual desire to avoid absorption into the squirearchy plays a role in Emily's ostensibly self-denying resolution to obey the canons of womanhood by refusing Arthur, Emily does not know it.

In spite of her short-lived rebellion, Emily is the true daughter of her Tory family—but Glencora is the liberal wife of a Liberal politician. Where Emily embraces the idea of male supremacy, Glencora scorns it. "What fools, what asses, what horrors men are!" she exclaims to a friend (17). Where Emily tries to submerge her own identity in her husband's, Glencora is proud of her independence: "I am the wife of the Prime Minister. . . and I am myself too,— Glencora M'Cluskie that was, and I've made for myself a character that I'm not ashamed of" (37). Where Emily tries to obey the men who have authority over her, Glencora secretly disobeys her husband and is unabashed when he catches her. Where the ideal of feminine delicacy has immense power over Emily, Glencora rejects it: "Why shouldn't she be vulgar, if she could most surely get what she wanted by vulgarity?" (19). Where Emily is domestic and retiring, Glencora's wildly aggressive behavior convinces her husband that she hopes to relegate him to the role of "nominal Prime Minister" (18) and to take on the job herself.

If we judge Emily and Glencora by Victorian standards, we must conclude that the former is infinitely superior to the latter. But as one reads *The Prime Minister,* it is impossible not to feel the contrast between Emily and Glencora as a contrast between stasis and motion, darkness and light. Emily's unremitting and unavailing attempts to govern her feelings produce a painful sense of physical restraint. When Lopez shocks her with his dishonesty, her mind recoils, though she is "very careful that he should not feel any such motion in her body" (25). She refuses to betray her love for Arthur "by a gleam of her eye, by the tone of a word, or the movement of a finger" (67). Emily never becomes the incarnate angel she aspires to be, but her struggles to obey the code do manage to turn her into "a monument of bereaved woe" (70), who will not even go out of doors. She produces in the reader the same sense of recoil controlled by convention that she herself experiences.

Glencora's eye, on the other hand, is always gleaming, and her wit scintillates as well. Her words flow freely: "When affronted she would speak out, whether to her husband, or to another,—using irony rather than argument to support her cause" (6). She is always on the move; her fingers are constantly busy about her own business and everyone else's. "I should like to put the queen down . . . [and] make Buckingham Palace second rate," she claims outrageously (6). Readers might disapprove in theory of Glencora's ambition, vulgarity, dishonesty, and insubordination, but the delight they feel whenever she appears on the scene, the sense of lifting oppression as they move from Emily's presence to hers, tells another tale. Emily actually senses it herself. For when Glencora tells her an indiscreet joke and grimaces comically, Emily "could not refrain from smiling" (77)—her only spontaneous smile in the entire novel! It is no accident that Emily maddens even the small band of critics who (taking their cue from the narrator's conventional remarks) think Trollope wanted his readers to admire her. After arguing that Emily should be seen as a woman of impressive moral seriousness, Juliet McMaster admits guiltily that she "find[s] Emily a real pain, one of the most unpleasant characters in the novels."[15] In fact, McMaster's response to Emily demonstrates how effectively Trollope controls his readers.

Though *The Prime Minister* slyly denigrates Emily's passivity by contrasting it with Glencora's liveliness, it also shows that neither woman is really free. The novel examines the conflict that develops when Glencora decides to consolidate Plantagenet's position as prime minister through lavish hospitality. Glencora believes that her husband's social ineptitude will shorten his term in office, unless she creates the links to his supporters that he cannot forge. By the end of the novel Glencora's analysis of her husband's deficiencies has been fully validated, but her attempts to help him are not very successful. She cannot, as she hopes, make personal friends for him by proxy. The fastidious Plantagenet is disgusted by her vulgar guests and prohibits further political houseparties. Marital authority and the political system jointly resist Glencora's pretensions to power, but not before it has been shown that this popular woman might well make a better prime minister than her husband.

One of the *The Prime Minister*'s two plots, then, appears to end as romantic comedy should, in the happy marriage of a submissive woman. The other plot also seems to conclude with poetic justice, as a threatening woman's rebellion grinds to a halt. But the novel's conclusion, like its development of character, is less conventional than it appears. Emily gains love, but must settle for a constricting life she once rejected. As several critics have noted, the Wharton-cum-Fletcher world she enters is not so obviously superior to Lopez' world as its complacent inhabitants believe.[16] Plantagenet loses the prime ministership, and Glencora falls with him. But they too have love at the end: the love that has grown through the years of their difficult union. There is really not much difference between Emily's fate and Glencora's.

The Claverings subverts the superficially orthodox poetic justice with which it concludes by its unorthodox development of character and theme—and in doing so subverts romantic comedy itself. But *The Prime Minister* must be said to disrupt romantic comedy, rather than to subvert it. The ingenue's story tells of marriage, not romance; her feminine aspirations are shown to be at once impossible and destructive; her rebellious foil is infinitely the more attractive of the two. Because both women are ultimately defeated by a society that does not offer them the expanded possibilities they sought, one can hardly say that the ingenue is rewarded and the foil punished, even though the former does marry "Mr. Right." By exaggerating its use of a technique that had been employed more quietly in the early novels, this brilliant book distorts romantic comedy so cruelly that it becomes almost unrecognizable.

Progressive Romantic Comedy

Even in his later years, however, Trollope sometimes wrote enjoyable and coherent romances, but the romances he celebrated during this period were the ones that expressed his reservations about conventional marriage. In the subplot of *The Small House at Allington* that concerns Bell Dale's love affair with Dr. Crofts, Trollope first experimented with a new kind of romantic comedy, which I have called progressive comedy because its satisfying conclusion is premised upon unorthodox notions about woman's nature. The democratic, self-reliant Bell hopes to have a democratic marriage with a man who needs her labor. But Trollope is careful to keep Bell's convictions under wraps—just as Bell herself does. And he is careful to keep her slightly unconventional love affair at the periphery of his story.

But when Trollope came to write *The Belton Estate* in 1865, he centered it upon a more audacious progressive comedy. The lovable Will Belton is himself something of a feminist: he tries to cut off the entail that makes him the heir to Clara's family estate; he supports Clara's right to befriend a fallen woman; he wants to marry Clara even though he knows he was not her first choice. When Clara comes to share Will's views, the two marry. The comic celebration that concludes their story follows as convincingly from what preceded it as do the romantic climaxes of Trollope's earliest, and most conservative, comedies.

In his later novels, Trollope continued to write satisfying progressive comedies ending in marriages of comradeship and equality. Indeed, the women who do make happy marriages in these novels are frequently independent types like Violet Effingham,[17] who itches to "go in for everything [she] ought to leave alone" (*Phineas Finn*, 10), Nora Rowley, who offended Victorian readers by her desire to live in lodgings without a chaperone, or Isabel Boncassen, who takes no pains to conceal that she is much smarter than the man she loves. And the men these women marry are either very unconventional, very gentle, or—in the case of Nora's prospective husband—both at once. But of all progressive comedies in the later novels the most progressive is the romance of Phineas Finn and Madame Max Goesler. In *Phineas Finn* (1869), Madame Max makes good her claim to greater liberty than any other heroine achieves. In *Phineas Redux* (1874), she successfully challenges the powerful institutions of Victorian patriarchy. Trollope's extraordinary characterization of this privileged woman breaks down the barriers that separated men and women in Victorian theory and practice—and it points the way to the future. Madame Max's extended romantic comedy offers Trollope's most feminist revision of the genre. For this reason, I shall examine it closely in the following pages.

When Madame Max is introduced in *Phineas Finn*, the first words she speaks are, "Mr. Finn, what would I not give to be a member of the British Parliament?" (*Finn*, 60). The narrator's description of Madame Max stresses such masculine qualities as aggression, foresight, and courage: "She seemed to intend that you should know that she employed [her eyes] to conquer you, looking as a knight may have looked in olden days who entered a chamber with his sword drawn from the scabbard" (*Finn*, 60). Madame Max speaks, thinks, and lives like a man—but we do not dislike her for doing so. Shirley Letwin is right, I think, to assert that Madame Max is the most perfect gentleman in Trollope's novels.[18] But Trollope never subverted conventional notions about the sexes more radically than when he cast a woman in this role. Madame Max fits naturally into the modern, aristocratic milieu of the Palliser series, but in the earliest novels she would have appeared grotesque, like Madeline Neroni in *Barchester Towers*. Trollope's conception of womanhood has expanded: now a "masculine" woman is no longer monstrous, but tremendously attractive.[19]

The facility with which Madame Max evades convention in *Phineas Finn* proves how privileged she is. Her liberty tells us of new possibilities for women, not of existing realities. Madame Max claims a freedom of speech greater than that of the narrator himself. She asks the duke of Omnium straightforwardly, "Do you think I would be any man's mistress?" (*Finn*, 67)—but the narrator himself will not use the word, preferring such sickly euphemisms as "a complaisant friend." And Madame Max's thoughts are even freer than her speech. When Glencora begs her not to marry the duke, Madame Max knows Glencora is afraid that she will give the duke an heir. As she tells Glencora that her fears "are premature," there comes "a smile over her face which threatened to break from control and become laughter" (*Finn*, 61). Surely Madame Max, who has already been the wife of one aged husband, is thinking of the sexual failures to which old men are subject.

Madame Max's thoughts here move far beyond the bounds of propriety that restrict the Victorian novelist, and the narrator therefore cannot tell his readers anything about the farcical misadventure she visualizes. She thus becomes the first of Trollope's respectable, "serious" female characters to have access to a range of conjecture upon sexual matters greater than that of the narrator. In the earlier novels, hints concerning sex often come from characters like Sophie Gourdeloup and Mrs. Greenow who are disreputable, comic, or both. In *Can You Forgive Her?* only circumstantial evidence implies that Plantagenet's indifference to sex has caused his wife's infertility; neither Glencora nor the narrator explicitly makes this connection. By allowing Madame Max freedoms that, as the narrator of novels intended for family reading, he feels unable to claim, Trollope protests the restrictions to which society subjects both respectable women and respectable fiction.

Madame Max advocates the "ballot, manhood suffrage, womanhood suffrage . . . [and the] education of everybody" (*Finn*, 60)—not entirely in jest. And she chafes against the restrictions of custom, repeatedly asking the question that is becoming routine among Trollope's intelligent women: "What is there that I can do?" (*Finn*, 56). But Madame Max pursues her search for freedom with unprecedented self-confidence. Though she is only "the daughter of a small country attorney," Madame Max gains wealth and acceptance in the highest levels of London society "by her own resources" (*Finn*, 61). A woman's traditional method, marriage, gives her a start, but after her widowhood, Madame Max pursues her goals in a less feminine way. Though affectionate, she never gives in to emotion. Aware that the situation of an unprotected woman is precarious, she "would sit . . . for the hour together, resolving, or trying to resolve, what should be her conduct. She did few things without much thinking, and though she walked very boldly, she walked warily" (*Finn*, 60). Rational and ambitious, Madame Max will not look for love until she has achieved independence and wealth. She continues to manage her husband's business after his death, spending months at a time in Vienna, "sitting on a stool in a counting-house" (*Finn*, 64).

Madame Max confidently claims male privileges of sexual aggression. From the beginning of their love affair until they marry, Madame Max is Phineas' suitor. She pursues him quietly, but with a persistence that would have been unthinkable to the ingenues of Trollope's earliest novels, many of whom were ideally "feminine" in their refusal to love until a proposal authorized them to investigate their feelings. Madame Max seeks out Phineas; taking his hand, she offers him money; she hints broadly that she would like to marry him; when he fails to propose, she does so herself; though he rejects her, she continues to befriend him. In her circumstances, as well as in her behavior, she occupies the "male" position in this courtship. Several years older than Phineas, with a social position of her own, she intends to support him on the proceeds of her labor.[20]

But in *Phineas Finn*, even the independent Madame Max cannot find an activity that really challenges her. Like many women in Trollope's late novels, she is left with a sense of emptiness at the center. Though so much freer than other women, Madame Max still feels herself a "cabinned, cribbed, and confined creature" (*Finn*, 72). She longs for wider liberty and more significant action. In *Phineas Redux* she continues to surpass Trollope's other heroines by finding what she seeks—and love as well. The satisfying conclusion of her romance with Phineas is premised upon the defeat of male institutions and the male viewpoint at the hands of aggressive women.

In *Phineas Redux*, Glencora and Madame Max attack three powerful institutions that exclude direct participation by women: the political system, the legal system, and the police. Though their attack is not completely successful, their critique of these institutions is validated both by the novel's plot structure and by the narrator's commentary. And in the end, Phineas Finn, convinced that public life is tainted with dishonesty, partially withdraws from it—just as his efforts to gain government office have been crowned with success.[21] This novel tells the story of an ambitious man's disillusionment with male institutions and goals, and his decision to adopt a more feminine way of life. Its conclusion exalts an unorthodox domesticity based upon equality between the sexes.

When Phineas returns to England, the world he encounters is darker than the one from which he retired at the conclusion of *Phineas Finn*. Unfounded rumors destroy his chances of gaining office, and the idealistic Phineas learns how innuendo and malice affect political decisions. "In sober earnest one cannot tell how these things operate; but they do operate," he says sadly (*Redux*, 32). Phineas maintains a dignified silence as he watches the maneuvering of his rival, Mr. Bonteen. But his influential women friends, Glencora and Madame Max, do not share his respect for the autonomy of the political process and inaugurate a frankly personal campaign to get Phineas into office. Glencora's attempts to convince various powerful men to interfere are met by pious protestations that the system of choosing political appointees functions as it should, taking cognizance of merit, immune to personal pressure. "Never in my life have I asked for an appointment as a personal favor" (*Redux,* 37) says one friend; another states flatly that "I never interfere" (*Redux,* 37). When her husband repeats these very words—"My dear Glencora, I never interfere" (*Redux,* 37)—Glencora is exasperated, for she knows that "interference" caused Phineas' exclusion. "Who does interfere? Everybody says the same. Somebody interferes, I suppose" (*Redux,* 37), she retorts irritably, and of course she is right. But the Prime Minister is "firmly resolved that no woman's fingers should have anything to do with his pie" (*Redux,* 40), and he refuses to consider Phineas' claims.

When Phineas is accused of murdering Bonteen, however, Glencora and Madame Max are able to circumvent the legal system and the police; by these methods they achieve a complete success and pave the way for a resolution that is both comic and feminist. Though circumstantial evidence suggests that Phineas murdered Bonteen, the supposition is improbable, given Phineas' character. When an equally improbable accusation—supported by the same kind of evidence—was made against Josiah Crawley in *The Last Chronicle of Barset* (1867), men were divided from women in their response to the case. The former, almost to a man, were convinced of Crawley's guilt. The latter, almost to a woman, refused to believe that a man of Crawley's purity would stoop to crime—though they could not fault the evidence.[22] In *The Last Chronicle* feminine intuition proves correct, male rationality mistaken, when Crawley is vindicated by evidence that comes as a surprise to all concerned. But responses to the accusation against Phineas do not break down so cleanly by gender; the complex issues here are handled in a more subversive way.

Though the women who love Phineas instantly conclude that he is innocent, other women condemn him—while several of his oldest male friends readily credit his innocence on grounds of character. What separates the sexes here is their attitude toward the legal system itself. Plantagenet Palliser states the "male" case in favor of the law when he tells Glencora that "the jury will have means of arriving at a conclusion without prejudice, which you and I cannot have; and therefore we should be prepared to take their verdict as correct" (*Redux,* 63). Because they believe that the law can arrive at a "rational" conclusion superior to any individual judgment, Phineas' male supporters have no desire to sift the evidence for themselves. "I as your friend was bound to await the result [of the trial]" (*Redux,* 68), says one intimate—even as he protests that "personally" he believed Phineas innocent.

But Glencora and Madame Max feel no such commitment to the legal system and are unwilling to privilege its brand of rationality above their own inferences. When Glencora asserts that "if they find [Phineas] guilty, their verdict will be damnable and false" (*Redux,* 63), she is not arguing conventionally for feminine intuition against male rationality, but for belief in private judgment against faith in the rationality of institutions. It is this belief that the two women set out to vindicate, as they investigate the murder.

The Bonteen murder is a pretty pathetic whodunit; it is far more surprising that the police and lawyers should *fail* to solve this obvious crime, than that Glencora and Madame Max should succeed. The real murderer, Joseph Emilius, a disreputable man, has a clear motive for removing Bonteen. His shaky alibi hinges upon the fact that he had lent his latchkey to his landlady. It requires no great deductive powers to see that Emilius might have had a duplicate key made, as Glencora and Madame Max immediately do. But when Madame Max suggests this to Phineas' attorney, the professional man does not "think much of the unprofessional assistance which the lady proposed to give him" (*Redux,* 47). For the legal system, like the political system, is resistant to feminine influence.

Confronted with the hostility of Phineas' official defenders to her interference, Madame Max formulates her own complex and rational hypothesis, whose accuracy she soon establishes. Madame Max succeeds because she does not wear the blinders that prevent both lawyers and the police from investigating thoroughly. Phineas' attorney attempts to construct the best case he can, using the evidence available to him. Professionally this makes sense, for a lawyer succeeds by demonstrating his prowess in the courtroom and not through feats of detection. The police also have an approach peculiar to their profession. "So anxious [are] they not to be foiled in the attempts at discovery which their duty called upon them to make" that they convince themselves their remaining suspect must be guilty as soon as Emilius produces his alibi (*Redux,* 46).

When Madame Max conducts her own investigation, traveling all over Europe and dealing "out sovereigns—womanfully" (*Redux,* 56) in exchange for information, she has little trouble discovering the facts. "I wonder how it was," Glencora asks, "that nobody but women did see it clearly?" (*Redux,* 74). The answer is to be found not in feminine intuition but in feminine detachment from narrowly professional perspectives. Where the lawyers sought an acquittal and the police a conviction, only Madame Max sought the truth. The one piece of evidence that Madame Max fails to discover herself is the murder weapon, and it is significant that this weapon is found, quite near the scene of the crime, by a five-year-old child. The police are so sure the bludgeon in Phineas' pocket is the murder weapon that they have not even bothered to search. Their pretensions are exposed by the women and children who have been excluded from participation in—and corruption by—the professional point of view. Trollope realized that sleuthing is an attractive activity for women to whom other forms of endeavor are closed, offering a unique chance to discredit professionals on their own turf.[23] And so Madame Max becomes the first female detective in fiction.

Phineas' encounters with the seamy side of politics and the law enlighten him even as they traumatize. By the end of *Phineas Redux,* he has accepted the dark view of politics that the opening sections of the narrative document. "What does it matter who sits in Parliament?" he wonders. "The fight goes on just the same. The same falsehoods are acted. The same mock truths are spoken" (*Redux,* 68). For a man who was once "of all believers in Parliament . . . the most faithful" (*Redux,* 68), this is quite a change. Phineas rejects the office he once desired and begins to identify with the feminine perspective as he renounces his professional ambitions. One expects "from a woman," but not from a man, "both the truth and the discernment" (*Redux,* 70) that his female friends showed in judging his case, he says firmly. Phineas decides to live as women are told to do, preferring a clear conscience to success and power. And, like the ideal Victorian woman, he will be protected by his spouse from the impure world of professional competition. After rejecting office Phineas accepts a feminized identity as "Madame Goesler's husband" (*Redux*, 67).

Though Phineas loves Madame Max, he does not quite understand her. He feels it is only natural that "she should choose to be revenged for the evil which had befallen her, when she offered [him] her hand in vain" (*Redux*, 77) at the end of *Phineas Finn*—and he fears a spiteful rejection. But Phineas could escape these fears if he realized how courageously Madame Max has claimed male prerogatives. Though she was humiliated when Phineas rejected her, Madame Max felt sure that "she had in truth done nothing to disgrace herself" (*Redux*, 15) and was no angrier than a rejected male suitor would have been. So when Phineas visits Madame Max to ask for her hand, her reaction surprises him. "I have come," he begins, but Madame Max immediately interrupts him. "I know why you have come," she says. Certain that a lady would never admit that she expected a declaration, Phineas answers foolishly, "I doubt that. I have come to tell you that I love you." Again her response is surprising. "Oh Phineas;—at last, at last!" she cries, and rushes into his arms. Soon she tells Phineas that their marriage "must be an even partnership" (*Redux*, 79).

And it certainly is an even partnership. Phineas will remain in Parliament and will gradually begin again to do the world's work—for this work must be done. But he will be protected from the pressures of professionalism by his wife's money. Madame Max will continue to manage her Viennese business and will spend much time apart from her husband helping Glencora prosecute her wild schemes. This is the Victorian ideal transformed out of recognition, for instead of the wife's providing a sanctified refuge to which the husband can periodically withdraw, both spouses cultivate a mixture of involvement and detachment. The remaining Palliser novels show that the Finns share power, freedom, professional engagement, and the right to obey conscience on absolutely equal terms. As in Bell's subplot of *The Small House at Allington* and in the main plot of *The Belton Estate*, this satisfying comic conclusion is premised upon the rejection of convention by an exceptional husband and wife. But here the rejection is more complete, just as the wife is more exceptional. Though Will respects Clara's autonomy, she will stay at home and keep his house; but in the Finns' house there is no angel. The Finns are the precursors of the childless, two-career couple.

Feminist Tragedy

As the years passed, Trollope grew increasingly audacious in his attempts to modernize romantic comedy on behalf of the independent woman. One must be impressed by the ingenious ways Trollope used romantic comedy to articulate his reservations about the ideal of femininity, because the conventions of the form are restrictive: romantic comedy can do only so much, no matter how energetically one stretches it. At the conclusion of every romantic comedy, the heroine must make a promising marriage, even if there is reason to suspect that this marriage will not be ideal. What of the many women who fail to do this? How can fiction give shape to their predicament? These are questions that Trollope began to ask early in his writing career, but to which he later returned with increasing frequency.

As early as *The Bertrams,* Trollope realized that if comedy shows how men and women learn to get along with one another, then tragedy might be used to explore what happens when they fail to do so. But in the section of *The Bertrams* that deals with Henry Harcourt's ruin, Trollope ran into problems by trying to force an antifeminist interpretation on material that did not support it. Determined to make the powerless Caroline bear much of the blame for the powerful Henry's decline, Trollope failed in his attempt to use tragedy to explore the dark side of Victorian marriage. In spite of the narrator's shrill assertion that Caroline's coldness helped to destroy her husband, Henry's fall results from his ambition and dishonesty; it has little connection with his marital difficulties.

Like so much else in *The Bertrams,* however, this tragedy can support a more feminist reading than the one the narrator supplies. If we refuse to follow the narrator in seeing Henry as the tragic protagonist and instead look at the story as Caroline's tragedy, then we might view her as a heroine on the model of Antigone: a powerless woman faced with the necessity of obeying irreconcilable imperatives. Antigone cannot both obey the religious imperative to bury her brothers and Creon's order that she refrain from doing so. Caroline—less dramatically, but perhaps no less painfully—cannot obey the contradictory demands of the feminine code that she be at once loving and prudent. But Trollope pulls back from the tragic implications of Caroline's story by permitting a bittersweet comic conclusion in her eventual marriage to George.

Trollope missed his opportunity to write a woman's tragedy in *The Bertrams,* but he never made that mistake again. In the years that followed, as his view of society in general and the position of women in particular continued to darken, Trollope realized that tragedy could be given a feminist twist. In this he was not alone. As Jeannette King points out in her study of tragedy in the work of Eliot, James, and Hardy, many Victorian novelists were interested in a new kind of tragedy that portrayed the doomed struggles of ordinary people against a persistently hostile social environment. These novelists revealed "the new forms of barbarity which civilization gives rise to" by including such tragedies in their novels.[24] And they often used a woman as the tragic protagonist both because they saw that Victorian women were indeed the victims of civilized barbarity and because they realized that "womanhood . . . is the most immediate and overwhelming of deterministic factors" that prevent individuals from fulfilling their aims.[25]

In the novels that followed *Framley Parsonage,* Trollope began to explore the tragedies of Victorian women, stressing their helplessness in a society that denies them power, the difficulty of successful rebellion, and the irreconcilable demands with which they must deal. The first rebel whose rebellion brings about her tragic destruction is Lady Mason; the first heroine who fails to find happiness because the code of feminine behavior makes impossible demands upon her is Lily Dale—quickly followed by Julia Ongar. The stories of Lily and Julia do not end comically, but neither are they tragic, for both women achieve a measure of contentment. Building on the foundations laid in *Orley Farm, The Small House at Allington,* and *The Claverings,* Trollope's novels of the 1870s and 1880s turn with increasing earnestness to the tragedies of women.

But before he could return to the woman's tragedy, Trollope had to undertake a related project: debunking the notion of the male tragic hero that *The Bertrams* took so seriously. *He Knew He Was Right* (1868) clears the ground for the feminist tragedies of the later novels by suggesting that in a society where power is largely reserved for the male, men may willfully seek tragedy, but are far less likely than women to have it thrust upon them.[26]

He Knew He Was Right begins with the marriage of the rich and intelligent Louis Trevelyan to the beautiful Emily Rowley. But what initially looks like the celebratory marriage concluding a comedy turns out to be the commencement of a new sort of tragedy. Like many tragic heroes, the free and powerful Louis cannot resist the temptation to overreach himself. Louis is destroyed by two forces: the excess leisure with which a gentleman of fortune must deal and his sense of his powers and prerogatives as a man. Believing that he has a right to complete submission from his wife, with little to occupy his time, Louis becomes obsessed by Emily's friendship with an old crony of her father's, and his descent toward madness and death commences.

But the tragedy of Louis' deterioration is belittled when the narrator locates its genesis in nothing more significant than boredom and remarks that, had Trevelyan needed to labor for his bread, his naturally tyrannical temper would never have gotten out of hand. Trevelyan's desire to dominate his wife also has its importance in Trollope's cynical reconsideration of the male tragic hero. Such heroes get into trouble by attempting to claim a power that cosmic or social forces deny them. Sometimes they belong to a privileged class, which is in the process of losing its power but which will not give up without a struggle. Trollope, however, employs a very diminished modern analogue to this situation when he suggests that, in contemporary England, males are the privileged group trying to protect historic—but indefensible—privileges against the mildest sort of feminist revolt.

In *He Knew He Was Right* dissatisfaction with woman's social position has become so prevalent that, as P. D. Edwards remarks, "all the novel's heroines either share or sympathize with the feminine grievances that Emily Trevelyan voices."[27] But none of these her-

oines is by any means a radical feminist like the minor comic character, Wallachia Petrie. The heroines are willing to be mastered by
men, but they do insist on being mastered through argument. They
will not permit themselves to be treated as chattels. Yet this is
precisely the way Louis, with his slightly outdated definition of his
"power as a man" (79) tries to control Emily. "He was her master
and she must know he was her master" (5). Louis' initial tragic
error results from a pathetic desire, born of insecurity, to destroy
the autonomy of the only human being he loves.

Unlike the heroes of classical tragedy, who lose control of the
hostile social and cosmic forces they have inadvertently released,
Louis remains free, almost until the moment of his death, to change
his mind and choose comedy. He need only grant Emily the mod-
icum of independence she demands and all will be well. But because
Louis becomes enamored of himself in the role of tragic hero, he
continues to choose tragedy of his own free will. Yet tragedy freely
chosen is not real tragedy. Thus Louis' increasing sufferings, as
many critics have remarked, seem increasingly ridiculous as it becomes clear that his rigidity alone prevents a happy outcome. In
suggesting that rigid, mechanical behavior is the essence of farce,
Bergson reveals the reason why Trollope is able to present Louis'
grim decline in farcical terms.

When Louis delivers an ultimatum to Emily, the narrator comments that he does it with an air that is "comic with its assumed
magnificence" (69). His indignant anger is described as "almost
grotesque" (86), and he is mocked for referring, as a bona fide tragic
hero might almost do, "to the affairs of the last two years as though
they had been governed by an inexorable fate which had utterly
destroyed his happiness without any fault on his part" (92). By the
close of the story, Louis has been unmasked as something very
different from the tragic hero he pompously pretends to be—for
the novel, as Andrew Wright notes, invites its reader "to measure
the distance between cosmic tragedy and domestic obsession."[28]
But *He Knew He Was Right* does not lack real tragedy. Emily has
her faults, but unlike her husband, she did not freely choose the
deprivations of love, liberty, and reputation she undergoes. During
most of the novel, she can end the conflict with Louis only by

confessing—falsely—that she is an adulteress. Ostensibly a man's tragedy, the novel is in fact the tragedy of a woman. For in Victorian England, as a minor character remarks, "it's two to one the young 'ooman has the worst of it" (32), and those are not good odds. *The Bertrams* suggests that a powerful man can easily become the tragic victim of a powerless woman: *He Knew He Was Right* argues the opposite.

In the sections of *Phineas Finn* and *Phineas Redux* that concern the fate of Laura Standish and her husband Robert Kennedy, Trollope continues to explore the tragic possibilities of Victorian marriage. But he does not simply retell *He Knew He Was Right*'s story of a pseudo-tragic hero destroyed by his attempts to dominate a woman. Trollope's use of tragedy in the Phineas novels suggests that a woman's destruction does not always result from the tyranny of her spouse; its causes are likely to be more complicated than that. Not only Kennedy's conventional view of women, but Laura's as well, dooms him to madness and death, her to lasting unhappiness. For although Laura has a masculine manner, she is in fact much less rebellious than the other London ladies who figure in the Phineas novels. Accepting the feminine code, she thinks she can find happiness by obeying it. But she discovers that the code is far more contradictory and unrealistic than she had imagined. The male tragic hero falls when he claims excessive liberty, but Laura is destroyed by her belief that Victorian conventions offer women sufficient freedom.

When Phineas first meets Laura, she wields a power that few girls could have matched, but she takes her privileges for granted. Phineas is struck by the "unlimited confidence" that Laura's widowed father places in her: "She was much more mistress of herself than if she had been [his] wife instead of [his] daughter" (*Finn*, 4). When Laura wants to find Phineas a seat in Parliament, she need only ask one of her influential friends. Laura fails to see that because her independence and power depend on men, her position is highly precarious: "Lady Laura Standish had nothing of fear about her" (*Finn*, 4).

Though Laura jokes that "a woman's life is only half a life, as she cannot have a seat in parliament" (*Finn*, 6), she is in fact satisfied with her position and bitterly opposes the women's movement. "That women should even wish to have votes at parliamentary elections was to her abominable, and the cause of the Rights of Women generally was odious to her" (*Finn*, 10). It may seem surprising that a woman who gives the impression of looking "at the world almost as a man looked at it,—as an oyster to be opened" (*Finn*, 14) should oppose the rights of women. But there is no real contradiction—Laura's antifeminist views were shared by many aristocratic women. "The political hostess," the historian Brian Harrison explains, "enjoyed extensive influence without the vote. Indeed, woman suffrage would merely raise up rivals to her influence and she had no reason to support it."[29] Beatrice Webb notes that prominent women were unlikely "to have experienced the disabilities felt by many other women"[30] and so to feel that reforms were needed. Laura is not unusual in combining opposition to women's rights with the belief that she herself "might be useful . . . [and] politically powerful" (*Finn*, 10) through the influence her social position gives her. "A woman may do as much as a man" (*Finn*, 32), she tells her friends.

Serenely unconscious of danger, Laura sets out to make a life that will combine masculine power with traditional femininity. She sacrifices her fortune to pay the debts of her brother, for she feels, conventionally, that this wild rake can be reclaimed by feminine influence. Without fortune, Laura can no longer obey the imperative of the feminine code that a woman must marry for love, but she decides that she has a higher duty: to refuse Phineas and prudently accept her prominent suitor, Robert Kennedy. With Kennedy's help she hopes both to retain her influence on "the affairs of the world" (*Finn*, 14) and to become Phineas' guardian angel: "It should be her care to see that his life was successful" (*Finn*, 17). In return for Kennedy's support, she plans to make him an obedient wife.

But after her marriage, Laura discovers that her naïve optimism distorted the grim reality of her situation in a ludicrously wide variety of ways. Laura learns that a woman cannot escape guilt for disobeying one imperative of the feminine code, merely because she has done so in order to obey another. Such contradictions are not as easily absorbed as she believed: she is tormented by guilt for having married without love. And she learns that the sexual response to Phineas that, as a pure woman, she thought she could repress, is far stronger than she realized. "When I was young," she tells Phineas later, "I did not credit myself with capacity for so much passion" (*Redux*, 12).

After marrying Kennedy, Laura also discovers how foolish she was in expecting to retain the extraordinary freedom fortune had given her. She learns that she is only a woman, subject to disabilities whose injustice she tried to ignore. Kennedy is not a cruel man, but he is a husband according to the book, demanding every last one of his rights under a code whose authority the antifeminist Laura tacitly accepts.[31] "A wife's obedience was one of those rights which he could not abandon without injury to his self-esteem" (*Finn*, 51). "Having married a rich man in order that she might be able to do something in the world," Laura finds that he will permit her to "do nothing" whatever (*Finn*, 32).

When Kennedy's accusation that she loves Phineas provides her with a pretext for leaving him, Laura seizes it—but she is partly aware that this is not the real reason for her flight. In truth, she simply cannot accept her subordinate position. "There are moments, Robert," Laura tells her husband, "when even a married woman must be herself rather than her husband's wife" (*Finn*, 39). But when she accepted Kennedy she had intended to be his dutiful wife during every moment of every day. Kennedy has a point when he says that women like Laura "rebel against the yoke because it is a yoke. And yet they accept the yoke, knowing it to be a yoke" (*Redux*, 10).

After Laura's departure, Kennedy becomes obsessed with asserting his right to reclaim her. Kennedy's attempts to force Laura to keep her vows, whatever this may cost her, lead him along the same path of madness and physical decay that Trevelyan followed— and his decline, too, is described in terms that rob it of all dignity.[32] As in *He Knew He Was Right*, so in *Phineas Redux*, a debased tragedy is the fate of the husband who claims a submission that his self-respecting wife cannot grant. But unlike Emily Trevelyan's tragedy, Laura's destruction cannot be attributed solely to the powerlessness of a wife's position.

The influence of social convention on the tragic heroine herself is also to blame. Laura's naïve acceptance of the feminine code helped to undo her, and it is possible to argue that with more realism and caution she might have fared better. For this reason, she is not quite so blameless a victim as Emily. In the course of the two Phineas novels, Laura changes a lot. But when in *Phineas Redux* she congratulates herself on the "womanlike" passivity of her response to Phineas' arrest—and castigates Madame Max's active attempts to free him as "unfeminine" (*Redux*, 65)—we realize that she will never question the feminine code as radically as she ought. Laura's experience proves the position of even the most privileged Victorian woman to be tragically precarious—but it also proves the need for critical thinking if danger is to be surmounted.

In the Lucinda Roanoke subplot of *The Eustace Diamonds*, Trollope again considers the tragic consequences that can result from attempts to destroy a woman's autonomy. As in the two tragedies we have just examined, incurable madness punishes the character who cannot renounce the obsessive attempt to dominate a woman. But now the tyrant and the woman that tyrant hopes to destroy are one and the same. Laura initially hopes to obey the feminine code because she thinks it will be easy to do so. Lucinda feels sure that obedience will be impossible—and yet she knows that she must obey. As she tries to enforce her own obedience, her sanity crumbles.

I argued earlier in this chapter that in the dark world of *The Eustace Diamonds* women are commodities to be priced and traded with little sentimentality. Their value depends upon the externals of rank, wealth, and beauty, and not upon character. The endlessly—and almost aimlessly—dishonest Lizzie Eustace is the product and embodiment of this phenomenon. No real self underlies her externals; she is whatever she thinks it most advantageous to be. Lucy Morris resists being turned into a commodity. But she is saved only by the intervention of an author in search of romantic comedy from repudiation by her venal lover. Lizzie's inconclusive story is ironic, Lucy's technically comic. But Lucinda, the novel's third heroine, represents a tragic possibility. Though she tries to convert herself into a commodity, she discovers that her real self cannot be repressed.

Lucinda, a beautiful, penniless girl, is being hawked about in society by her aunt, the adventuress Mrs. Carbuncle. Though Lucinda often wishes she were a poor woman with some work to do, she has no practical way to avoid the marriage of convenience for which society destines her. But she cannot dissemble her contempt for the men her beauty attracts. She remains "silent, arrogant, and hard of approach" (36), incapable of putting herself "in the way of taking such good things as her charms" (36) might be traded for. In the absence of birth and fortune, Lucinda's inability to flatter leaves her with nothing but her beauty to trade—and for this quality alone only the contemptible Sir Griffin Tewett is willing to marry her. Lucinda forces herself to accept him and tries to force herself to marry him. But no matter how she strives, she cannnot conquer her hatred or the sexual repulsion he arouses. "When he touches me my whole body is in agony" (69), she tells her aunt.

As Mrs. Carbuncle presses Lucinda to honor her engagement, she reminds herself that it is the common fate of female flesh to be traded, that girls must suffer, and that she herself has suffered. Like many women whose lives have been deformed by social pressure, she gets a perverse pleasure from watching other women undergo the same fate.[33] Because she loves Mrs. Carbuncle and because other options are simply not there, Lucinda earnestly endeavors to keep her contract with Sir Griffin: "Dear Aunt Jane . . . I have struggled so hard,—simply that you might be freed from me" (69). But Lucinda's attempt to convert herself into an object of exchange does not succeed—the self that she attempts to deny is broken by her struggles.

On the morning of her wedding, with her eyes fixed on the Bible—a reminder of the moral world which has been closed against her—Lucinda wears on her face "a look of fixed but almost idiotic resolution" (70), as she promises that Sir Griffin "shall never touch [her] again alive" (70). Another loser in the battle of the sexes has been driven mad. But where men like Trevelyan and Kennedy actively court madness as they attempt to break their wives' wills, Lucinda goes mad as, in obedience to the dictates of society and to pressure from other women, she tries to break her own. Her tragedy is particularly frightening because its sources are so diffuse;

the only villain at whom one can point a finger is society itself. P. D. Edwards remarks that although Trollope "usually sees a trace of absurdity in the display of strong emotion" and therefore tends to mock his self-styled tragic characters, Lucinda is an exception, "an extreme case, and . . . a particularly bitter one."[34] In Victorian England, Trollope suggested with increasing assurance and frequency as the years passed, the most authentic tragedy is the tragedy of the helpless woman.[35]

Conclusion

Trollope began his career as an unreconstructed believer in the doctrine of separate natures and separate spheres. By the time he completed *The Belton Estate,* however, he had decided that this doctrine and the code of behavior based upon it were making life difficult for women. The novels that follow *The Belton Estate* amply acknowledge the suffering of women under the rule of custom— it could indeed be said that they are obsessed with this suffering. But Trollope's later novels also suggest, through their handling of genre, that the problems of women resist easy solutions.

By undercutting conservative romantic comedy, Trollope hints that Victorian marriage is not a happy destiny for many women. When he affirms progressive comedy, on the other hand, he may seem to be offering a solution to the woman's problem: let men and women of goodwill join in marriages of equality, and all will be well. Marriage is still the only answer for women, these comedies seem to imply, but a new kind of marriage is needed. This way of looking at Trollope's progressive comedies, however, is both too simple and too optimistic.

In *He Knew He Was Right,* no fewer than three progressive comedies end with genuine rejoicing. "It is as if three Elizabeths married three Darcys," James Kincaid observes, and surely nothing could be more delightful than that.[36] These unconventional marriages take place over the objections of the older generation; all three husbands value the strength, not the pliability, of their prospective brides.[37] When these comedies are balanced against the tragic destruction of the Trevelyans' ultra-conventional marriage, the message seems clear: if prospective husbands emulate the novel's comic heroes, their brides will find fulfillment in matrimony.

But *He Knew He Was Right* complicates this issue by suggesting that its comic and tragic heroes are innately different from one another. Louis is one of those men who are "absolutely unfitted by nature to have custody or guardianship of others" (27), while the comic heroes are men of great natural sweetness. Hugh Stanbury has "the sweetest temper that was ever given to a man for the blessing of a woman" (4); Charles Glascock possesses "a disposition as sweet as an angel's" (63); Brooke Burgess sports "as sweet a mouth as ever declared the excellence of a man's temper" (31). These men desire marriages of equality because of their innate sweetness— and in defiance of what they have been taught by a society that endorses male supremacy. But if we can feel sure of a woman's happiness only when she marries an exceptionally kind man, then reform of the customs that encourage men to tyrannize over their powerless wives is needed to protect women who do not draw such prizes in the matrimonial lottery. The "solution" offers little hope to the wife of an ordinary man, who is likely to treat her more or less as custom suggests, and it offers even less hope to the wives of naturally tyrannical men like Trevelyan.

Trollope frequently, though not invariably, balances the progressive comedies in his later novels against plots that are ironic or tragic, thus suggesting that the power of convention makes such comedies difficult to achieve. The balancing of Violet Effingham's progressive comedy against Laura Standish's tragedy in *Phineas Finn* is a case in point, as is the paralleling of Isabel Boncassen's joyous match with Mabel Grex's wasteful destruction in *The Duke's Children*. Nothing is more remarkable in Trollope's later novels than the way he manages to create delightful romantic comedy within the context of a world that, for women at least, has become essentially tragic.

By sidelining even progressive comedy while emphasizing the woman's tragedy, Trollope's later novels imply that reform is badly needed. Yet women who argue for radical change are cruelly caricatured in these very novels: comically doctrinaire feminists appear in *He Knew He Was Right, Is He Popenjoy?* (1878), and the novella

Kept in the Dark (1882), though such characters are absent from Trollope's earlier work. In explaining this apparent contradiction, I would like to enlarge upon Kincaid's suggestion that *He Knew He Was Right* ridicules the feminist Wallachia Petrie because she is too optimistic and not because she is too feminist. "Feminism is burlesqued here, certainly," Kincaid argues, "but the burlesque is conducted in terms that exactly invert those of the usual attack. Ordinarily we are assured that there is no dilemma after all, and that the feminists are proposing radical solutions for non-problems. Here we are led to believe that the dilemma is far too deeply rooted and basic ever to be touched by the feminists' solutions: they are too easy."[38] By caricaturing doctrinaire feminists, Trollope implies that no sensible woman would seriously propose the immediate abolition of long-established customs. Although many intelligent, moderate women in Trollope's later novels are just as dissatisfied with their position as the feminist rebels those novels ridicule, they hesitate to offer drastic solutions.

Neither individual reform, nor the radical social reforms proposed by feminists can solve the problems of Victorian women. But there is hope in the possibility—perhaps even the probability—of gradual social reform. The comic heroes of *He Knew He Was Right* grant their wives greater liberty than custom recommends not only because they are innately generous but also because they understand better than the conventional Louis Trevelyan what women are really like. "If I were married . . . I fancy I shouldn't look after my wife at all. It seems to me that women hate to be told of their duties," Hugh Stanbury tells Louis, revealing a view of female nature that diverges dramatically from the ideal of the submissive angel (19). And Stanbury's view of women is the one that emerges from Trollope's later fiction.

Trollope believed that shifts in public opinion would be followed by the gradual reform of custom and law. This combination of stability and flexibility was, in his view, the greatest virtue of the English social and political tradition. The process of reform was not always orderly or rational, Trollope's novels suggest, but it was usually effective in the long run. In the course of the Phineas novels, for example, the need for a law protecting Irish tenant rights is felt by the Irish themselves, then publicized by a few maverick MP's, and finally acknowledged by Parliament. In this flexible society, a more realistic assessment of woman's nature and needs should eventually produce the adjustments needed to accommodate it. Perhaps Trollope hoped that his sympathetic portrayals of independent women would contribute to the process of reform.

Notes
Editions Cited
Index

Notes

All citations to Trollope's novels, autobiography, letters, travel books, and short fiction that are incorporated into the text refer to the editions listed in the Editions Cited.

Introduction

1. See, for example, Bill Overton, who argues that Trollope's early novels do not question the "official" Victorian attitude towards the angel in the house, *The Unofficial Trollope* (Totowa, New Jersey, 1982); or P. D. Edwards, who thinks that Trollope treated the ingenue conservatively in all the novels that precede *He Knew He Was Right* (1868), *Anthony Trollope* (New York, 1977). Critics who believe that Trollope exalts the angel in the house in *both* his early and his later novels include A.O.J. Cockshut, *Anthony Trollope: A Critical Study* (London, 1955); Q. D. Leavis, *Fiction and the Reading Public* (London, 1932); Charles Blinderman, "The Servility of Dependence: The Dark Lady in Trollope," in *Images of Women in Fiction*, ed. Susan Cornillon (Bowling Green, Ohio, 1972); and Shirley Letwin, *The Gentleman in Trollope* (Cambridge, Mass., 1982).

2. Critics who have explicitly noted the gradual liberalization of Trollope's attitude toward women—though they date and describe this development in a variety of ways—include Juliet McMaster, *Trollope's Palliser Novels* (London, 1978), p. 166; Robert Polhemus, *The Changing World of Anthony Trollope* (Berkeley, 1968), pp. 89–121; and Richard Barickman, Susan MacDonald, and Myra Stark, *Corrupt Relations: Dickens, Thackeray, Trollope, Collins, and the Victorian Sexual System* (New York, 1982), pp. 195–235. In the works cited above, Overton and Edwards also admit, by implication, that a change occurred, when they argue that one or another of Trollope's later novels demonstrates feminist sympathies, after claiming that his early novels do not. R. C. Terry argues that Trollope treats his ingenues conservatively, but subverts the Victorian ideal of separate spheres in his disenchanted treatments of marriage. In developing the latter point, however, Terry generally cites novels written during the second half of Trollope's career. *Anthony Trollope: The Artist in Hiding* (London, 1977).

3. In addition to the books cited in notes 1 and 2 above, the following critical works also note the sympathy for dissatisfied women expressed in one or more of Trollope's later novels: James Kincaid, *The Novels of Anthony Trollope* (Oxford, 1977); Robert Tracy, *Trollope's Later Novels* (Berkeley, 1978); Peter K. Garrett, *The Victorian Multiplot Novel* (New Haven and London, 1980); Geoffrey Harvey, *The Art of Anthony Trollope* (London, 1980); and Andrew Wright, *Anthony Trollope: Dream and Art* (Chicago, 1983). Recently a number of articles have made similar arguments about several of the later novels.

4. Of the two novels I do not discuss, one, *The Struggles of Brown, Jones, and Robinson,* is a spoof of the advertising mentality which shows little concern with the position of women; the other, *Castle Richmond,* a retrospective "sociological" novel about the Irish potato famine, is not really comparable to the other novels of this period, all of which deal with middle-class characters in contemporary England.

1. The Woman Question

1. John Ruskin, "Of Queen's Gardens," *The Literary Criticism of John Ruskin,* ed. Harold Bloom (Garden City, N.Y., 1965), p. 195.

2. [James Davies], A review of two books on women, *Quarterly Review,* 119 (1866), p. 50. Quoted in Joan N. Burstyn, *Victorian Education and the Ideal of Womanhood* (New Jersey, 1980), p. 37.

3. Ruskin, "Of Queen's Gardens," p. 193.

4. William Rathbone Greg, "Prostitution," *Westminster Review,* 53 (1850), p. 457.

5. E.B. Leach, "Woman: What Is her Appointed Position and Work?", *Girl's Own Paper* (March 1884), p. 340. Quoted in Deborah Gorham, *The Victorian Girl and the Feminine Ideal* (London, 1982), p. 120.

6. Ruskin, "Of Queen's Gardens," p. 194.

7. "The Model Daughter," *Punch,* 14 (1848), p. 230. Quoted in Burstyn, *Victorian Education,* p. 38.

8. Mrs. Ellis, *The Daughters of England* (London, 1843), p. 73.

9. Edward Tilt, *The Elements of Health, and Principles of Female Hygiene* (London, 1852), p. 15. Quoted in Gorham, *The Victorian Girl,* p. 102.

10. "Feminine Wranglers," *Saturday Review,* 18 (1864), p. 112. Quoted in Burstyn, *Victorian Education.*

11. Juliet McMaster has listed a number of instances in Trollope's novels where characters discuss this issue. *Trollope's Palliser Novels,* p. 167.

12. "Queen Bees or Working Bees?", *Saturday Review,* 8 (1859), p. 576. Quoted in Burstyn, *Victorian Education,* p. 51.

13. W. Nicholson, *How to Be a Lady* (Wakefield, c. 1850), p. 253. Quoted in Gorham, *The Victorian Girl,* p. 115.

14. Burstyn, *Victorian Education,* p. 27.

15. Barbara Bodichon, "Married Women and the Law," (1854), in Janet Horowitz Murray, ed., *Strong-Minded Women* (New York, 1982), p. 119.

16. Caroline Norton, "An Indissoluble Sacrament," in Erna Hellerstein, Leslie Hume, and Karen Offen, eds., *Victorian Women* (Stanford, 1981), p. 259.

17. Norton, "An Indissoluble Sacrament," p. 259.

18. Sarah Ellis, *Education of the Heart* (London, 1869), p. 15. Quoted in Burstyn, *Victorian Education*, p. 60.

19. Maria Grey, "The Women's Educational Movement," in Theodore Stanton, ed., *The Woman Question in Europe* (New York, 1884), p. 31.

20. Trollope discussed this movement in *North America* (Philadelphia, 1862), pp. 284–85.

21. Frances Hoggan, "Women in Medicine," in Stanton, *The Woman Question*, p. 67.

22. Anthony Trollope, "Novel Reading," *Nineteenth Century*, 5 (1879), p. 26.

23. Critics tend to overestimate the play's sympathy for feminism, because they are interested in its links to the far more feminist novel *Can You Forgive Her?*. See, for example, the introduction by Michael Sadleir, reprinted in the Arno Press edition of *The Noble Jilt* (New York, 1981).

24. As the above discussion indicates, the authors of *Corrupt Relations* radically oversimplify when they assert that Trollope "defended antifeminist taboos in his personal life." Barickman, MacDonald, and Stark, *Corrupt Relations*, p. 11.

25. Anthony Trollope, "Higher Education for Women," (1868) in *Four Lectures*, ed. Morris Parrish (London, 1938), p. 74.

26. Trollope, "Higher Education," p. 76.

27. Trollope, "Higher Education," pp. 75–76.

28. For a more extended discussion of the role Trollope's childhood played in shaping him as an artist, see Andrew Wright, *Anthony Trollope: Dream and Art*, pp. 13–27.

29. David Skilton, *Anthony Trollope and His Contemporaries* (London, 1972).

30. Sandra M. Gilbert and Susan Gubar, *The Madwoman in the Attic* (New Haven, 1979), p. 49.

31. Patricia Thompson, *The Victorian Heroine: A Changing Ideal 1837–1873* (Westport, Conn., 1978), p. 111.

32. The critical work taking this approach to which I am most deeply indebted is James Kincaid's outstanding book, *The Novels of Anthony Trollope*. Peter K. Garrett's *The Victorian Multiplot Novel*, Bill Overton's *The Unofficial Trollope*, and Geoffrey Harvey's *The Art of Anthony Trollope* also discuss the form of Trollope's novels. Critics who argue that the tension among formal elements in some of the novels implies greater sympathy with women than their narrators express include Barickman, MacDonald,

Stark, *Corrupt Relations;* Rajiva Wijesinha, *The Androgynous Trollope* (Washington, D.C., 1982); Terry, *Anthony Trollope: The Artist in Hiding;* and McMaster, *Trollope's Palliser Novels.*

33. McMaster, *Trollope's Palliser Novels,* p. 179.

34. Barickman, MacDonald, and Stark, *Corrupt Relations,* p. 200.

35. Robin Gilmour, "A Lesser Thackeray? Trollope and the Victorian Novel," in *Anthony Trollope,* ed. Tony Bareham (Plymouth and London, 1980), p. 194.

36. Kincaid, *The Novels of Anthony Trollope,* p. 32.

37. Robert Polhemus, *Comic Faith: The Great Tradition from Austen to Joyce* (Chicago, 1980), p. 197.

38. Kincaid, *The Novels of Anthony Trollope,* pp. 34–35.

39. Garrett, *The Victorian Multiplot Novel,* p. 183.

40. Garrett, *The Victorian Multiplot Novel,* p. 9.

41. Kincaid, *The Novels of Anthony Trollope,* p. 27.

42. Kincaid, *The Novels of Anthony Trollope,* p. 30.

43. Kincaid, *The Novels of Anthony Trollope,* pp. 31–32.

44. Garrett, *The Victorian Multiplot Novel,* p. 5.

45. Kincaid, *The Novels of Anthony Trollope,* p. 28.

2. Affirming the Ideal

The sections in this book dealing with *Barchester Towers* were published in a slightly different form in Jane Nardin, "Conservative Comedy and the Women of *Barchester Towers,*" *Studies in the Novel,* 18 (1986), pp. 381–94.

1. Several critics have argued that the narrator of *Barchester Towers* is among Trollope's most complex and manipulative, making a variety of assertions that need to be assessed in the light of what actually happens in the novel. See, for example, Robert Polhemus, *Comic Faith,* p. 197; and Kincaid, *The Novels of Anthony Trollope,* pp. 34–36. They may well be right in general, but on the issue of woman's place, the narrator's commentary is not radically undermined by the events of the novel.

2. U. C. Knoepflmacher discusses *Barchester Towers's* conservative vision. But although Knoepflmacher agrees that the novel is conservative in its treatment of sex roles, he sees the "status quo ante" differently from the way I do, arguing that in the end "women will still retain their old mastery over men." *Laughter and Despair: Ten Readings in Novels of the Victorian Era* (Berkeley, 1971), p. 42. I think the comic subplot concludes with men resuming their old mastery over a woman.

3. Quoted in Kincaid, *The Novels of Anthony Trollope,* p. 105.

4. Kincaid ignores the praise Eleanor often receives from the narrator. He is certainly right that the narrator's "rhetorical instructions . . . move the reader away from" Eleanor and Arabin in various ways, but this is only part of the story. *The Novels of Anthony Trollope,* p. 105.

5. Kincaid, *The Novels of Anthony Trollope*, p. 112.

6. Kincaid sees the ivy metaphor—the plant is "clinging but deadly," he claims—as implying that Eleanor's inability to stand alone is a serious flaw. *The Novels of Anthony Trollope*, p. 111. But ivy is not in fact deadly to the oak, and the image was a conventional one at the time. For a discussion of its use in genre painting, see Helen Roberts, "Marriage, Redundancy or Sin," in Martha Vicinus, ed., *Suffer and Be Still* (London, 1972), pp. 48–49. I hope to show that *Barchester Towers* uses the image with little irony.

7. W. David Shaw argues that only Grantly's "fantastic suspicions" of a romance between Eleanor and Slope force her to defend him. "Moral Drama in *Barchester Towers*," *Nineteenth Century Fiction*, 19, 1 (June, 1964), p. 47. But Eleanor became Slope's champion long before Grantly interfered.

8. P. D. Edwards agrees, arguing that Eleanor fails "to display the womanly tenderness that would have averted a misunderstanding" with Arabin. *Anthony Trollope*, p. 18.

9. Knoepflmacher views Susan as one of the novel's domineering women, who only pretends to be a "pattern of obedience." *Laughter and Despair*, p. 36. Edwards agrees, seeing Grantly as a victim of "petticoat government . . . badgered by his wife." *Anthony Trollope*, p. 22. But whatever Susan's ends may be, she pursues them in traditionally feminine ways. Her advice never becomes nagging, and she never challenges her husband's authority.

10. Here again both Knoepflmacher and Edwards see Miss Thorne as domineering. The former accuses her of arranging "the manly sports her brother neglects." *Laughter and Despair*, p. 36. The latter claims she is a "natural man tamer" with an abnormal "passion for muscular medieval sports." *Anthony Trollope*, p. 26. These discussions of Susan and Miss Thorne suggest that even in the 1970s male critics often expressed disapproval of female characters whose submission to men was less than total.

11. Critics often view Madeline's role as very subversive. See, for example, Barickman, MacDonald, and Stark, who argue that, although Trollope was ambivalent about Madeline, he uses her primarily to "satirize the values implicit in the story of his conventional heroine." *Corrupt Relations*, p. 55.

12. Kincaid, *The Novels of Anthony Trollope*, p. 71.

13. Nearly every critic who has ever mentioned the novel notices its Dickensian qualities. See, for example, Tony Bareham, "Patterns of Excellence: Theme and Structure in *The Three Clerks*," in *Anthony Trollope*, ed. Bareham, pp. 57–59; and Edwards, *Anthony Trollope*, pp. 84–87.

14. Edwards discusses the "strain on Trollope's emotional vocabulary" imposed by the novel's "absence of restraint." *Anthony Trollope*, p. 84.

15. Two other critics agree that the novel is elaborately patterned around contrasts among the six main characters, but identify a different pattern. Bareham sees a contrast between characters dominated by the head and

those ruled by the heart. "Patterns of Excellence." Harvey sees a contrast between prodigality and prudence. *The Art of Anthony Trollope*, p. 20.

16. Polhemus, *Changing World*, p. 53.

17. Hugh Hennedy is the only critic who talks of it at all, so far as I know. *Unity in Barsetshire* (The Hague, 1971), p. 60.

18. Kincaid, *The Novels of Anthony Trollope*, p. 114.

19. A notice of the novel published in the *Saturday Review* remarked upon "the trifling inconsistency of praising a man for being disinterested in the first place, and paying him 300,000£. for his disinterested conduct immediately afterwards." Quoted in Bill Overton, *The Unofficial Trollope*, p. 126.

20. Kincaid, *The Novels of Anthony Trollope*, p. 74.

21. Polhemus, *Changing World*, p. 63.

22. Jane Austen, *Mansfield Park* (London, 1923), p. 109. There are enough similarities between *The Bertrams* and *Mansfield Park* to make it likely that Austen's novel served as a rough model for Trollope's—whether Trollope was conscious of this or not. Both are novels about the need for firm moral principles and a sense of vocation in establishing a stable center of self; both contrast ambitious characters with characters who are content with tranquillity; both turn on the issue of ordination; both contain characters named Bertram and Price; and both are dark comedies that end with less than complete rejoicing. The point of the parallel for Trollope would, I suspect, be that the world where his novel takes place is even darker than the already threatened pastoral world of *Mansfield Park*.

23. Several critics argue that *Framley Parsonage* is about the vanity of ambition and that Lady Lufton, no less than Mark, must learn the lesson. Mary Hamer suggests that Lady Lufton must recognize that "the proper scope of her power" is limited. "*Framley Parsonage*: Trollope's First Serial," *Review of English Studies*, New Series, 26, 102 (May, 1975), p. 160. Other critics agree with me that Lady Lufton, though temporarily frustrated, ultimately gets her own way. Thus Edwards claims that though "breaches are made in the defense of [Lady Lufton's] citadel, they are nearly all closed by the end of the novel." *Anthony Trollope*, p. 40.

24. A possibility that Russell A. Fraser overlooks when he remarks that *Framley Parsonage* "seems to deny the possibility of a full-fledged hero." "Anthony Trollope's Younger Characters," *Nineteenth Century Fiction*, 6, 2 (Sept., 1951), p. 98.

25. Edwards argues that Lady Lufton's objection to Lucy is "an all-too-familiar expedient for stringing out the story, rather than a pointer to any real conflict of principles." *Anthony Trollope*, p. 41. Edwards is right, I think, that there is no real reason for Lady Lufton to reject Lucy—but this is precisely what Lady Lufton needs to learn.

26. In my treatment of *Framley Parsonage* as a pastoral idyll, I am indebted

to Kincaid's valuable discussion in *The Novels of Anthony Trollope,* pp. 120–25.

3. *Subverting the Ideal*

1. Though he does not enlarge on the suggestion, Geoffrey Harvey agrees that *Orley Farm* attacks "the Victorians' profound belief . . . in the sanctity of womanhood as the regulator of moral conduct in the home." *The Art of Anthony Trollope,* p. 97. Laura Hapke, on the other hand, believes that *Orley Farm* is completely conventional in its treatment of women, though it takes a female felon as its heroine. "The Lady as Criminal: Contradiction and Resolution in Trollope's *Orley Farm,*" *Victorian Newsletter,* 66 (Fall, 1984), pp. 18–21.

2. I think Polhemus is going too far when he asserts that Sir Joseph, "though nominally [Lady Mason's] husband, was actually more of a father figure to her," a "kind and protective" figure, who treats her almost as well as Sir Peregrine does. *Changing World,* p. 77.

3. Both Harvey and Polhemus misread the novel on this point. Harvey asserts that Lady Mason voluntarily seizes the land and thus "re-enacts her original crime." *The Art of Anthony Trollope,* p. 105; Polhemus argues that Lady Mason "legally reclaims the land for [Lucius] at his coming of age." *Changing World,* p. 77. Both critics display an interesting unwillingness to admit how limited Lady Mason's freedom of action really is.

4. Coral Lansbury argues that Mrs. Orme is "the social conscience of *Orley Farm* . . . the woman that Lady Mason might have been in altered circumstances." *The Reasonable Man* (Princeton, New Jersey, 1981), p. 170. But this overlooks both Lady Mason's superiority in force and intelligence and the fact that Mrs. Orme only becomes the novel's conscience after Lady Mason has altered *her* life.

5. Harvey, *The Art of Anthony Trollope,* p. 91.

6. Edwards quotes Sadleir in *Anthony Trollope,* pp. 107–8.

7. In discussing the Furnivals' marriage, Polhemus again shows a tendency to take the husband's side: Furnival "finds himself tied to an ignorant, jealous old woman whom he no longer loves." *Changing World,* p. 83. Furnival, as Trollope explicitly notes, is no younger than his wife—and her jealousy is the direct result of his behavior.

8. Robert Martin Adams calls this a "pointless episode lifted from *L'Ecole des Femmes.*" "*Orley Farm* and Real Fiction," *Nineteenth Century Fiction,* 8, 1 (June, 1953), p. 36. But insofar as this episode subverts the comic subplot, it does have a point.

9. Kincaid sees the comic subplot involving Madeline in a similar manner: "There is no essential comic rhythm, and the slight comic counterplot actually heightens this fact." *The Novels of Anthony Trollope,* p. 79.

10. Several critics have remarked that *The Small House at Allington* is the first of Trollope's novels to take a disenchanted look at the realities of love and the first to take a real interest in its romantic heroine. Polhemus notes that in the series of novels from *The Small House* through *The Claverings*, Trollope "gets at the perils of love—the run-of-the-mill, yet heartbreaking difficulties of love and marriage." *Changing World*, p. 91. Judith Weissman remarks that Lily is Trollope's first interesting ingenue. "'Old Maids Have Friends': The Unmarried Heroine of Trollope's Barsetshire Novels," *Women and Literature*, 5, 1 (Spring, 1977), p. 16.

11. See McMaster for an extended discussion of Lily as a masochist: *Trollope's Palliser Novels*, pp. 3–19. Sarah Gilead describes Lily as a "self-pitying, self-glorifying" character, a "fleur du mal." "Trollope's *The Small House at Allington*," *The Explicator*, 42, 2 (Winter, 1984), p. 13.

12. Weissman notes that Lily's "love for Crosbie is influenced by some unfortunate cultural commonplaces," but does not enlarge on the suggestion. "Old Maids Have Friends," p. 17. Kincaid takes the opposite tack, arguing that Lily's "true virtue" lacks a cultural context and "therefore is unsupported and can depend only on itself. It is thus very likely to appear or become perverse." *The Novels of Anthony Trollope*, p. 126. Wright takes an intermediate position, suggesting that some of Lily's views about love are standard, others, like her insistence that betrothal is as binding as marriage, unusual. *Anthony Trollope: Dream and Art*, p. 63. I would call Lily's views on betrothal exaggeratedly conventional, rather than unconventional.

13. *The Compact Edition of the Oxford English Dictionary* (Oxford, 1971), p. 2298.

14. Wright takes a similar approach to Lily, whom he calls "a sentimental heroine in a less than sentimental world." *Anthony Trollope: Dream And Art*, p. 63.

15. Hennedy sees this quite differently, arguing that Amelia is "a female social climber, a kind of female Crosbie." *Unity in Barsetshire*, p. 95.

16. Kincaid holds that "the major action of the novel," Lily's unfortunate romance, is "more idealized" than the main actions of the earlier novels, and therefore the narrator is forced to create some tension with his cynical stance. I think that the narrator's cynical stance, in conjunction with the damaging evidence that her story itself contains, informs the reader that Lily's behavior is not as ideal as it seems. *The Novels of Anthony Trollope*, p. 36.

17. Cockshut, *Anthony Trollope*, p. 111.

18. Arthur Pollard, *Anthony Trollope* (London, 1978), p. 138. Shirley Letwin is also an admirer of Luke, whom she sees as an ideal gentleman. *The Gentleman in Trollope*, pp. 116-18. I hope to show that Luke is not totally admirable.

19. Kincaid, *The Novels of Anthony Trollope*, p. 83.

20. Cockshut, *Anthony Trollope*, p. 111.

21. Edwards, *Anthony Trollope*, p. 59.

22. Polhemus, *Changing World*, p. 99.

23. Edwards notes that "the novel also sketches in the clerical and commercial as well as the strictly political 'politics' of the town." *Anthony Trollope*, p. 59. Edwards does not, however, notice that *Rachel Ray*'s "politics" are related thematically to its love story—as I shall attempt to demonstrate.

24. Mrs. Cornbury resembles Arabella Greenow of *Can You Forgive Her?*, another woman who has the magical power to solve problems that most of the women in the novel find agonizing and irresolvable.

25. The critics who have discussed *Can You Forgive Her?* are sharply divided in their estimates of Grey. Those who think Grey is a perfect gentleman and admirable human being include McMaster, *Trollope's Palliser Novels*; Letwin, *The Gentleman in Trollope*; Wright, *Anthony Trollope: Dream and Art*; and Polhemus, *Changing World*. Those who see Grey's treatment of Alice as repressive include Kincaid, *The Novels of Anthony Trollope*; Barickman, MacDonald, and Stark, *Corrupt Relations*; George Levine, "Can You Forgive Him? Trollope's *Can You Forgive Her?* and the Myth of Realism," *Victorian Studies*, 18, 1 (Sept., 1974), pp. 5–30; and, up to a point, Edwards, *Anthony Trollope*, p. 93.

26. For a somewhat different analysis of the ways in which the narrator evokes sympathy for his female characters, see Garrett, *The Victorian Multiplot Novel*, pp. 182–85.

27. Both McMaster, *Trollope's Palliser Novels*, and David S. Chamberlain, "Unity and Irony in Trollope's *Can You Forgive Her?*, *Studies in English Literature*, 8, 4 (Autumn, 1968), pp. 669–80, notice that the novel's three main plots deal with a maid, a wife, and a widow. But they have not seen how systematically Kate, George's ex-mistress Jane, and the unnamed prostitute extend the range of women's experience with which the novel deals. Kincaid suggests that *The American Senator* offers an anatomy of English country society. *The Novels of Anthony Trollope*, pp. 234–36.

28. Several critics see the unrealistic nature of Alice's aspirations as proof that Trollope believes women cannot wield power responsibly and is attacking the feminist belief that women can function outside the home. See, for example, Edwards, *Anthony Trollope*, p. 94; McMaster, *Trollope's Palliser Novels*, p. 164; and Levine, "Can You Forgive Him?," p. 15. But if Trollope's intention had been to show that feminist aspirations are misguided, he would, presumably, have made Alice a real feminist. That he did not do so suggests a somewhat different point.

29. For a more extended discussion, see Arthur Pollard, "Trollope's Idea of the Gentleman," in John Halperin, ed., *Trollope's Centenary Essays* (London, 1982), pp. 86–94.

30. The contrast between Grey and Palliser, on the one hand, and Vavasor

and Fitzgerald, on the other, is often defined as an opposition of prudence to passion. See, for example, Chamberlain, "Unity and Irony." But it is hard to make this scheme work, because Trollope is most explicit about Alice's passionate attraction to Grey. A more complex scheme is needed.

31. A number of critics see Glencora's pregnancy in symbolic terms: as proof that her husband has finally made a commitment to domesticity. This works, of course, but there is a physical cause as well—and Trollope hints at it in a surprisingly broad way, considering when the novel was written.

32. I am indebted to Deborah Morse's unpublished dissertation on women in the Palliser novels, *Am I Not Doing It All for Him?*, (Northwestern University, 1986) for the idea that Glencora's triumphant production of an heir carries with it this ironic consequence.

33. Kincaid may see the ending for Kate in more positive terms than the text warrants, when he argues that she "eventually resists her brother's demands" and so achieves independence. Kincaid, *The Novels of Anthony Trollope,* p. 186. Kate does resist George, and does liberates herself—into nothingness.

34. McMaster notes that Alice's behavior is "curiously at odds with her character," but does not hypothesize that this may result from Alice's having no satisfactory way to express her character, given the limited options available to women. *Trollope's Palliser Novels,* p. 23.

35. The two critics who have written most interestingly about *Miss Mackenzie,* P. D. Edwards and James Kincaid, both see the work as a straightforward comedy—albeit a dark one. Edwards argues that Trollope uses comic form "to shield himself from the grimmer implications of the old maid's plight," which he fears to encounter in their full grimness. *Anthony Trollope,* p. 64. Kincaid believes that the "new and darker problems" the novel explores are appropriate to its particular brand of comedy: "a fable of rejuvenation and rebirth, not of natural growth." *The Novels of Anthony Trollope,* p. 87. But of course there is always the possibility that the novel's dark content undermines its comic form.

36. Polhemus sees this as the novel's central scene: "The drama of the novel lies in this private victory of life over Victorian repression." *Changing World,* p. 113. But the "triumph" is compromised by Margaret's failure to find the fulfillment she is daring enough to desire. One might argue that "Victorian repression" has the last laugh.

37. Kincaid, *The Novels of Anthony Trollope,* p. 86.

38. Edwards, *Anthony Trollope,* p. 63.

39. Kincaid, *The Novels of Anthony Trollope,* p. 87.

40. Geoffrey Chaucer, *The Canterbury Tales,* translated by Nevill Coghill (Baltimore, 1952), p. 371.

41. Edwards believes that the purpose of the parallels is "to distance those elements in the heroine's situation that the reader is likely to find

most affecting and most worrying, to lend them a faint but comforting air of the fantastic . . . a sentimental filter for the intense boredom and frustration Miss Mackenzie suffers." *Anthony Trollope*, pp. 63–64. But can such grim stories as Mariana's and Griselda's really act as "sentimental filters"? Comparing Margaret's experience with theirs stresses its dark side.

42. Several critics note tensions of this sort in *The Claverings*, although some of them attribute these tensions to a failure of Trollope's art.

43. Wright, *Anthony Trollope: Dream and Art*, p. 128. More than one critic senses what Wright articulates here.

44. See Cockshut, *Anthony Trollope: A Critical Study*, pp. 86–87, for a discussion of the hypocrisy with which characters in *The Claverings* react to death.

45. Three critics precede me in suggesting that the human tendency to idealize love and domesticity is a theme in *The Claverings*: Harvey opines that Harry Clavering is "caught in the clash between society's inflexible idealizations of romantic love and the reality of unpredictable human passions," *The Art of Anthony Trollope*, p. 117; Wright thinks that the book exposes the "sentimental conventions of fiction" which its characters and readers accept, *Anthony Trollope: Dream and Art*, p. 133; and Polhemus says that the novel is about "the mental strains" that the characters' attempts to "uphold the Biedermeier love ideal" impose upon them, *Changing World*, p. 113.

46. Critics who discuss the unfairness of Julia's punishment and the surprising way Trollope rehabilitates her include Overton, *The Unofficial Trollope*, pp. 159–61; and Harvey, *The Art of Anthony Trollope*, pp. 120–24.

47. See, for example, Polhemus, *Changing World*, p. 114; Edwards, *Anthony Trollope*, pp. 69–71; and Harvey, *The Art of Anthony Trollope*, p. 122.

48. Critics who agree that Trollope subtly denigrates Florence even as he idealizes her include Polhemus, *Changing World*, p. 116; Wright, *Anthony Trollope: Dream and Art*, p. 129; and Edwards, *Anthony Trollope*, p. 70.

49. Critics who think that Harry should have married Julia include Polhemus, *Changing World*, p. 118; Pollard, *Anthony Trollope*, pp. 125–26; and Edwards, *Anthony Trollope*, p. 71.

50. John Halperin argues that the theme of *The Belton Estate* is "desire mediated, controlled, and directed by the responsiveness of its object." This is certainly true of Aylmer's desire for Clara, but Halperin's attempt to apply the concept to Will—whose "pursuit of Clara predictably grows more tenacious when he learns he has a rival in the field," in Halperin's view—is unconvincing. Introduction to *The Belton Estate* (New York, 1986), p. vii and p. xi. Will never wavers in his passionate desire to marry Clara. It does not increase when he learns about Aylmer, and it does not decrease, as Aylmer's does, when Clara tells him she loves him.

51. Polhemus sees "the Winterfield doctrines" as the source of Clara's unsatisfactory attitudes about sex. *Changing World*, p. 127. Those doctrines

may, of course, have influenced Clara in spite of her conscious rejection of her aunt's teaching, but her approach to sex is, as I hope I have shown, typical of the time, neither exceptionally puritanical nor in need of special explanation.

52. Edwards, *Anthony Trollope*, p. 66.

53. Edwards thinks that because Trollope hedges his approval of Mrs. Askerton with so many qualifications suggesting that her case is unusual, we must conclude that he is not "at all disposed to question the accepted sexual code." *Anthony Trollope*, p. 67. Trollope was not prepared to exonerate the "average" adulteress, of course, but the fact that he would exonerate *any* adulteress means he did question the code. Pollard's position is closer to mine. He argues that the good characters in *The Belton Estate* are unconventional in judging Mrs. Askerton not "by a code . . . [but] by what she is." *Anthony Trollope*, p. 142.

4. *Comedy, Tragedy, and the Position of Women*

1. Levine, "Can You Forgive Him?," p. 7.

2. Edwards, *Anthony Trollope*, pp. 62–63.

3. Terry, *Anthony Trollope: The Artist in Hiding*, p. 107.

4. Kincaid, *The Novels of Anthony Trollope*, p. 79.

5. Kincaid, *The Novels of Anthony Trollope*, p. 28.

6. Quoted in Edwards, *Anthony Trollope*, p. 103.

7. Overton notes that in "his unrevised state," Tregear is "over-clever, conceited, and unwilling to advance himself by his own efforts." *The Unofficial Trollope*, p. 77.

8. McMaster argues that Mary "has neither Glencora's sparkle, nor her pliability. . . . [She is] the immovable object." *Trollope's Palliser Novels*, pp. 132–33.

9. Kincaid agrees, arguing that in *The Eustace Diamonds* "'faith in virtue, constancy, and honesty'. . . will no longer support even the righteous. . . . The heroine is almost forgotten." *The Novels of Anthony Trollope*, p. 203.

10. Thus Polhemus, who thinks Lucy is an unsuccessful character, "a bloodless figure of affirmation," nonetheless reads this subplot as if Trollope hoped to produce an undisturbed romantic comedy expressing his "faith in human will and independence." *Changing World*, p. 177, and p. 176.

11. Overton, *The Unofficial Trollope*, p. 177, and p. 168.

12. Kincaid agrees, arguing that Frank "does more than touch pitch lightly; he wallows in it. His marriage to the heroine does little to alter the novel's sombre tone." *The Novels of Anthony Trollope*, p. 203.

13. See, for example, Polhemus, *Changing World*, p. 202; Harvey, *The Art of Anthony Trollope*, p. 36; Tracy, *Trollope's Later Novels*, pp. 53–54; and McMaster, *Trollope's Palliser Novels*, p. 120, for negative assessments of Emily.

14. Harvey argues forcefully, and in some detail, that "Lopez is hated because he lives as the world lives, not as it pretends to live." *The Art of Anthony Trollope*, p. 154. Garrett argues, more generally, that "eccentric" figures like Lopez or Melmotte "serve as an extreme embodiment of the general tendencies of [Trollope's] world." *The Victorian Multiplot Novel*, p. 218.

15. McMaster, *Trollope's Palliser Novels*, p. 120. Tracy has exactly the same reaction. *Trollope's Later Novels*, pp. 53–54.

16. See Harvey, *The Art of Anthony Trollope*, pp. 152–56.

17. Kincaid argues that "Violet is as rebellious as her lover," which— considering that Chiltern's rebellion has made him almost a social outcast— is saying a lot. *The Novels of Anthony Trollope*, p. 196.

18. Letwin, *The Gentleman in Trollope*, pp. 74–81.

19. McMaster agrees, arguing that "in making this bold Jewish adventuress one of the most sympathetic women in the Palliser series, Trollope shows himself to have become much more liberal in his racial and sexual attitudes than he was in the Barsetshire series." *Trollope's Palliser Novels*, p. 56.

20. McMaster makes a similar point, when she notes that "the difference of sex is not nearly so noticeable a component in Phineas's relation with Marie Goesler as it is in those with his other women." *Trollope's Palliser Novels*, p. 56. It could be argued that Trollope went so far with Madame Max that he frightened himself. In *Phineas Finn*, she is over thirty, while Phineas is twenty-eight. But in *Phineas Redux*, the age difference has disappeared.

21. Polhemus also discusses professional disillusionment as a theme in *Phineas Redux*. See *Changing World*, p. 181.

22. See Kincaid's discussion of this aspect of *The Last Chronicle of Barset*, *The Novels of Anthony Trollope*, p. 135.

23. Polhemus seems to have something similar in mind, when he argues that *Phineas Redux* shows Trollope's understanding of "the antisocial sentiment which has created . . . the fiction of private detectives." *Changing World*, p. 182.

24. Jeannette King, *Tragedy in the Victorian Novel* (Cambridge, 1978), p. 69.

25. King, *Tragedy in the Victorian Novel*, p. 74.

26. Among the critics who argue that Trollope does not take *He Knew He Was Right*'s putatively tragic protagonist, Louis Trevelyan, seriously are Garrett, *The Victorian Multiplot Novel*, pp. 203–16; Edwards, *Anthony Trollope*, p. 114; and Kincaid, *The Novels of Anthony Trollope*, p. 150.

27. Edwards, *Anthony Trollope*, pp. 116–17.

28. Wright, *Anthony Trollope: Dream and Art*, p. 136.

29. Brian Harrison, *Separate Spheres* (New York, 1978), pp. 81–82.

30. Quoted in Harrison, *Separate Spheres*, p. 83.

31. As Wright puts it, Kennedy has a "copybook notion of marriage, the copybook consisting of maxims of male dominance and female submission." *Anthony Trollope: Dream and Art,* p. 101.

32. Edwards notes that Kennedy's fall is presented "semi-comically." His attempt to kill Phineas is "slightly ridiculous, a bumbling and stagy means of expressing emotion." *Anthony Trollope,* p. 162.

33. As Overton remarks, "it's perversely apt that a woman who has had to school herself to accept disadvantage should require that others too should submit." *The Unofficial Trollope,* p. 174.

34. Edwards, *Anthony Trollope,* p. 180.

35. As I read various critical works dealing with Trollope's later novels, I noted that the terms "tragedy" and "tragic" were used to describe the fate of many female characters, far more than I had space to discuss here.

36. Kincaid, *The Novels of Anthony Trollope,* p. 149.

37. Terry notes that the successful people in *He Knew He Was Right* show "a healthy scepticism towards society and convention" and reject the "conventional Victorian concept of [female] submission and male dominance." *Anthony Trollope: The Artist in Hiding,* p. 138.

38. Kincaid, *The Novels of Anthony Trollope,* p. 154.

Editions Cited

An Autobiography. Oxford: Oxford University Press, 1980.
An Editor's Tales. New York: Arno Press, 1981.
Barchester Towers. London: Chapman and Hall, 1887.
The Belton Estate. Oxford: Oxford University Press, 1986.
The Bertrams. Leipzig: Bernhard Tauchnitz, 1859.
Can You Forgive Her?. London: Oxford University Press, 1973.
The Claverings. New York: Dover Publications, 1977.
Doctor Thorne. London: Oxford University Press, 1926.
Dr. Wortle's School. London: Oxford University Press, 1928.
The Duke's Children. London: Oxford University Press, 1973.
The Eustace Diamonds. London: Oxford University Press, 1973.
Framley Parsonage. London: Chapman and Hall, 1888.
He Knew He Was Right. New York: Dover Publications, 1983.
La Vendée. New York: Arno Press, 1981.
The Letters of Anthony Trollope. Edited by N. John Hall. 2 vols. Stanford, California: Stanford University Press, 1983.
Miss Mackenzie. New York: Arno Press, 1981.
The Noble Jilt and Did He Steal It?. New York: Arno Press, 1981.
North America. London: Chapman and Hall, 1862.
Orley Farm. New York: Alfred A. Knopf, 1950.
Phineas Finn. London: Oxford University Press, 1973.
Phineas Redux. London: Oxford University Press, 1973.
The Prime Minister. London: Oxford University Press, 1973.
Rachel Ray. New York: Dover Publications, 1980.
The Small House At Allington. London: Chapman and Hall, 1889.
The Three Clerks. New York: Dover Publications, 1981.
The Way We Live Now. London: Panther Books, 1969.

Index

Jane Nardin is Professor of English at the University of Wisconsin-Milwaukee, where she teaches eighteenth- and nineteenth-century British literature, as well as a variety of courses in women's studies. She is the author of *Those Elegant Decorums: The Concept of Propriety in Jane Austen's Novels* (State University of New York Press) and *Barbara Pym* (G.K. Hall). Her articles on English and American prose fiction have appeared in *Women and Literature, Genre, Mosaic, Studies in the Novel, The Denver Quarterly,* and other journals.